I0795926

POSTCARD HISTORY SERIES

New Albany

IN VINTAGE POSTCARDS

(front cover): New Albany celebrated its centennial October 12–16, 1913. Among the festivities was a parade held on October 14, 1913, that included 108 floats. Dimestore retailer F.W. Woolworth created a whimsical float featuring a girl in a crescent moon-shaped carriage pulled by festively dressed horses. Note the numbers "5" and "10" on the wheels of the carriage. In about 1923, Woolworth Store opened its first cafeteria in the country in New Albany at 220 Pearl Street. The store was later moved to the northwest corner of Pearl and Market Streets. Woolworth Store left New Albany in the early 1970s.

(back cover): Another part of the centennial celebration was a Made in New Albany exhibit that included wares manufactured in New Albany. Some 90 companies were represented in the exhibit, including at least four that still exist today: Kaiser's, Vernia's, The New Albany Ledger, and The New Albany Tribune.

POSTCARD HISTORY SERIES

New Albany

IN VINTAGE POSTCARDS

David C. Barksdale and Robyn Davis Sekula

ARCADIA
PUBLISHING

ISBN 978-0-7385-3386-5

Published by Arcadia Publishing
Charleston, South Carolina

Printed in the United States of America

Library of Congress Catalog Card Number: 2004118162

For all general information contact Arcadia Publishing at:
Telephone 843-853-2070
Fax 843-853-0044
E-mail sales@arcadiapublishing.com
For customer service and orders:
Toll-Free 1-888-313-2665

Visit us on the Internet at www.arcadiapublishing.com

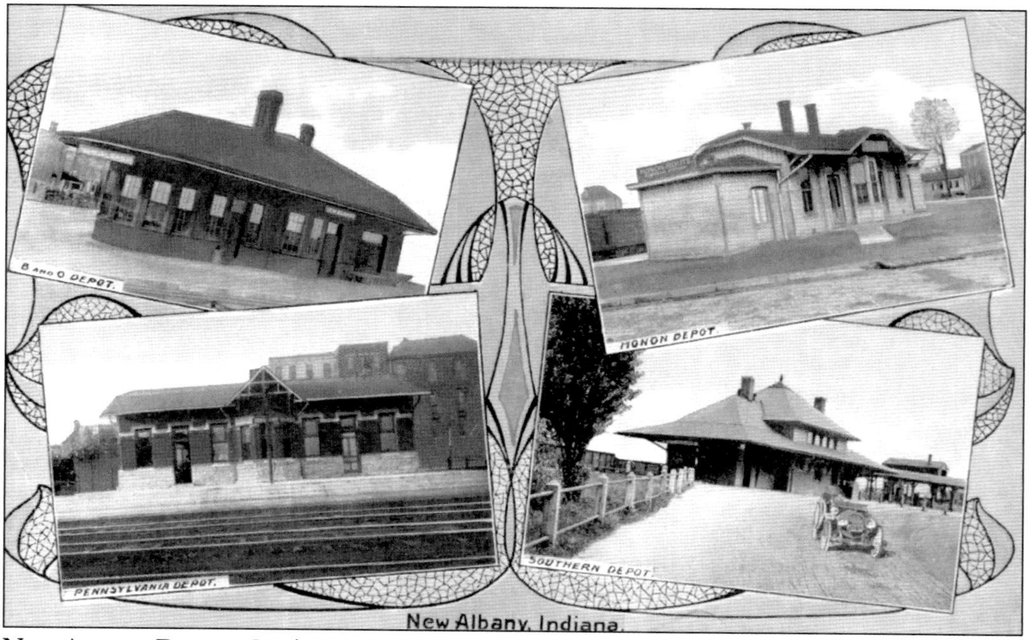

NEW ALBANY DEPOTS. In about 1910, New Albany was home to the four railroad depots shown on this card. Pictured on the top right is the Monon Passenger Depot, which was built in 1884 for the Louisville-Chicago-New Albany Railroad and located on the northeast corner of Vincennes and Main Streets. It was used for rail passengers until 1937 and was torn down in 1959. On the bottom right is the Southern Railroad Depot, which was built sometime between 1898 and 1905 on the northwest corner of West First and Water Streets. It has since been destroyed. On the bottom left is the Pennsylvania Passenger Depot, which was built in 1883 one block south of Main between State and Pearl. The Baltimore & Ohio Railroad Depot was built in 1893 at 230 Vincennes Street. It burned in 1981.

Contents

Acknowledgments

The authors wish to dedicate this book to the memory of Mrs. John A. Cody Jr., whose life-long love of New Albany and its rich history inspired this book. Though she is no longer with us, her research and postcard collection is a legacy that was extremely valuable in the production of this book. The authors also wish to thank Robert Real, Paul Graf, and Don Noble Smith for generously loaning us postcards that are featured throughout the book. Also, several area residents provided information to the authors as they helped compile the information featured in the captions. Those local residents were Bebe Cody, Paul Graf, Bunnie Hammer, Maggie Oster, Jane Steinert, Lana Aebersold, and Ann Robinson. Members of the New Albany-Floyd County Public Library staff, namely Lynn Rueff, Betty Menges, Patricia Foster, Cynthia Froman, and Sharon Bundy, were very helpful in assisting the authors during their research. Tom Reaugh of the National Weather Service was gracious in digging up detailed historical weather information for the authors. And last, but not least, are our long-suffering spouses, Greg Sekula and Debra Barksdale, who have put up with long nights of research and writing, and Carrie Barksdale, who allowed the authors liberal use of her computer. Thanks to all.

INTRODUCTION

New Albany, Indiana, is a nearly 200-year-old, scenic river town that lies along the banks of the Ohio River, opposite Louisville, Kentucky. The city is approaching its bicentennial, having been founded in 1813 by Joel, Abner, and Nathaniel Scribner, who purchased land on which to found the town. The Scribners divided the land into lots and sold it, advertising New Albany as an ideal place for relocation. They touted its location below the treacherous Falls of the Ohio and the impending construction of a saw mill, a grist mill, and a flour mill. New Albany soon became a bustling settlement, mostly due to shipping and boat-building interests, but other industries followed. The city was officially incorporated in 1839. By the mid-1800s, New Albany was the largest city in Indiana. Some of the city's most notable residences were built in these years and are still standing along the city's Main Street in downtown. The city's first school was organized in 1822, thanks to a generous donation of $5,000 from the Scribners to start a public school. Various church denominations followed, including Catholics, Baptists, Presbyterians, and Methodists, helping to bolster the city's population. In 1902, the city saw its first hospital constructed, St. Edward Hospital, and began building its first permanent library building, which was a Carnegie, both important milestones in the city's history. In 1913, with great fanfare, the city observed its centennial, which included a well-documented parade. Part of the celebration included the arrival of Scribner descendants, who traveled by boat down the Ohio River and were welcomed by thousands of locals. Just four years after New Albany celebrated its centennial, the city was ravaged by a tornado in March 1917, which cut a swath through the town nearly three miles long and a half-mile wide, killing 45 people. The city survived its worst flood in 1937, bouncing back to become the small but bustling town it is today. Earmarks of its past dot the town, with some of its most notable structures celebrated as museums, including the Carnegie Library, the Joel Scribner house, and the Culbertson Mansion. Though steeped in history, New Albany is a modern city with various industries, a reviving downtown, and a thriving university, Indiana University Southeast. The images shown in the postcards on these pages highlight its rich historical legacy, as well as point toward its future.

One

Views and Roads

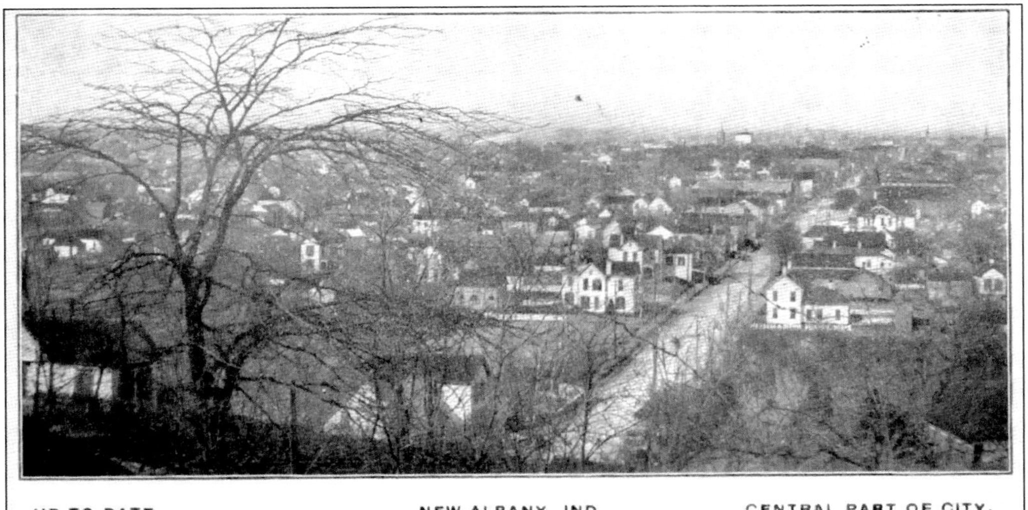

Central Part of the City. Looking east from Silver Hills, the residential area of western New Albany, mostly on West Main Street, is shown in this 1905 view. The Ohio River is on the right side of the card. Today, the area is a mix of homes and commercial establishments.

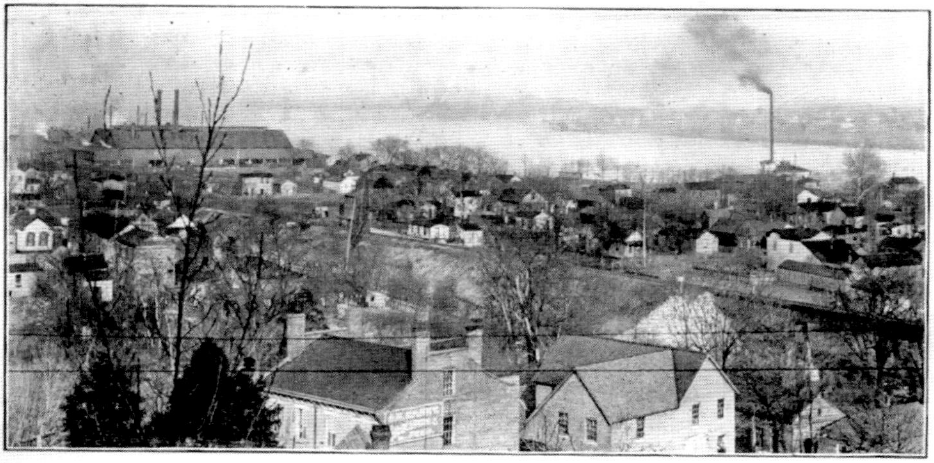

SOUTHERN PART OF NEW ALBANY, INDIANA

SOUTHERN PART OF NEW ALBANY. Industry lined New Albany's riverbanks at the turn of the century. This card shows what was then called "Lower Albany," which included mostly residential areas. The postcard is from about 1905.

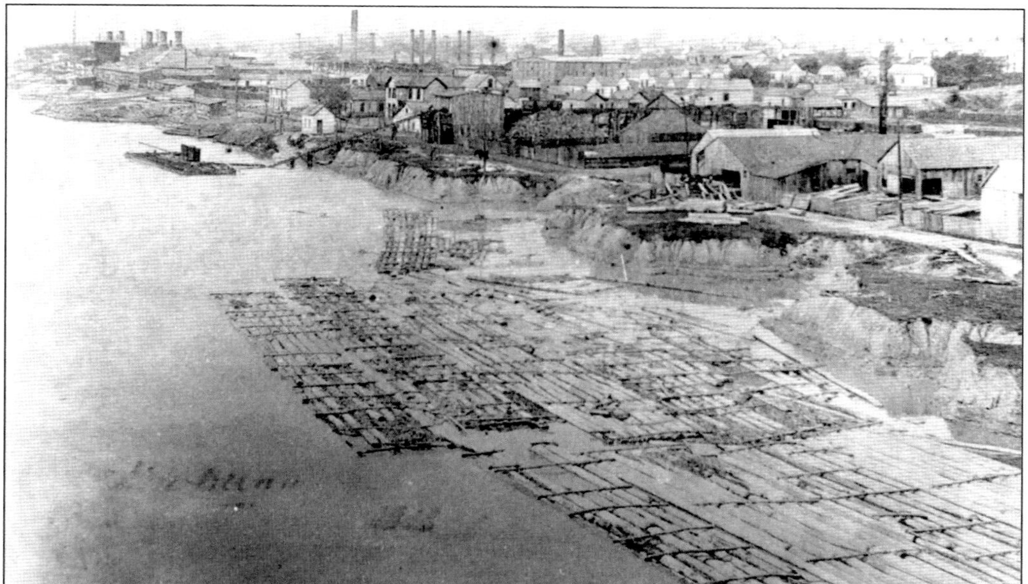

VIEW OF NEW ALBANY RIVERFRONT. Logs waiting for processing at nearby manufacturing plants occupy a stretch of New Albany's Ohio River shoreline in about 1905. The view shown in this postcard is taken from the Kentucky and Indiana Railroad Bridge looking west. Just a few blocks away was a residential area.

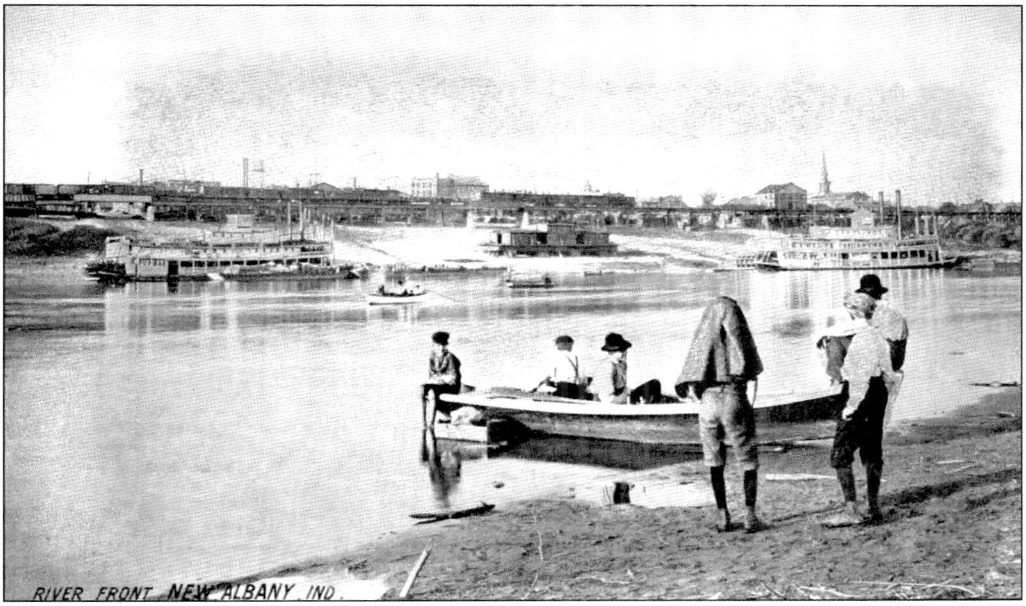

River Front. A group of boaters look across the Ohio River from Louisville to New Albany in this postcard from about 1910. The levy is shown in this image, along with two steamboats docked at the wharf in New Albany.

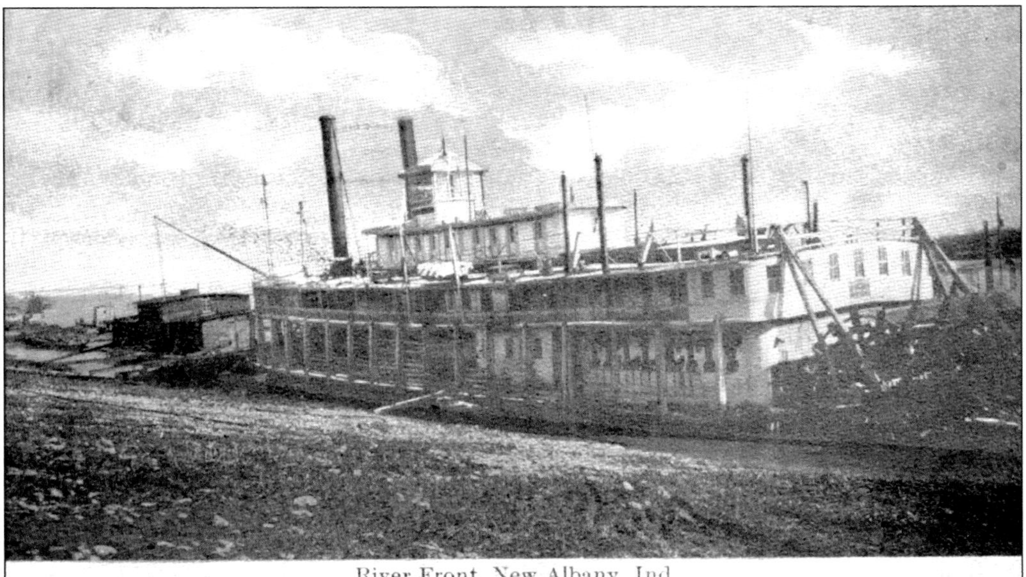

Tell City Steamboat. Steamboats were used both for ferrying goods and people at the time this postcard was made about 1910. The boat shown here is the Tell City Steamboat, which was built in 1889 in neighboring Jeffersonville. Although this is not a New Albany boat, hundreds of steamboats were built through the years in New Albany. Those boats included the first *Robt. E. Lee*, winner of the Great Steamboat Race against the Natchez.

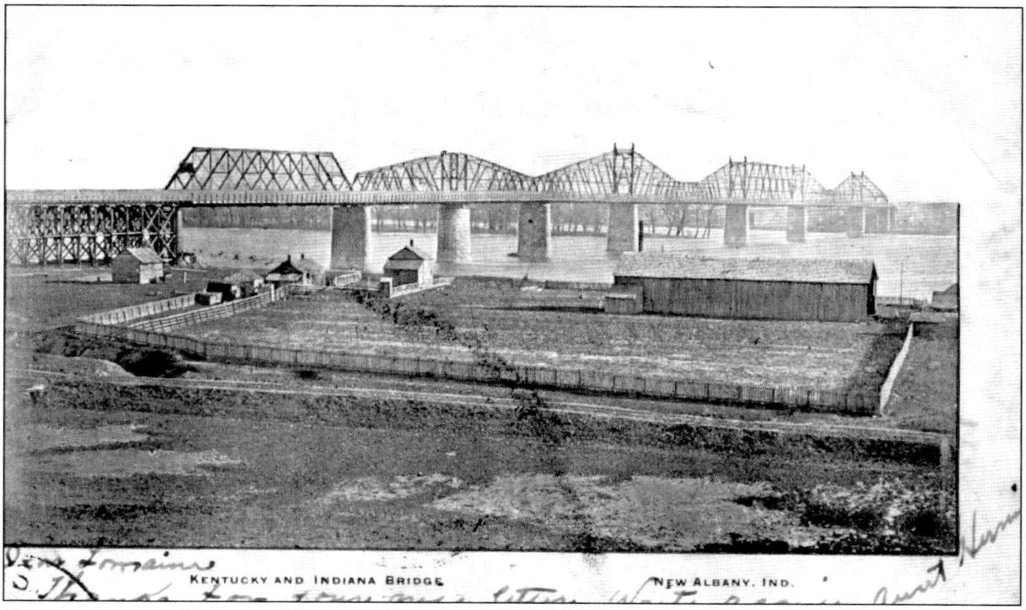

KENTUCKY AND INDIANA BRIDGE. Spanning the Ohio River and connecting Louisville with New Albany, the Kentucky and Indiana Railroad Bridge was built in 1886 at a cost of about $1.5 million. Business leaders in New Albany were eager to see the bridge constructed to both receive supplies by railway and to sell merchandise via rail freight. This card is from about 1905.

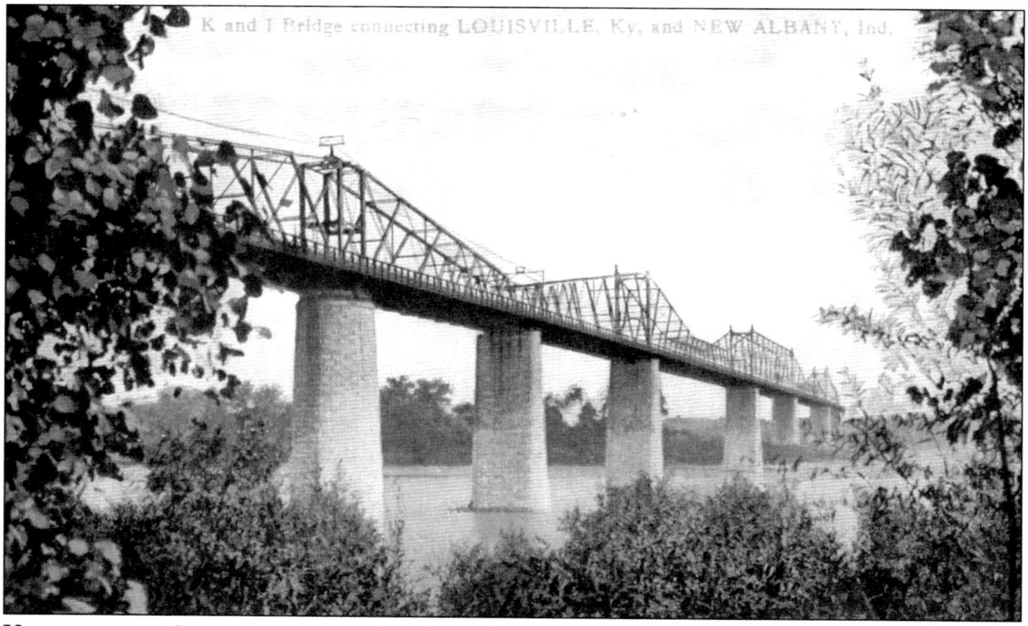

KENTUCKY AND INDIANA BRIDGE. The Kentucky and Indiana Railroad Bridge was also important to Louisville, as demonstrated by this card, which shows the same bridge from the Louisville side of the Ohio River. The card was made in about 1910.

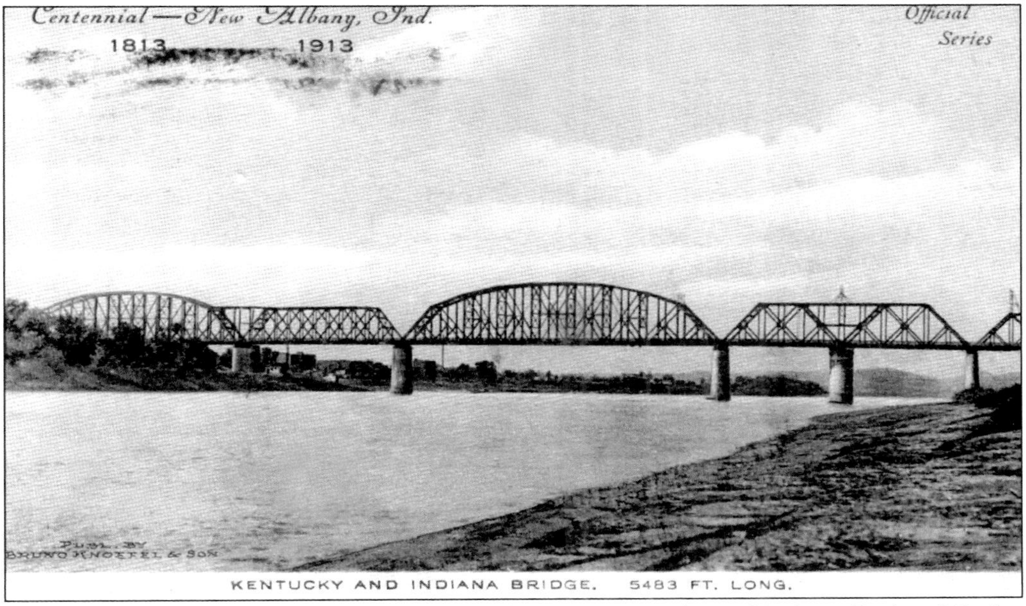

The New Kentucky and Indiana Bridge. The 1886 Kentucky and Indiana Railroad Bridge was replaced with a new, $5 million bridge in 1912, just in time for New Albany's centennial one year later. It was 5,483 feet long. This view looks downstream from the New Albany shoreline of the Ohio River. This same bridge is still used today by railroads.

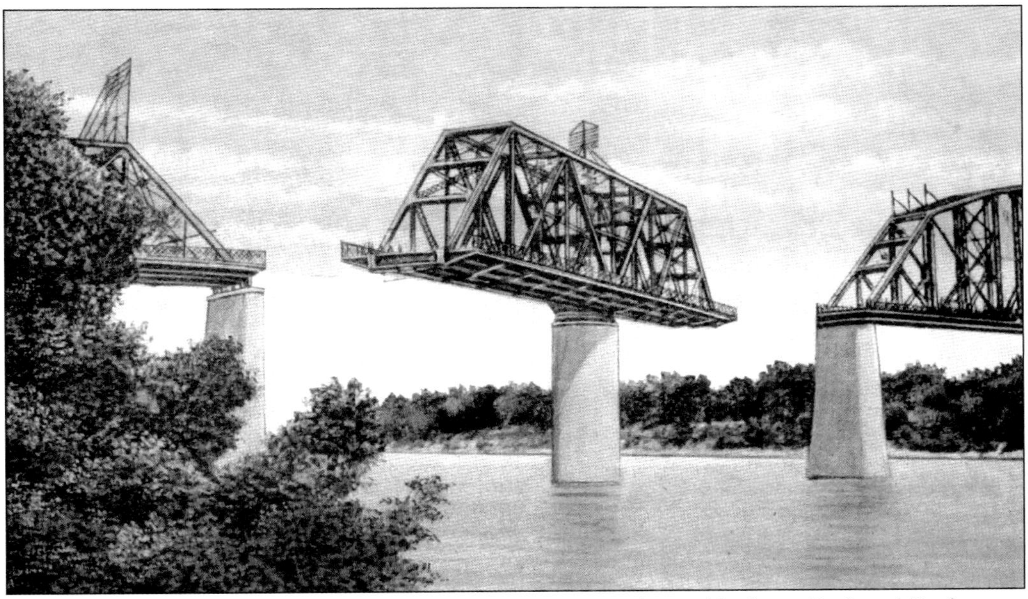

The Open Draw Span of the Bridge. The 1912 Kentucky and Indiana Railroad Bridge was built as a draw span so it would not block traffic from tall boats. The draw span was opened for the first time to much fanfare on July 7, 1913. It was only opened a few times. The postcard notes that it took 45 minutes to open and close in low gear and 20 minutes to open and close in high gear. The span itself was 420 feet long and weighed 2,400 tons.

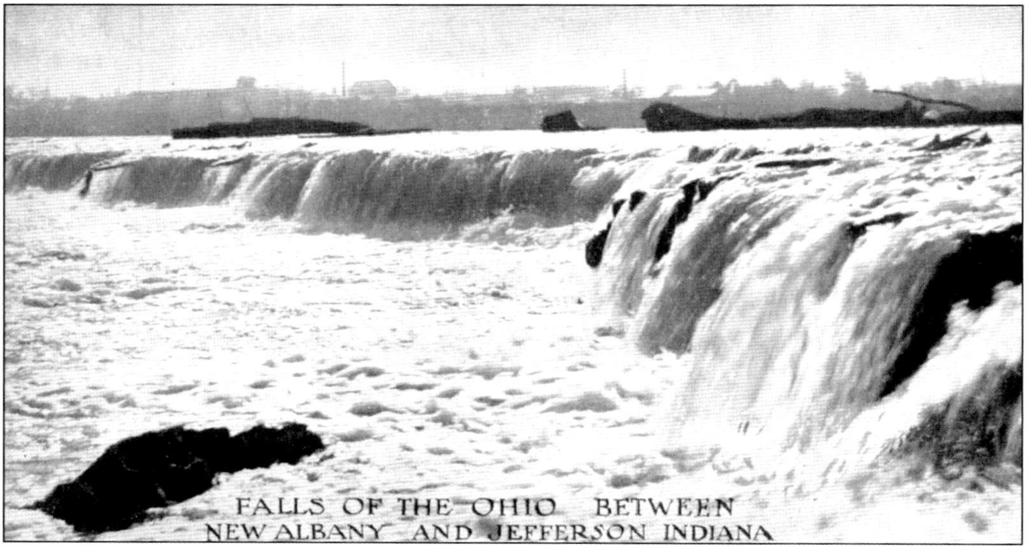

FALLS OF THE OHIO. Historical records indicate that the Falls of the Ohio were the only navigational barrier on the Ohio River for explorers. The river drops 26 feet over the two-and-a-half mile stretch of the Falls. Among the famous historical figures who have encountered the Falls are Gen. George Rogers Clark, Mark Twain, James Audubon, and Walt Whitman. This postcard is from about 1910.

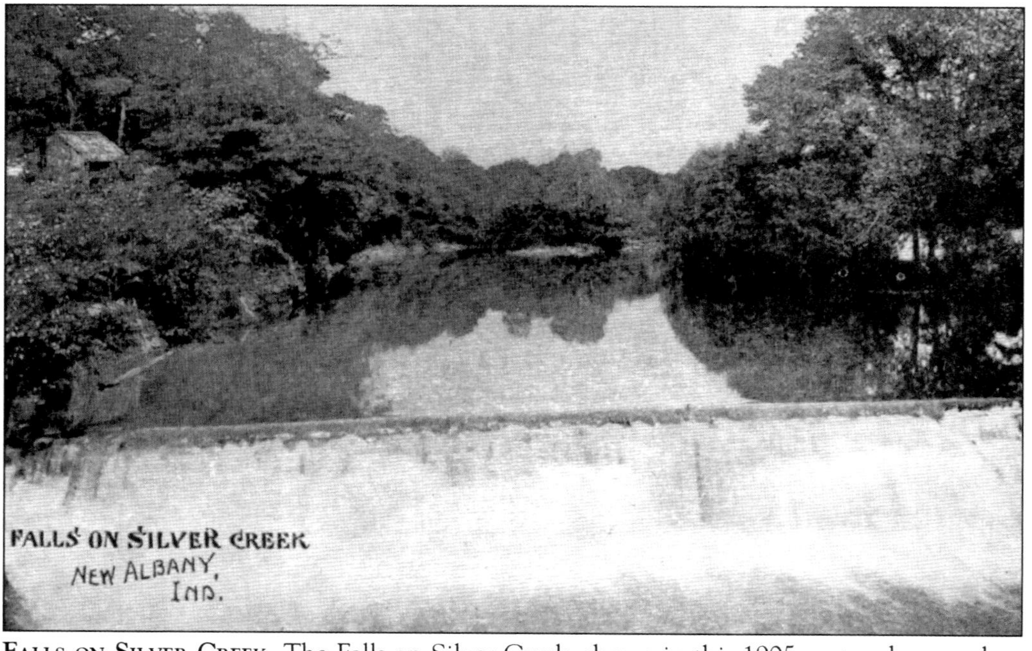

FALLS ON SILVER CREEK. The Falls on Silver Creek, shown in this 1905 postcard, were close to Glenwood Park, which today is a residential neighborhood. Silver Creek begins in Clark County and feeds into the Ohio River, and also forms the boundary between Floyd and Clark counties. The falls were created when the creek was dammed so that people could use it for recreation, including fishing and boating.

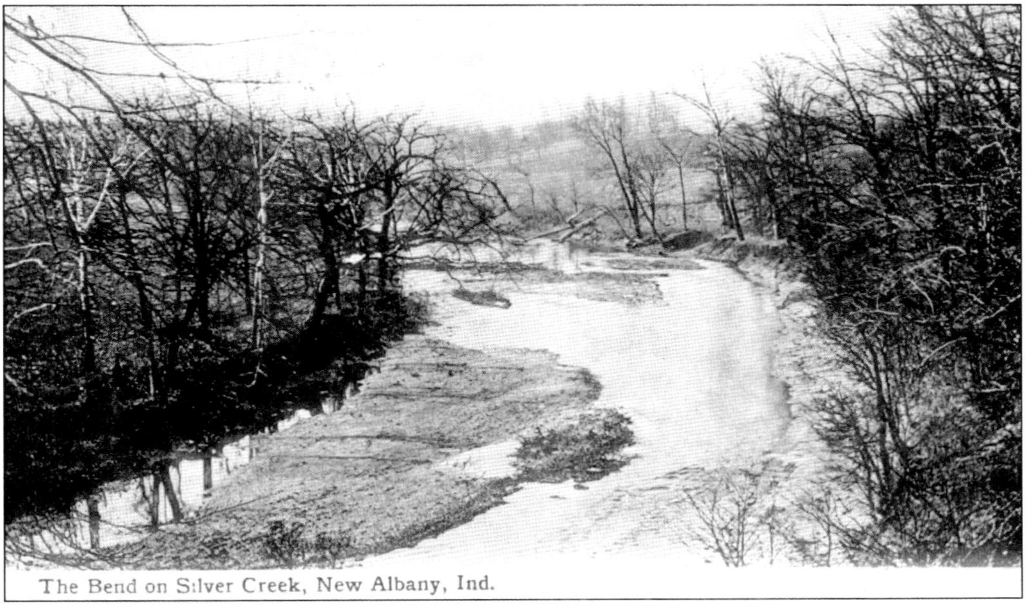

Bend on Silver Creek. Valued for its scenic views, Silver Creek was primarily used for recreation, including swimming and boating. This postcard is from about 1910.

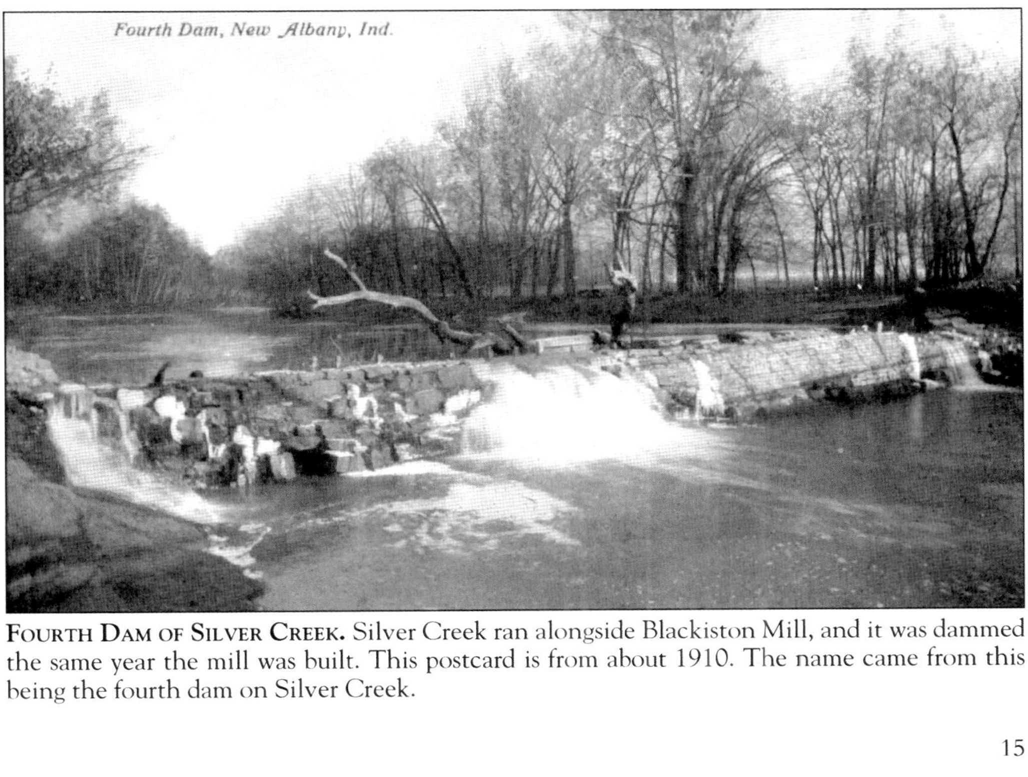

Fourth Dam of Silver Creek. Silver Creek ran alongside Blackiston Mill, and it was dammed the same year the mill was built. This postcard is from about 1910. The name came from this being the fourth dam on Silver Creek.

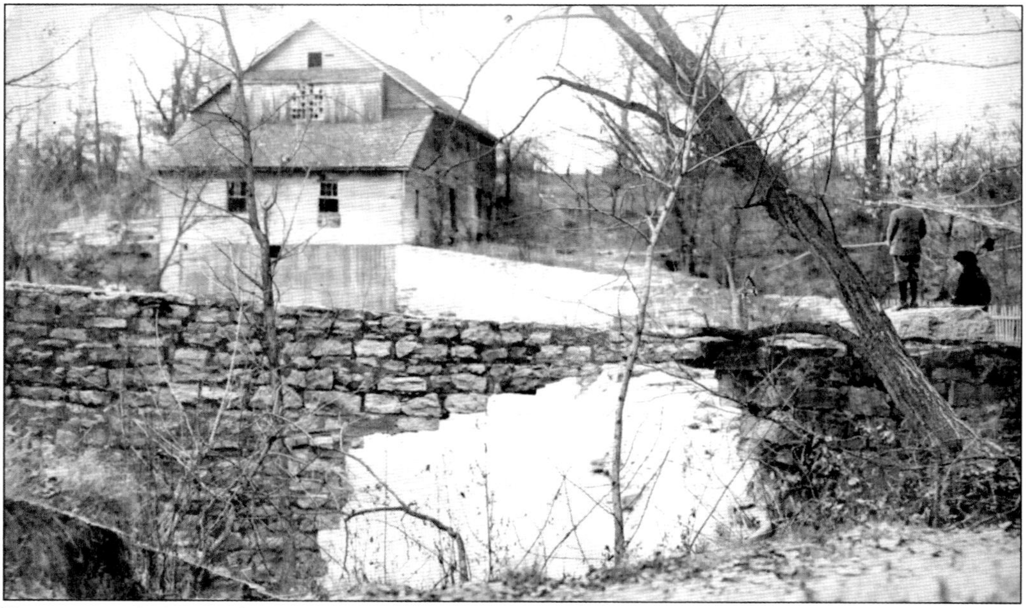

BLACKISTON'S MILL. One important commercial establishment that operated from the creek's banks was Blackiston's Mill, seen in this 1910 postcard. The mill is no longer standing, but a road named for it is a main corridor from New Albany to Clarksville. The historical spelling of the name is "Blackiston's," as opposed to the spelling of "Blackistone," seen in the next postcard on this page. The mill was built in 1853 and razed sometime in the 1990s.

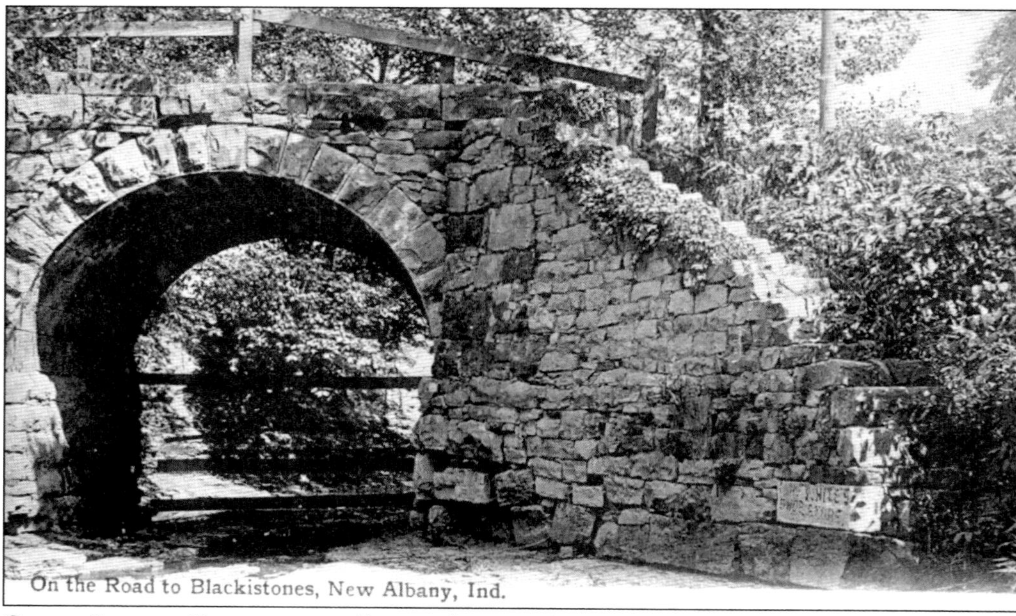

ON THE ROAD TO BLACKISTONES. Even at the turn of the century, the road leading to Blackiston's Mill was viewed as a crucial and scenic country road for both commercial traffic from the mill and Sunday drives. This postcard is from about 1910.

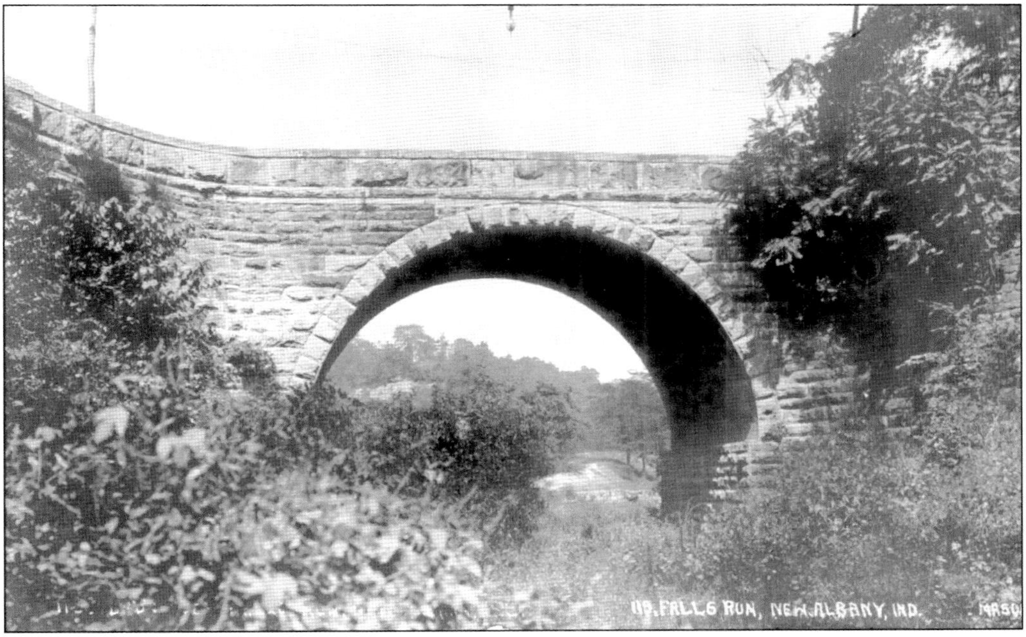

FALLS RUN BRIDGE. A rustic stone bridge with an arch took travelers over Falling Run Creek in western New Albany. The bridge was on West Main Street and was replaced in 1935. This postcard is from about 1905.

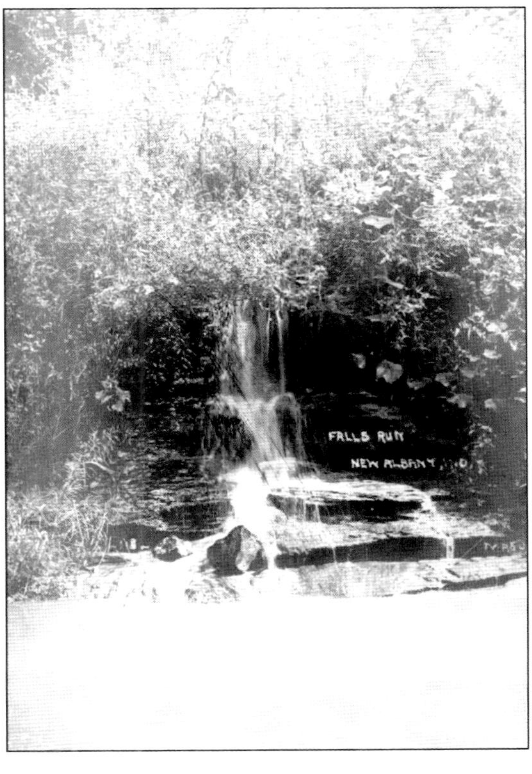

FALLS RUN. Falling Run Creek empties into the Ohio River within a half-mile of the stone bridge shown in the other postcard image on this page. This card is from about 1905.

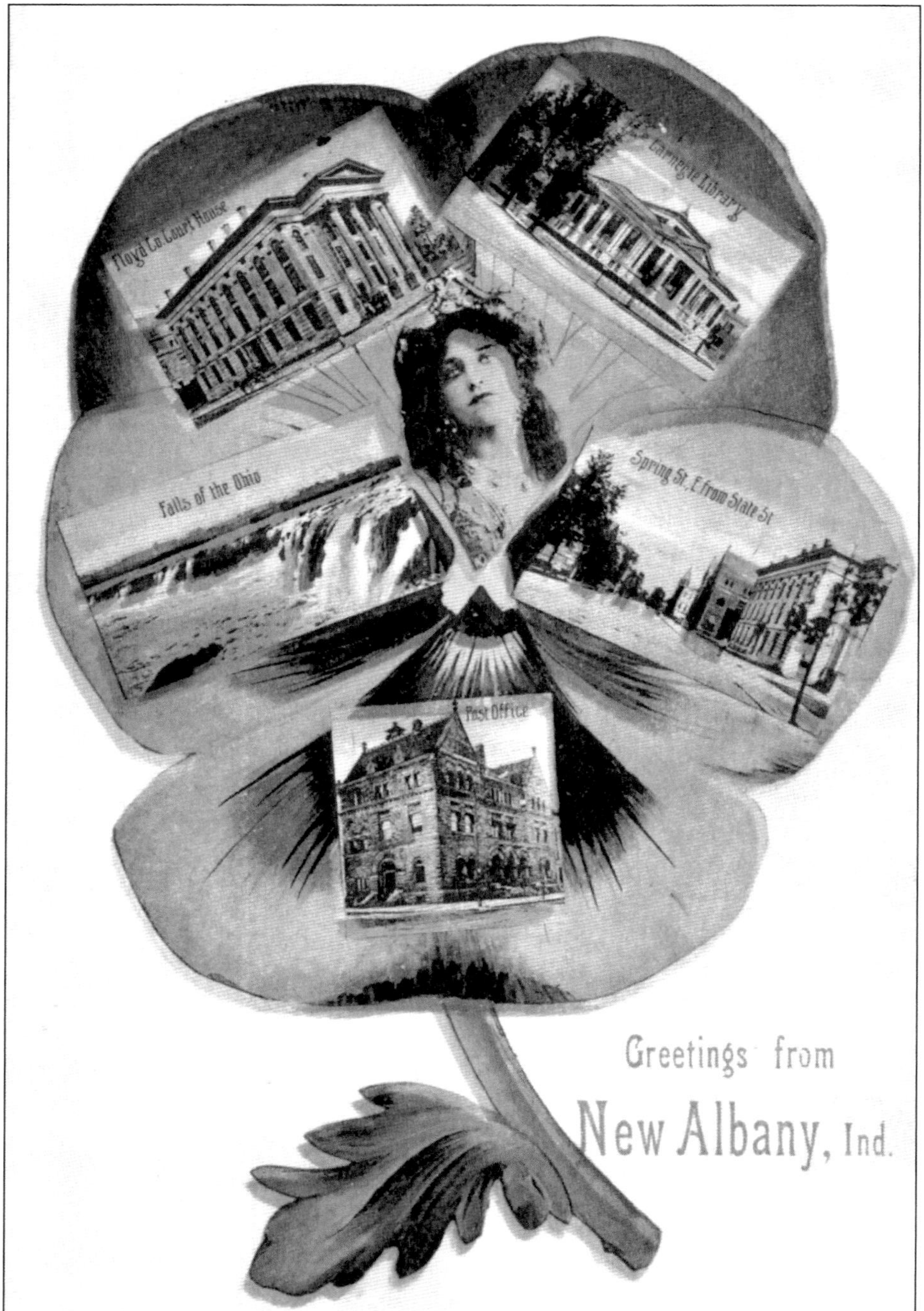

Greetings from New Albany. Five scenes depicting life in New Albany around 1910 are shown on this souvenir card. Clockwise from top left, the scenes are: the Floyd County Courthouse, the Carnegie Library, Spring Street looking east from State Street, the U.S. Courthouse and Post Office, and the Falls of the Ohio. The color postcard was printed in Germany and sold at Conner's Cut-Rate Drug Store in New Albany.

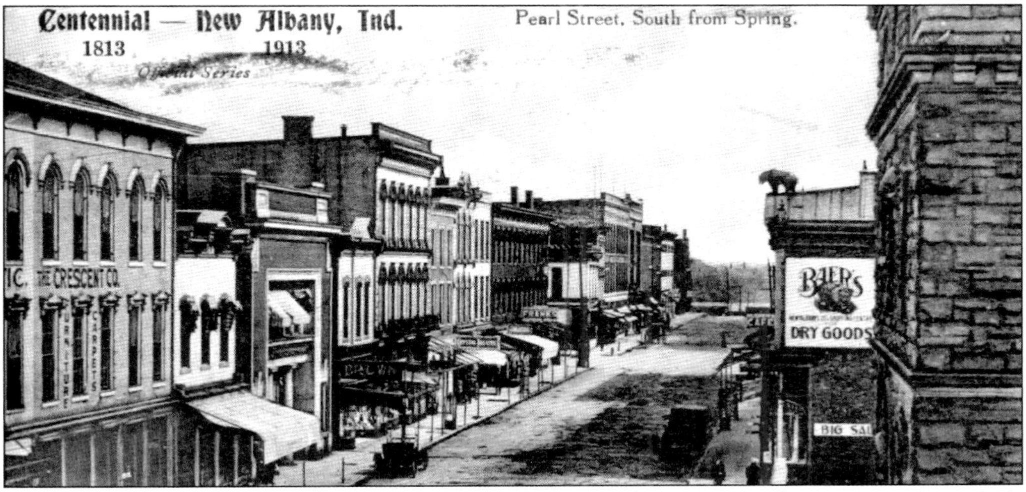

PEARL STREET, SOUTH FROM SPRING STREET. This postcard, created for the centennial in 1913, shows Pearl Street looking south from Spring Street. On the left hand side of the street is Washington C. DePauw's Ledger Block building, in which The New Albany Daily Ledger was housed. Adjacent to the Ledger Block is the 1886 Kaiser building, which still houses Kaiser's Tobacco Shop, New Albany's oldest continuous business, established in 1832. Kaiser's also holds the honor of being a state-recognized centennial business. Continuing down the street is the Mutual Trust Bank building, followed by another Kaiser family building, housing at the time of this card the C.C. Brown Merchant Tailor, and finally the 1860 Hieb building. Built for John Hieb, the building contained the first American-made plate glass windows in its store front. The glass was made at Captain John B. Ford's New Albany Glassworks. On the right-hand side of the street are the U.S. Courthouse and Post Office and the Baer's Dry Goods store building with its distinctive bear statue on the roof.

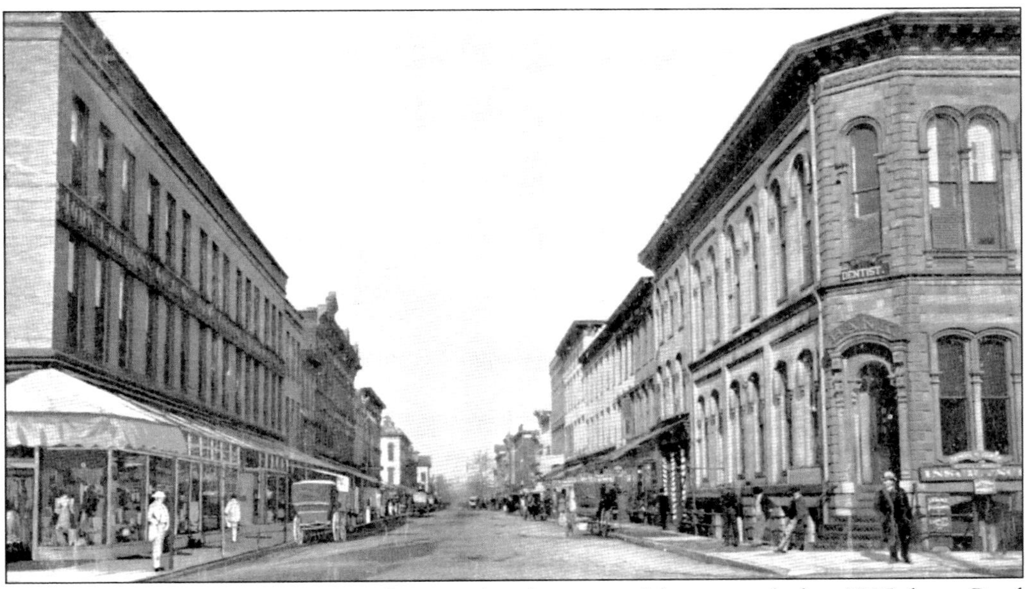

PEARL STREET, NORTH FROM MAIN STREET. Another view of downtown before 1905 shows Pearl Street looking north from Main Street. The 1903 John J. Morgan building is shown to the left.

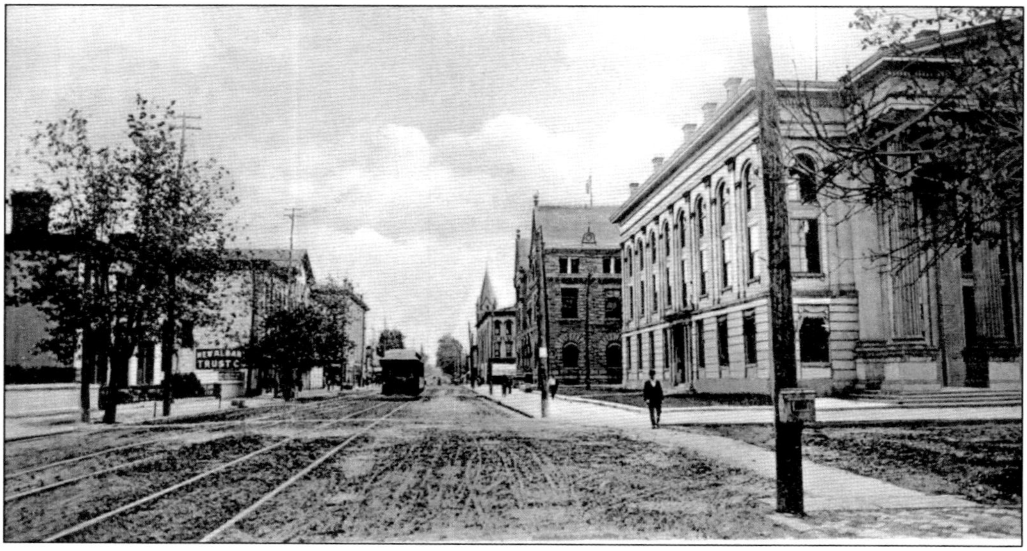

Spring Street Looking East from State Street. A variety of both civic and commercial structures are shown in this postcard from about 1905. On the left side of the card is the Floyd County Jail, which was built by Isaac P. Smith in 1859. The Floyd County Courthouse is on the right. The streets appear to be unpaved in this view, and streetcar tracks are clearly visible. A mule-drawn street railway system was established in 1867, turning to electric power for the same system in 1893. The street railway system was abolished in 1945.

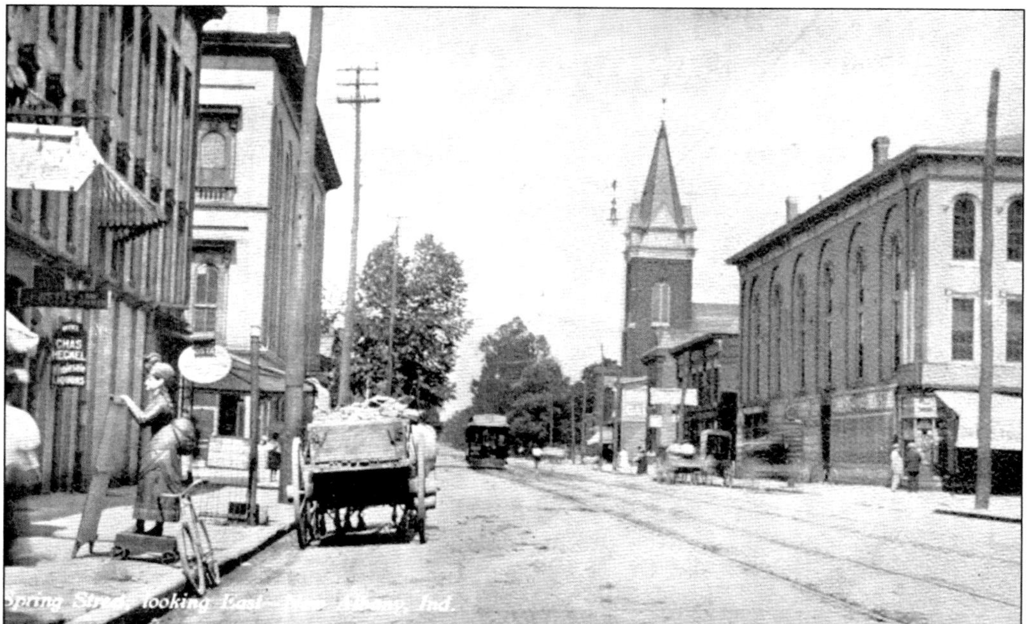

Spring Street Looking East from Pearl Street. P. Vernia's Masonic building and the 1866 Opera House are shown on the left side. The Ledger Block building is on the right, as is the former St. Mark's Church building, which has since been replaced with a modern structure. This postcard is from about 1910.

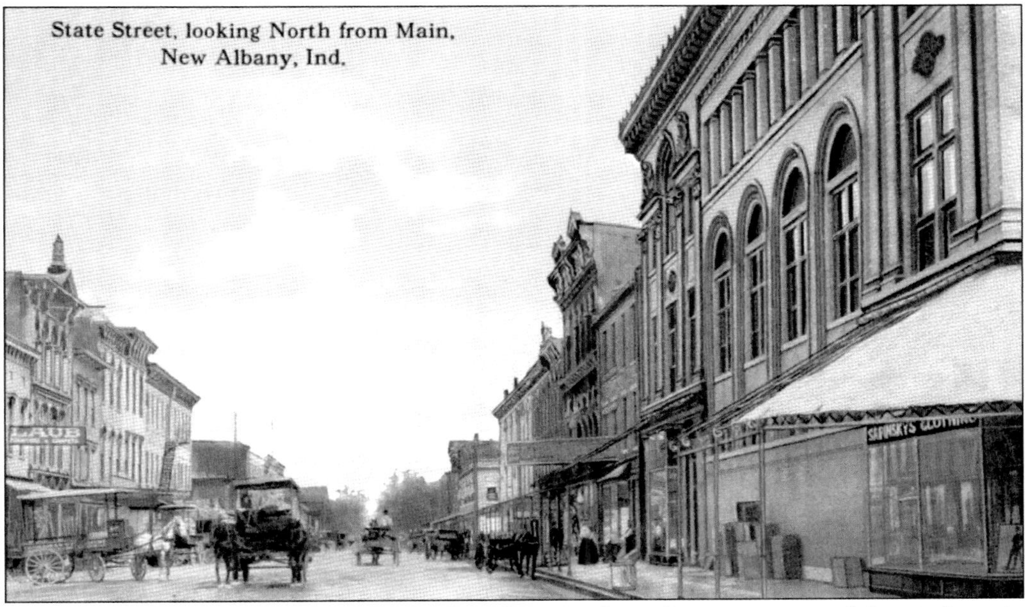

STATE STREET LOOKING NORTH FROM MAIN STREET. State Street was one of the city's main commercial streets in 1910, as it is today. This view shows State Street looking north from Main Street. The 1897 Sapinsky building, built by S. Day & Sons, is shown on the right.

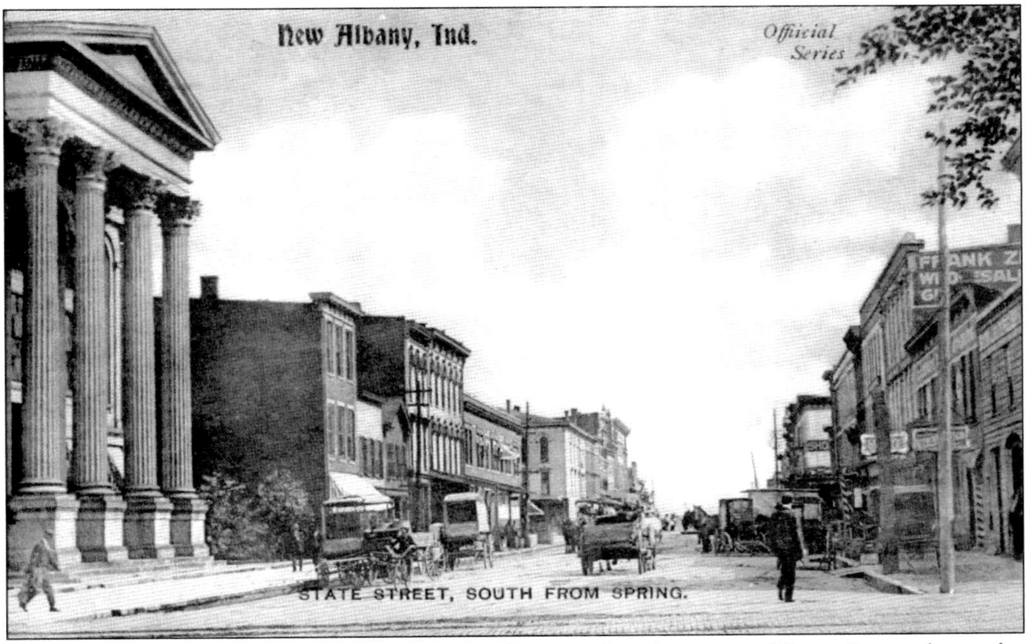

STATE STREET LOOKING SOUTH FROM SPRING STREET. Another view of State Street shows the Floyd County Courthouse on the left and the Frank Zinsmeister and Co. Wholesale Grocery on the right. This card was created for the city's 1913 centennial.

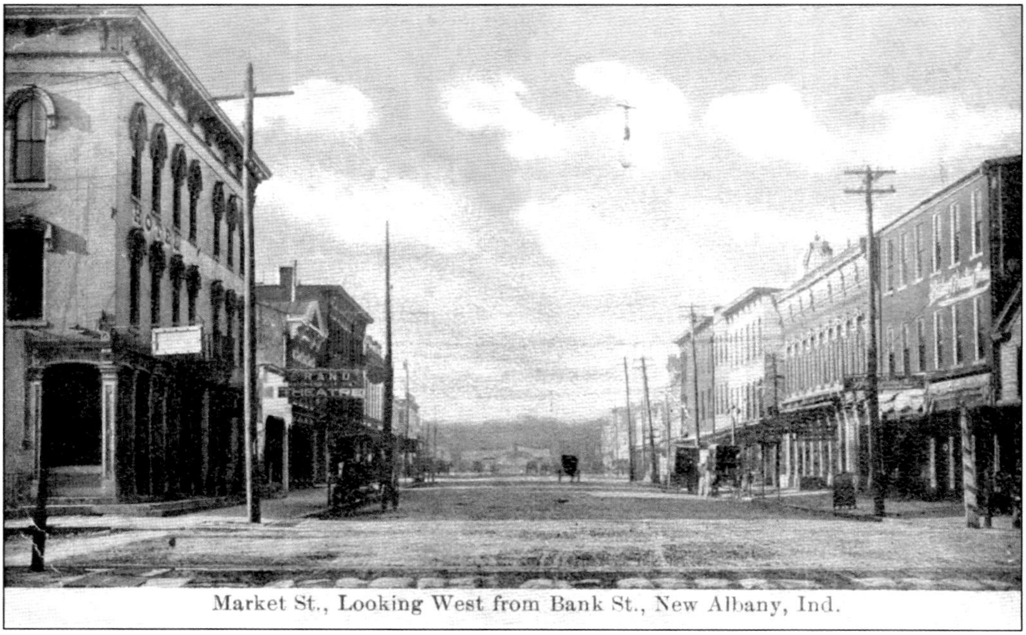

MARKET STREET LOOKING WEST FROM BANK STREET. In the foreground of the left side of this postcard is the Ashland Hotel, and next to it is the original Grand Theater building, which was designed by Louisville, Kentucky, firm Joseph and Joseph. This postcard is from 1910.

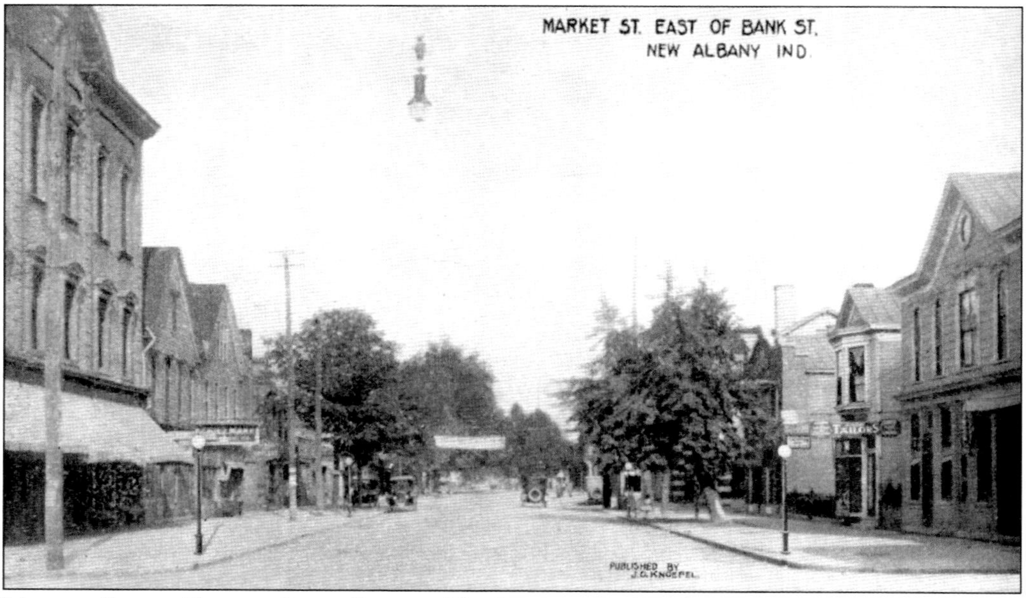

MARKET STREET EAST OF BANK STREET. The International Order of Odd Fellows still meets in the 1878 building shown on the left-hand side of this 1920 card. The IOOF is the New Albany Lodge No. 1, the first Odd Fellows lodge in Indiana.

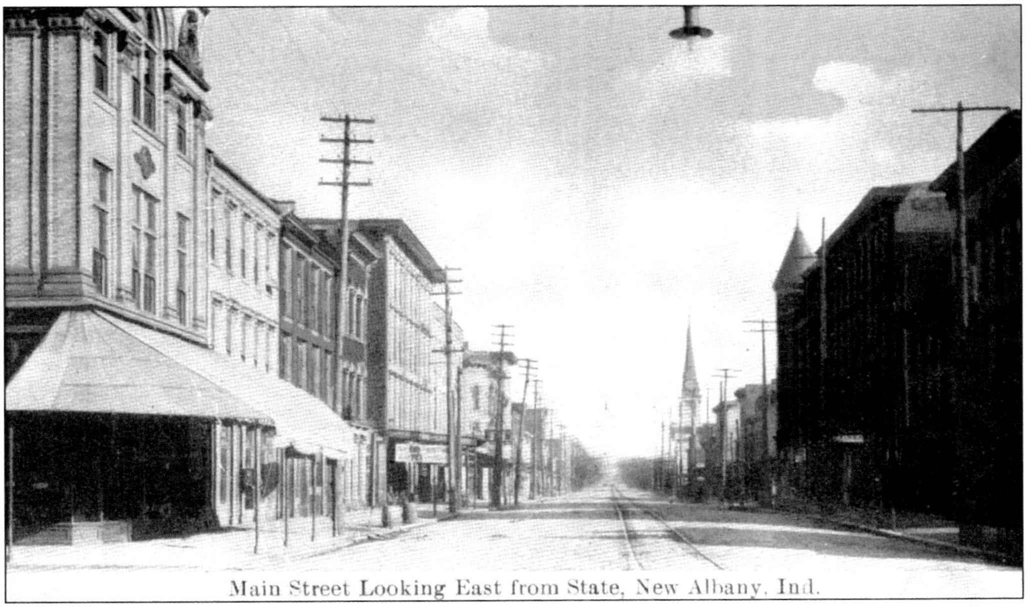

Main Street Looking East from State Street. This 1910 view of downtown New Albany shows the Sapinsky building on the left and the 1868 Clapp Block building on the right, along with the 1822 Dr. Clapp house, the Kerrigan Theater, and the YMCA. The steeple of Second Baptist Church or, more colloquially, the "town clock church," can be seen on the right. In this image, the church has its original steeple, which was destroyed by a lightning strike in 1914 and never replaced.

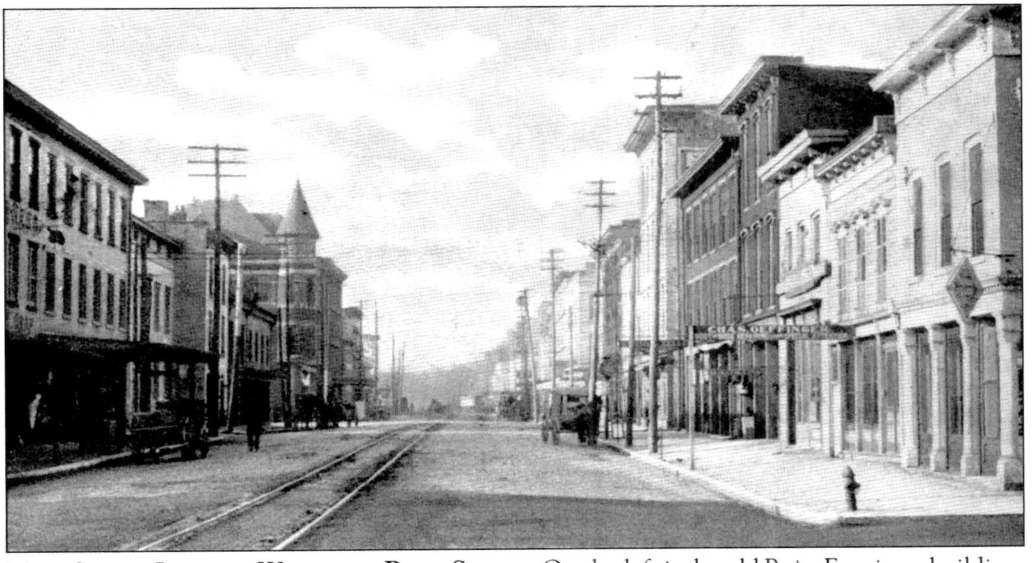

Main Street Looking West from Bank Street. On the left is the old Reisz Furniture building, which at the time of this postcard housed the Frank A. Kraft Funeral Director and Embalmer business. Farther down the street is the YMCA building, which has since been demolished. On the right, the two-story John E. Noyes building is shown, along with the Charles Oeffinger Boot and Shoe Repair business, in this 1910 postcard.

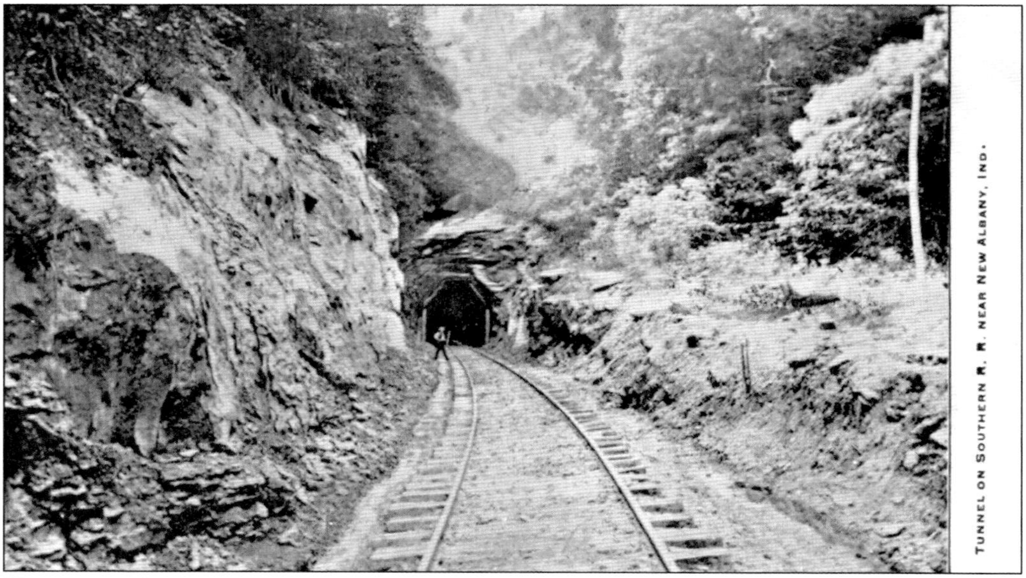

TUNNEL ON SOUTHERN RAILROAD. The Louisville-New Albany-St. Louis-Airline Railroad ran through this tunnel, which was 4,689 feet long, and took the train through the Knobs. The tunnel, shown in this 1905 postcard, was built as part of a railroad route, and was completed in 1881 at a cost of $1 million. The route was opened to Milltown the next year.

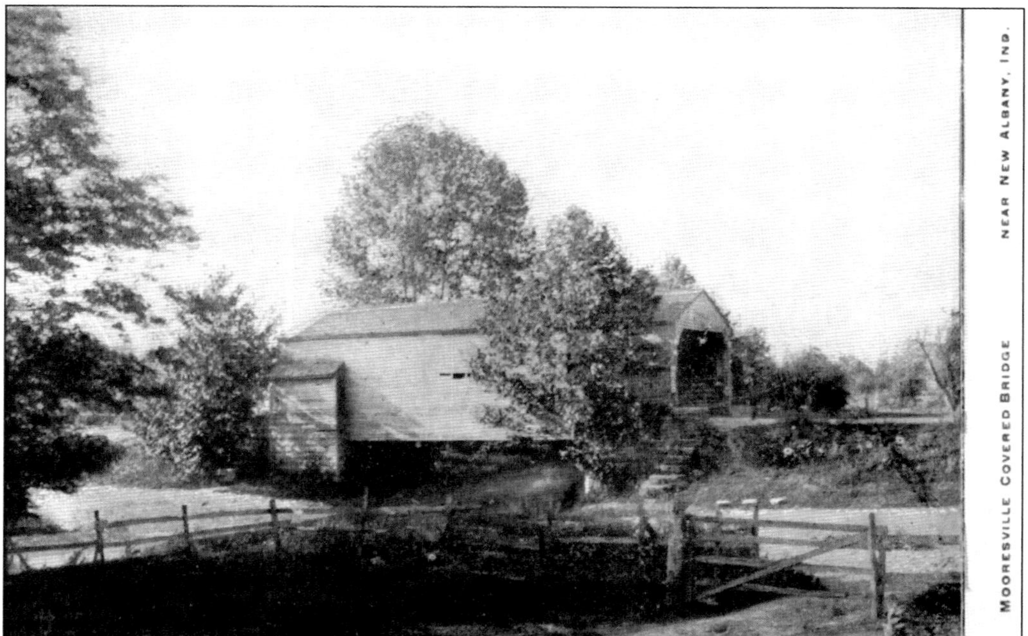

MOORESVILLE COVERED BRIDGE. Historical sources indicate that the Mooresville Covered Bridge was the first covered bridge built in the state of Indiana. It was a double-tunnel bridge, which could accommodate two vehicles at a time. It was built on Paoli Pike in 1820 and demolished in 1913. Mooresville was later renamed Floyds Knobs. This postcard is from about 1905.

Two

Public Buildings and Meeting Houses

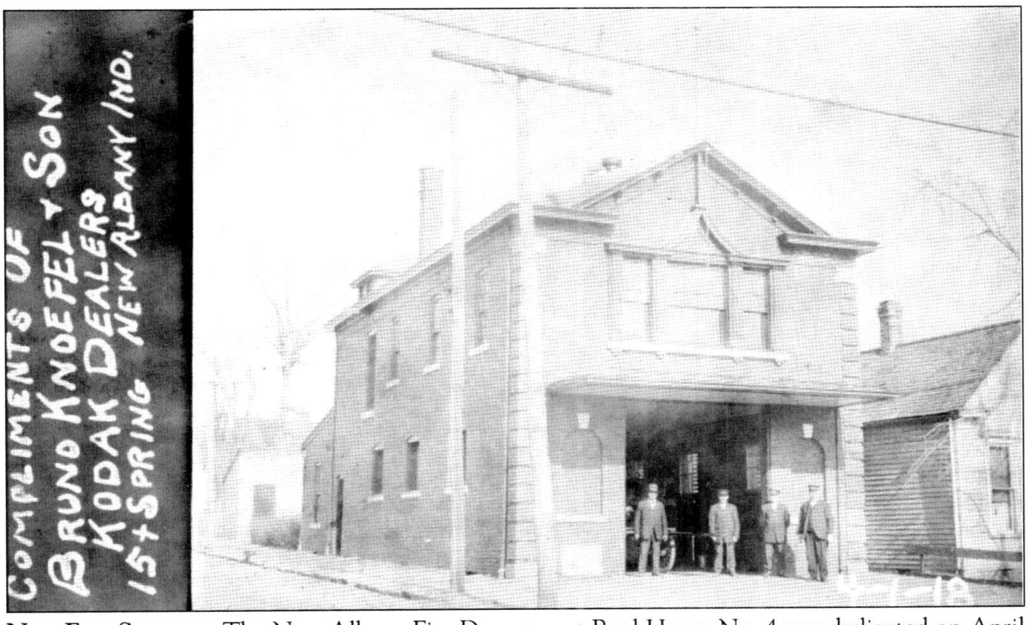

New Fire Station. The New Albany Fire Department Reel House No. 4 was dedicated on April 1, 1918, to replace a previous firehouse, which was destroyed in the tornado of 1917. The building is located on the southeast corner of State and Union Streets. This image shows a group of four firefighters standing in front of it. The card was used to advertise the drugstore of Bruno Knoefel and Son, who were also Kodak dealers, on the northwest corner of East 15th and Spring Streets.

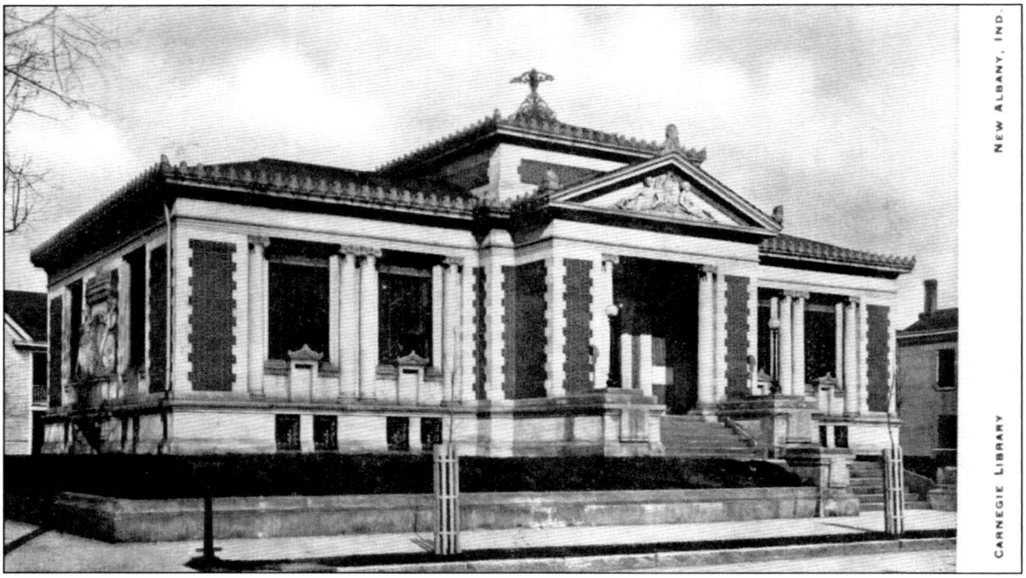

CARNEGIE LIBRARY. New Albany's grand Carnegie Library, shown in this 1905 postcard, was a source of great civic pride. It was built between 1902 and 1904 at 201 East Spring Street in the Neoclassical style. Andrew Carnegie gave $35,000 toward the construction of the building, and the New Albany City Council contributed the site for the building and $3,500 annually toward the project. Paul Emil Mosemiller of New Albany was the architect. The building housed the New Albany-Floyd County Public Library until November 1969. It underwent an extensive restoration in 1998. Today, it is the Carnegie Center for Art and History, a division of the New Albany-Floyd County Public Library.

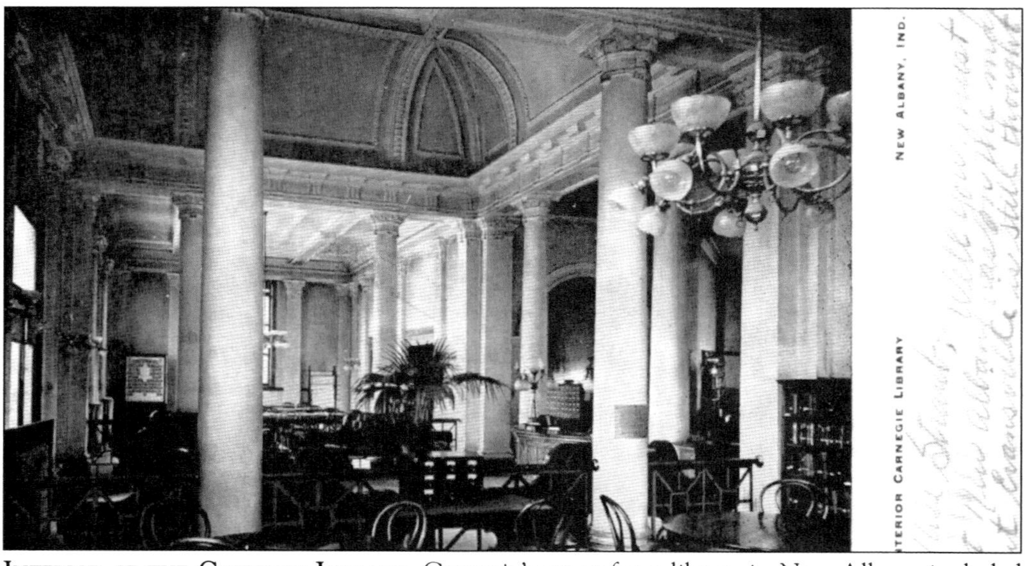

INTERIOR OF THE CARNEGIE LIBRARY. Carnegie's grant for a library in New Albany included $5,000 for furnishings, book stacks, and other interior equipment. This image of the interior, from about 1905, shows the rotunda, including the skylight and columns. The library was furnished in the Arts and Crafts style popular at the time.

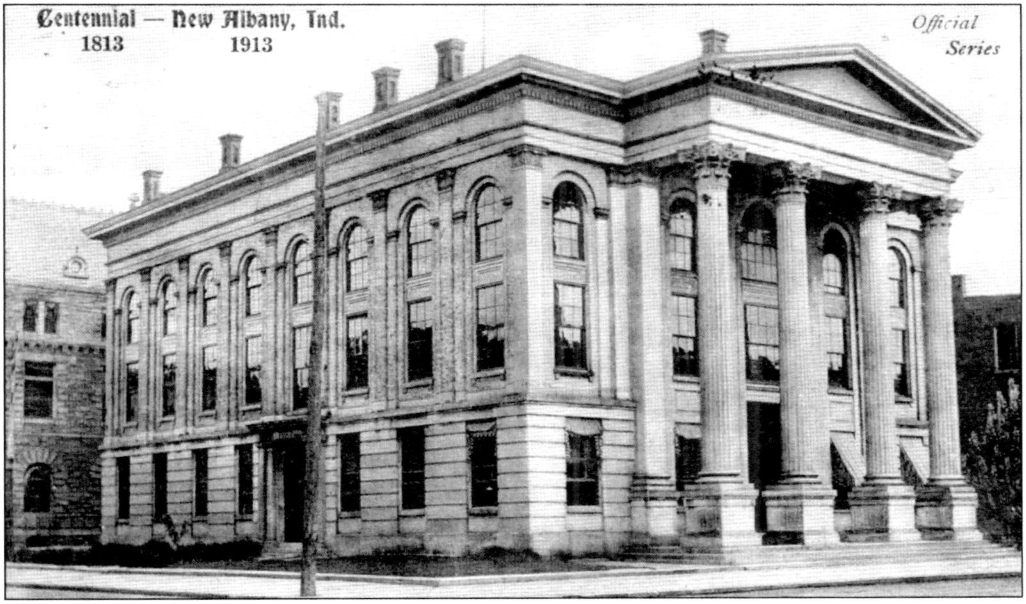

FLOYD COUNTY COURTHOUSE. Among downtown's most significant losses was the demolition of the Floyd County Courthouse. The Greek Revival building was constructed in 1866 at the southeast corner of Spring and State Streets of limestone from quarries in nearby Bedford, Indiana, at a cost of $127,700; it was the third courthouse for the county. The three-story building was demolished in 1963, and it was replaced by a bank on the site. City and County offices were moved to a new structure, still standing and used today, at Hauss Square and West Spring Street. It was the first municipal building in Indiana that combined city and county governments. This postcard is one created for the centennial in 1913.

GOVERNMENT BUILDING AND POST OFFICE. The three-story Federal Building was constructed in 1889 in the Romanesque Revival style at a cost of $100,000 on the southwest corner of Spring and Pearl Streets. Newspaper accounts indicate 5,000 people attended an opening reception in February 1889. It was demolished in 1970 and replaced by a separate U.S. Courthouse and a separate U.S. Post Office at different locations.

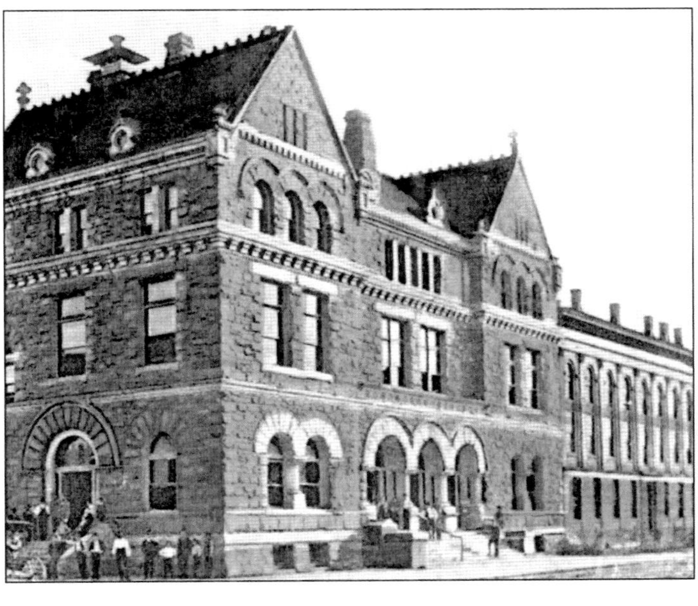

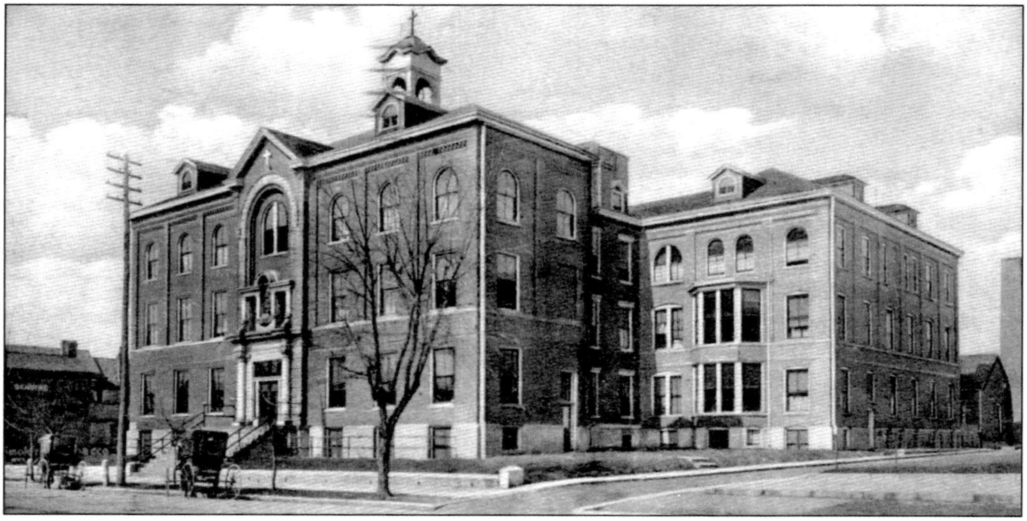

St. Edward Hospital. New Albany's first hospital was St. Edward Hospital, which was built by S. Day & Sons on the northeast corner of East Seventh and Spring Streets. When it opened in 1902, the hospital boasted 61 private rooms and 12 wards. The Rev. Edward M. Faller donated his personal funds to build the hospital. It was a city hospital, but run by a group of Catholic nuns who belonged to the sisters of St. Francis of the Perpetual Adoration. Its volume steadily increased, with the hospital treating 168 patients in 1902 and 11,353 in 1950. The building was transformed into the Providence Retirement Home in 1963 and today is a housing complex. This image is from 1913.

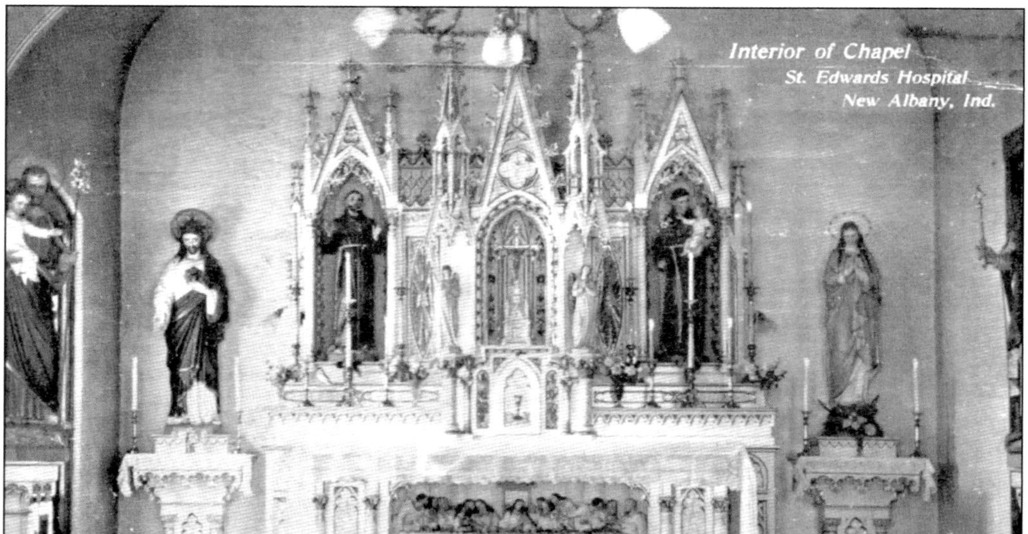

Interior of Chapel. Being a Catholic facility, St. Edward Hospital housed a small chapel for the use of patients and the sisters who ran the hospital. It seated about 50 people and was on the third floor of the building. A series of eight stained glass windows in the chapel depicted saints. This postcard is from about 1910.

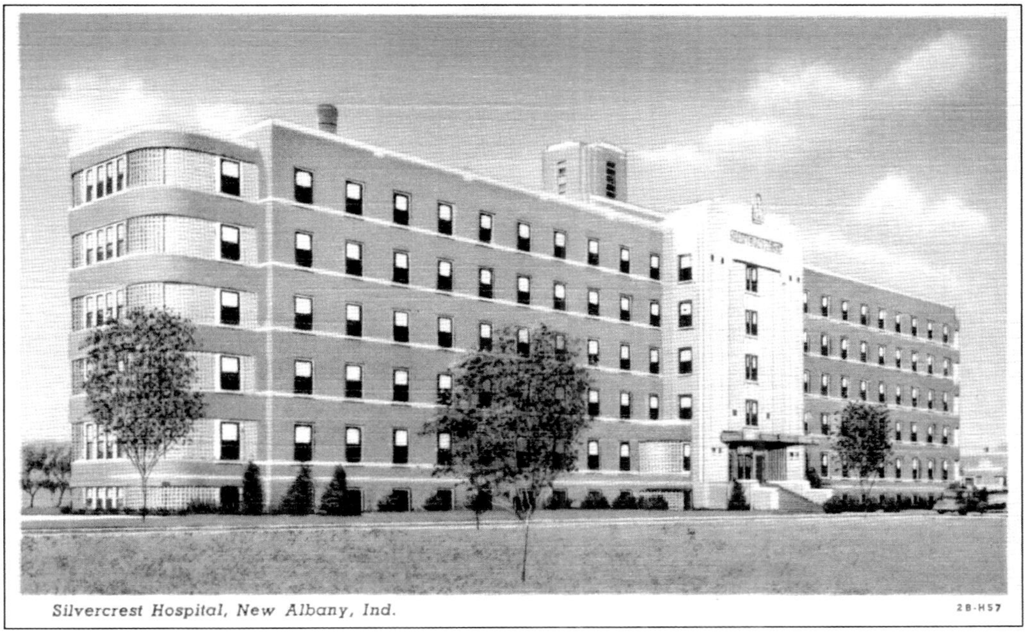

SILVERCREST SANITORIUM. Built in the Art Moderne style, the $1 million Silvercrest Sanitorium was completed in 1940 and could accommodate 150 patients. The hospital claimed to be one of the most modernly equipped hospitals of its kind in the U.S. The building is still in existence, but is no longer a tuberculosis hospital.

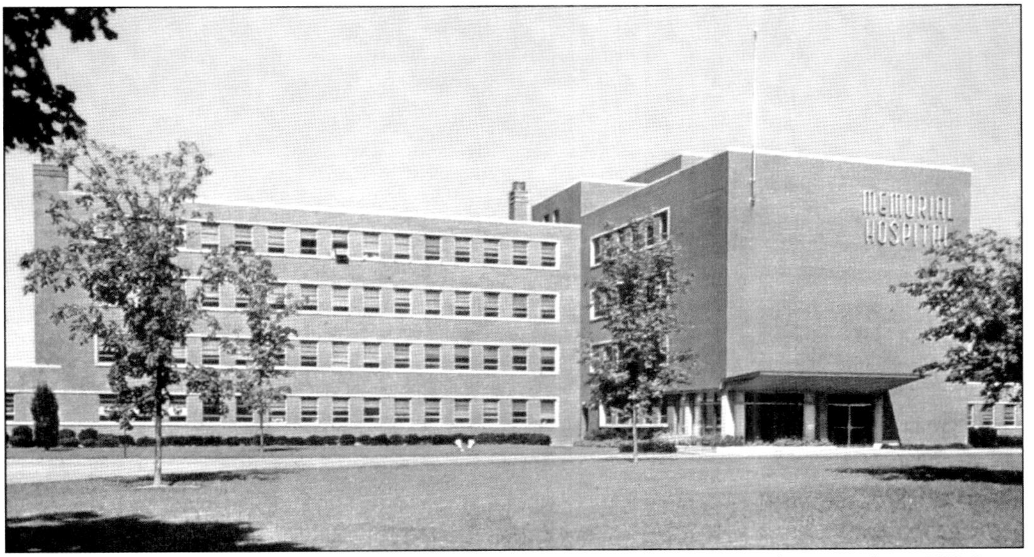

MEMORIAL HOSPITAL. Still serving the community today, Floyd Memorial Hospital at 1850 State Street began its life in 1953. A group of local businessmen began pushing for the construction of a county hospital in 1946 and raised funds from the public to put towards the construction. Newspaper accounts indicate that the public donated $265,000 to see the hospital come to fruition. The New Albany architectural firm Hawkins and Walker designed the building with future growth in mind.

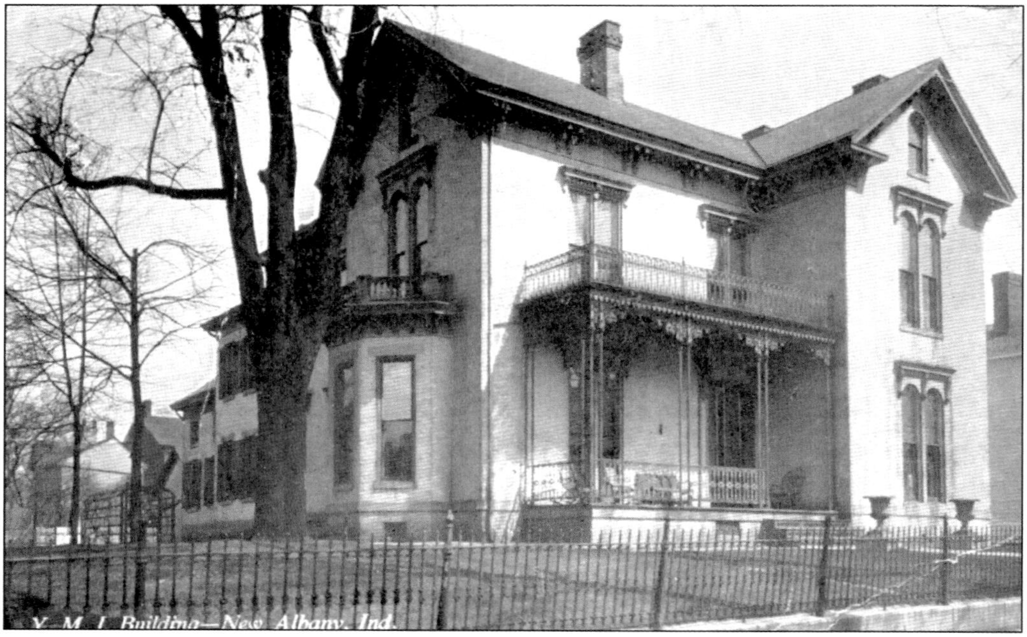

YMI BUILDING. The Young Men's Institution building was home to a Catholic organization at 805 East Main Street. The structure was originally built as a home to William A. Culbertson, who was the son of William S. Culbertson, builder of the Culbertson Mansion. The house was later home to the John F. Gebhart family. The Knights of Columbus razed the house in 1958 to create room for a parking lot for their own facility at the rear of the lot. This postcard is from about 1910.

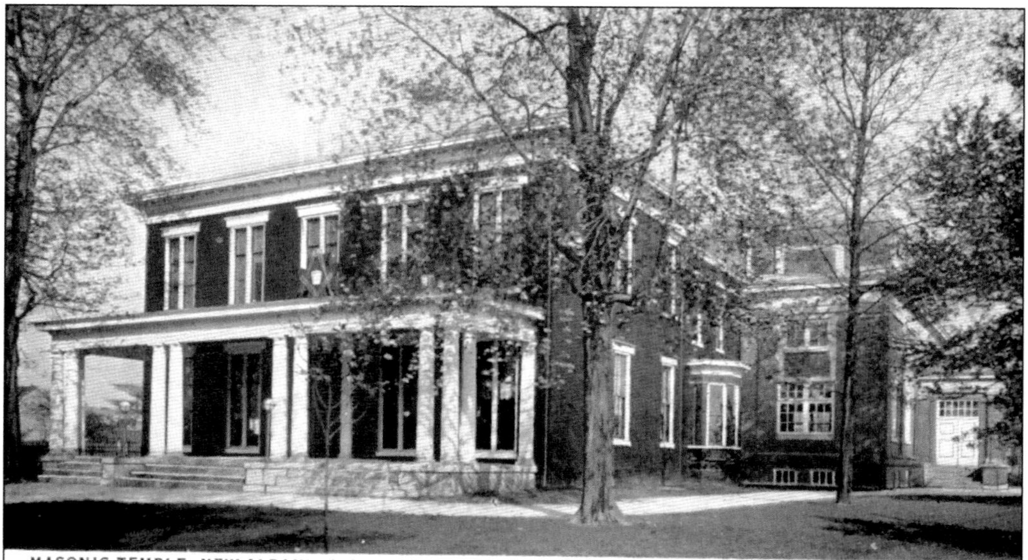

MASONIC TEMPLE. Formerly known as the Conner-Woodward house, this structure became the Masonic Temple for New Albany in 1916. It is located at 805 East Market Street and is still used as a Masonic Temple today. This postcard is from about 1920.

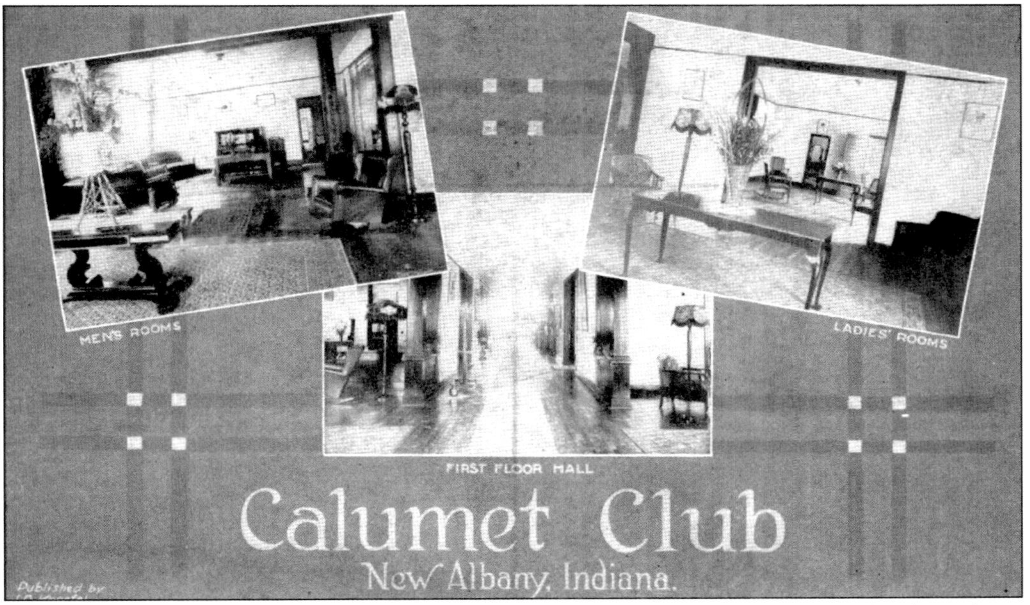

CALUMET CLUB. At its height in the 1920s, the Calumet Club had a total membership of 800 men aged 18 and older. The club completed a new meeting facility at 1614 East Spring Street in 1920 at a cost of $60,000. This card shows three images of the interior, including, left to right: the men's rooms, first floor hall, and ladies' rooms. The building included a bowling alley and basketball court. The building is still standing. This postcard was created shortly after the building was completed.

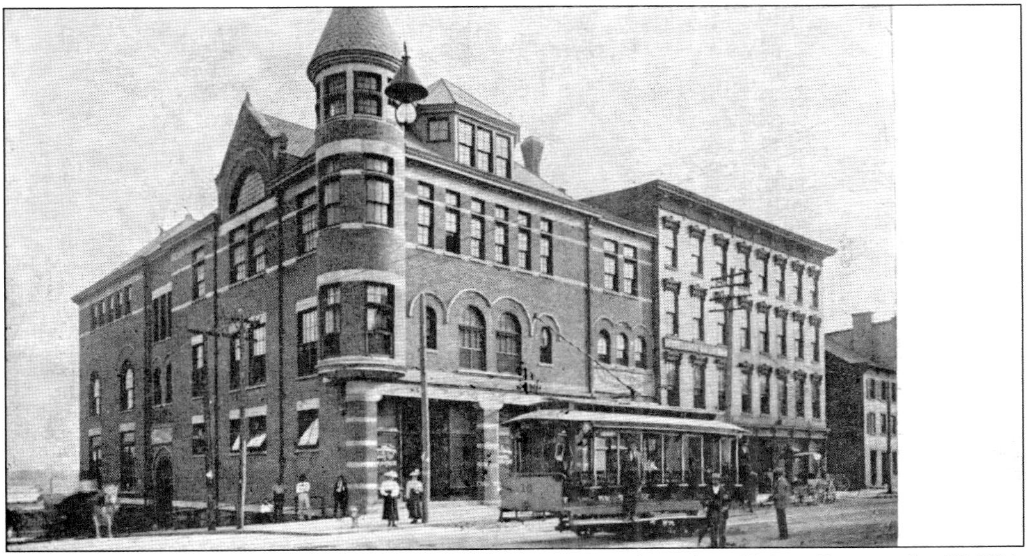

THE YMCA BUILDING. Located on the southwest corner of Pearl and Main Streets, the YMCA building was constructed in 1893. The building included two gyms, a swimming pool, reading rooms, a chapel, and dressing rooms. In 1922, the state purchased the building for the Indiana National Guard. It was razed in 1954. The Guard occupied the building for a short time and it was subsequently used by Goodwill Industries

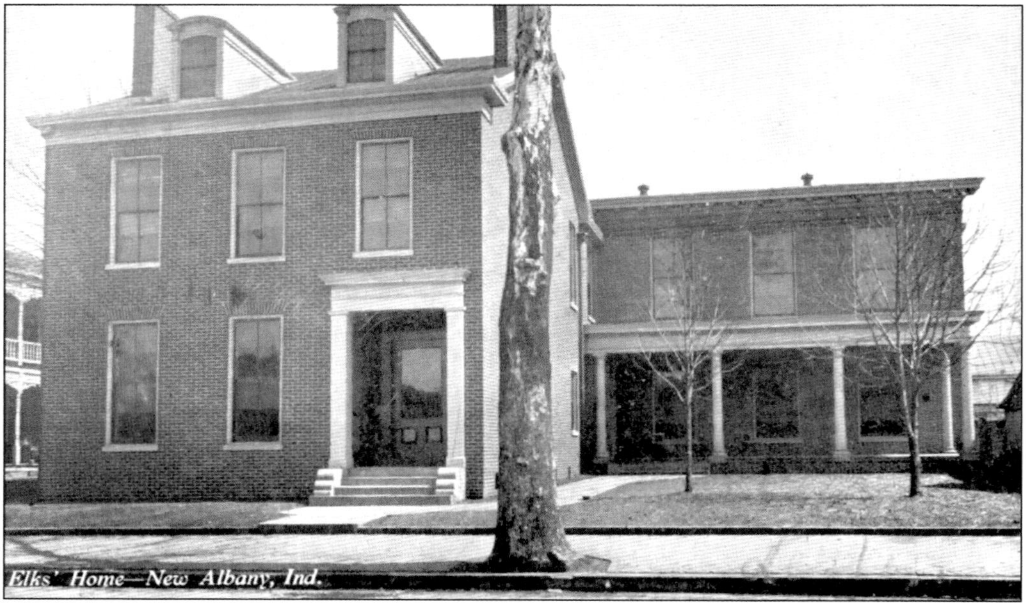

ELKS' HOME. This house at 430 Pearl Street had a notable history with ties to at least one of New Albany's most famous residents. William S. Culbertson lived in it until his mansion was completed in 1869. It later became the Elks' Lodge, but was demolished in 1921 for a new Elks building. This postcard is from about 1910.

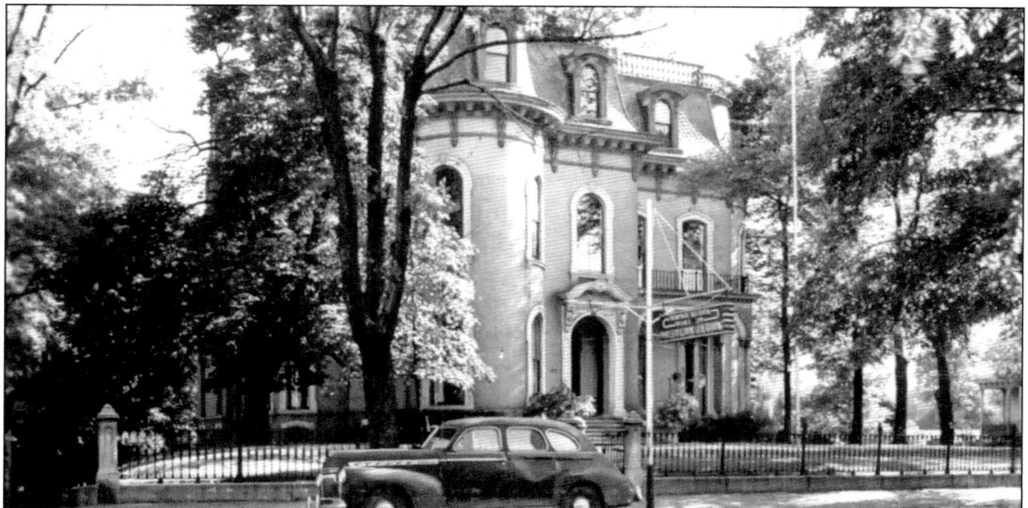

AMERICAN LEGION POST #28. The Culbertson Mansion State Historic Site is the current name for this structure, which was the American Legion Post when this card was created in 1947. It is located at the southwest corner of East Tenth and Main Streets. The home, in the Second Empire style, was built for William S. Culbertson in 1869, and became the residence of John S. McDonald and family in 1899. It was the McDonald family home until the American Legion bought it in 1946. Historic New Albany Inc. bought the house in 1964 and deeded it to the state of Indiana in 1976.

Three

Churches and Cemeteries

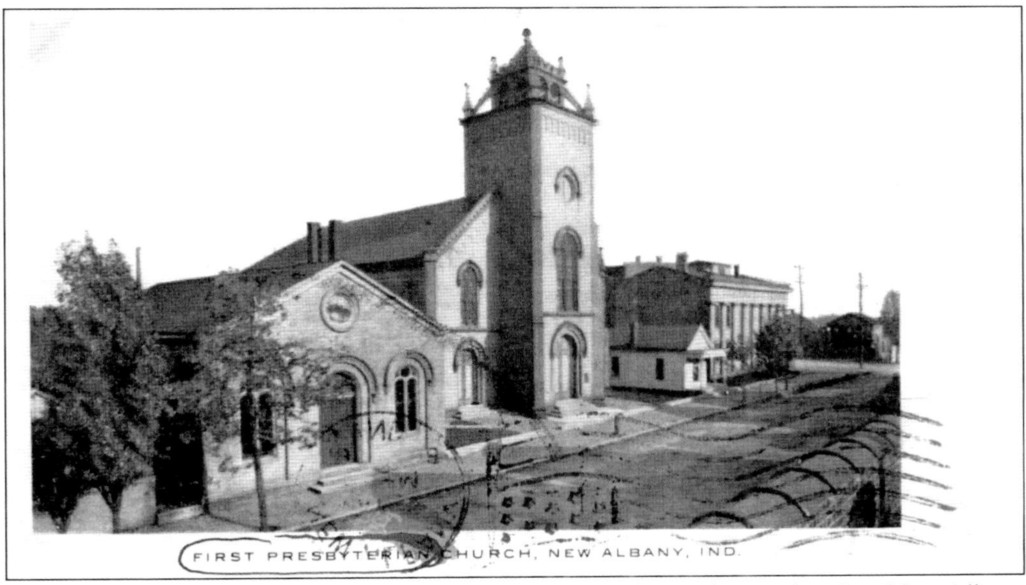

First Presbyterian Church. The Presbyterians were the first to form a church in New Albany after its settlement. First Presbyterian Church was established as the Union Church in 1816, with its name changed the next year to First Presbyterian Church of New Albany. The building shown in this 1905 postcard was completed in 1854 on the east side of Bank Street between Main and Market Streets and heavily damaged by fire in 1898. The building was restored in the same style but with a shorter steeple after the fire. In 1969, First Presbyterian merged with Hutchinson Memorial Presbyterian Church at East Thirteenth and Elm Streets to later become St. John United Presbyterian Church. The First Presbyterian Church building was razed and the space used as a parking lot.

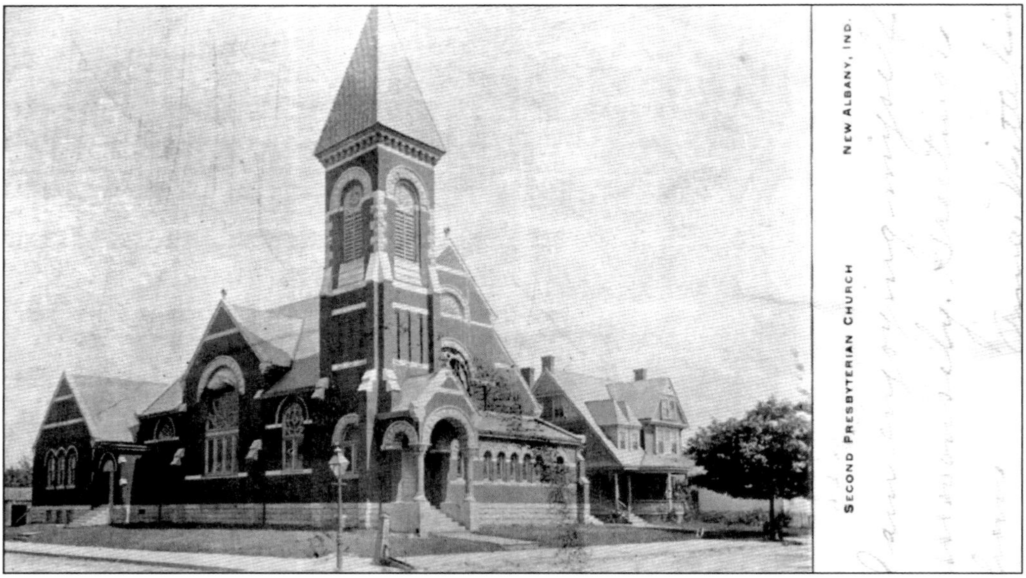

SECOND PRESBYTERIAN CHURCH. Established in 1837 with 103 former First Presbyterian members, Second Presbyterian Church's first permanent building was a Greek Revival structure located on the southeast corner of East Third and Main Streets. The congregation worshipped there until 1889. Its new church, shown in this 1905 postcard, was completed in 1890 on the northeast corner of East Thirteenth and Elm Streets in the Romanesque Revival style and is today known as St. John United Presbyterian Church. The former church building in downtown is now Second Baptist Church.

THIRD PRESBYTERIAN CHURCH. Organized in 1853 by 24 members from Second Presbyterian Church, Third Presbyterian Church built its most notable structure in 1868 on the northwest corner of East Ninth and Spring Streets in the Norman Gothic style. The congregation remained in the church until 1917, when Second and Third Presbyterian merged to create Hutchinson Presbyterian Church, named for Third Presbyterian's long-time pastor, Dr. Charles Hutchinson. The newly formed congregation chose to meet at East Thirteenth and Elm Streets, which was then the building of Second Presbyterian. In 1929, the name was changed to Hutchinson Memorial Presbyterian Church. First Presbyterian Church joined the two churches in 1969, and the name was changed to St. John United Presbyterian. This postcard is from about 1905.

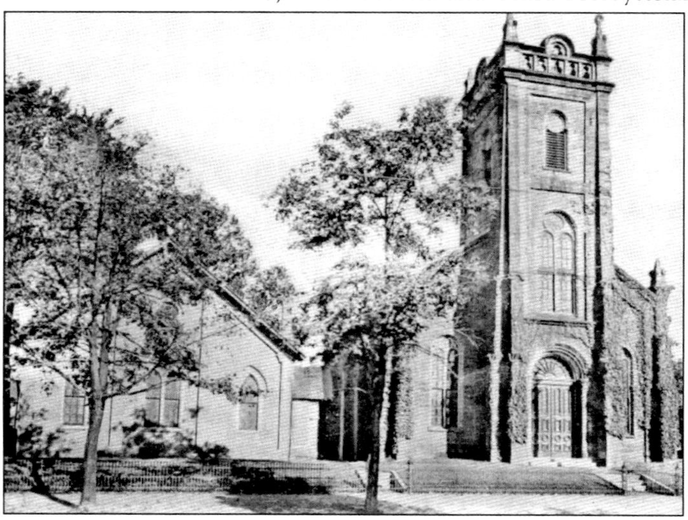

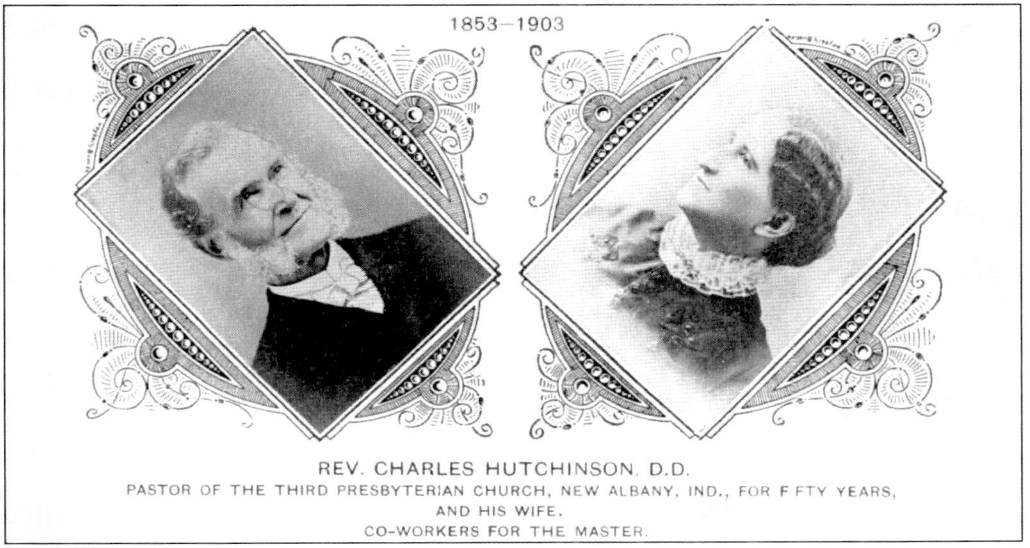

REV. CHARLES HUTCHINSON, D.D. The Rev. Charles Hutchinson was pastor of Third Presbyterian Church for 50 years, serving from 1853 to 1903. When Second and Third Presbyterian churches merged in 1917, the name of the new merged church was Hutchinson Presbyterian Church to honor Rev. Hutchinson.

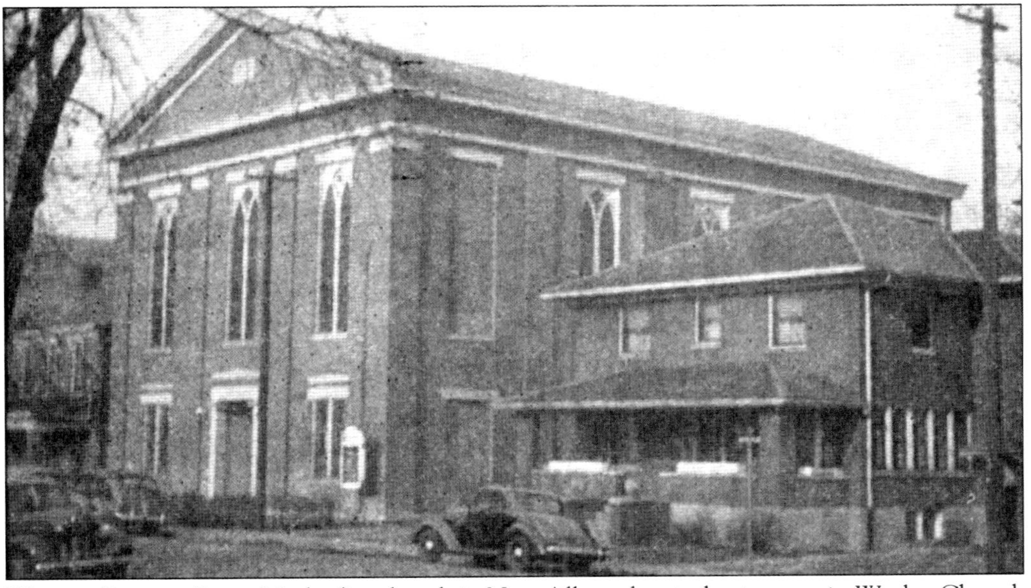

WESLEY CHAPEL. Every Methodist church in New Albany has its beginnings in Wesley Chapel, which was formed in 1817. Its first home was a one-story wood frame building on Lafayette Street that was used for its first decade. A one-story brick structure on the southeast corner of West First and Market Streets was affectionately called "the old ship" and used until 1854. The structure shown in this 1950s-era postcard was built in 1854 at West Second and Market Streets. The parsonage is seen on the right. The building shown here was demolished in 1964 and a new church built on State Street, where it is today.

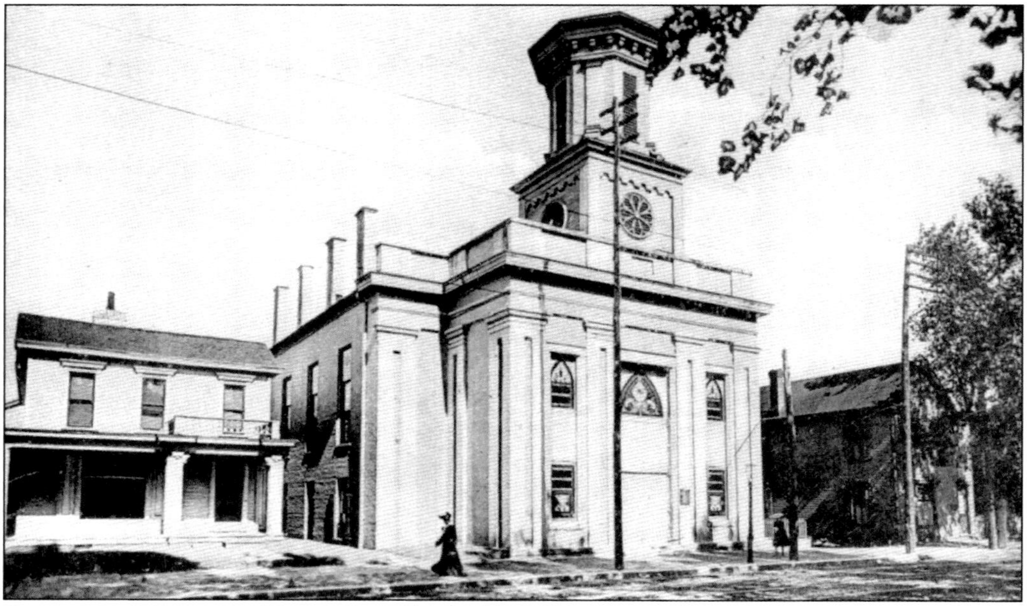

CENTENERY METHODIST EPISCOPAL. The building shown in this 1905 postcard, located on the northeast corner of East Third and Spring Streets, is the only structure that Centenery has ever used. The church was founded in 1839, exactly 100 years after the beginning of the Methodist faith in England, hence the name "Centenery." The building was dedicated in 1841 and has seen many modifications since then, including the loss of a steeple that was struck by lightning on May 5, 1900, and never replaced. The church's parsonage at that time is seen on the left-hand side of the postcard.

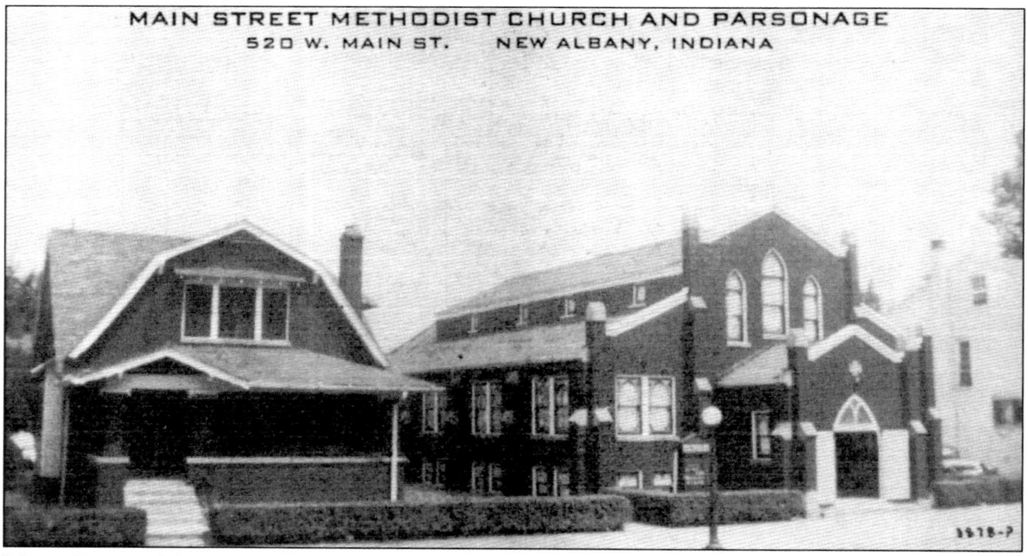

MAIN STREET METHODIST CHURCH AND PARSONAGE. This particular church was established in 1850 as "The Western Charge." The building shown in this postcard was built in 1923 in the 500 block of West Main Street after a 1922 fire destroyed the previous church. This image is from about 1940.

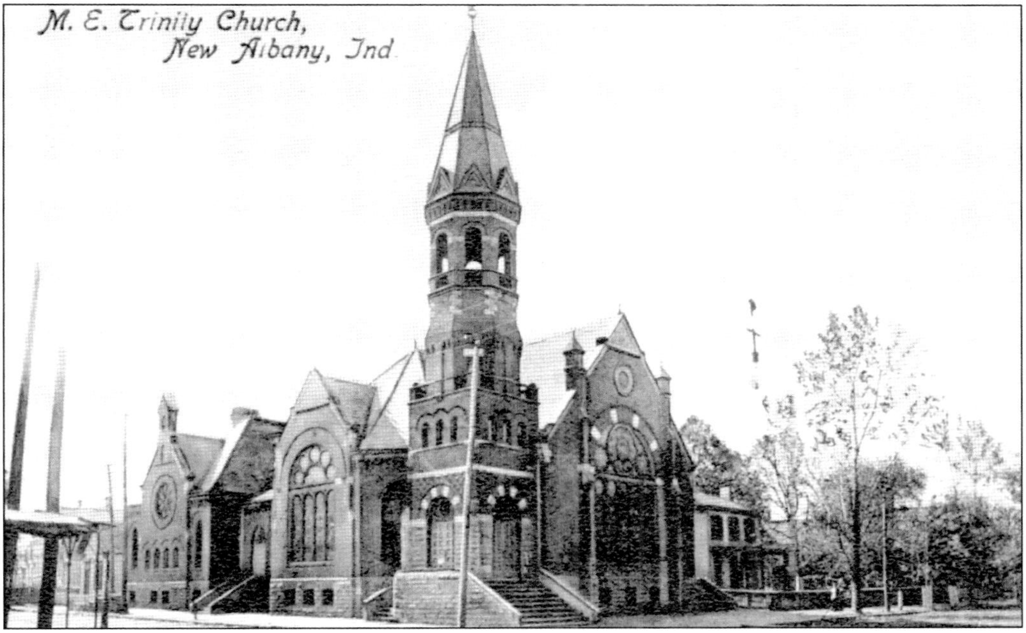

TRINITY METHODIST EPISCOPAL CHURCH. This 1905 image shows the former building of Trinity Methodist Episcopal Church located on the southwest corner of East Thirteenth and Spring Streets. The church began in 1854 as the John Street Church just a few blocks away at East Eleventh and Spring Streets. The John Street Church merged with two others in 1890 to become Trinity. The building shown in this picture has since been demolished and the church moved to Charlestown Road.

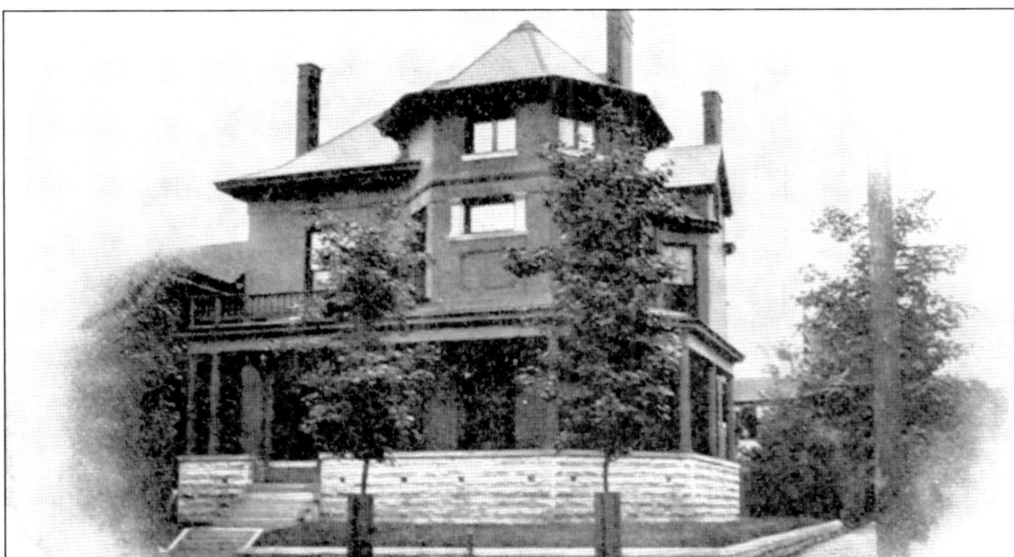

TRINITY PARSONAGE. The former John Street Church site was used to build a parsonage for Trinity in 1901 on the southeast corner of East Eleventh and Spring Streets. The parsonage is still standing, but is no longer church property. This postcard is from about 1905.

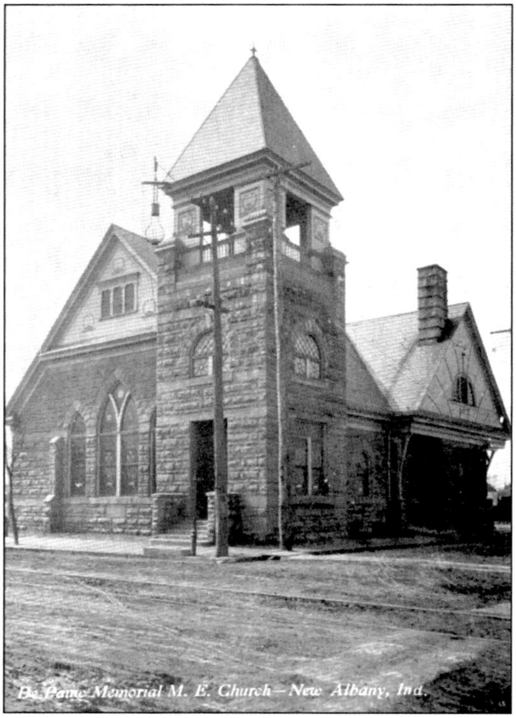

DePauw Memorial Methodist Episcopal Church. This 1910 image shows the former building of Jennie DePauw Memorial Methodist Episcopal Church on the southwest corner of Beeler and Vincennes Streets. The church was founded as the Kingsley Mission. Washington C. DePauw purchased the lot and relocated the former German Evangelical Church building to the site. That building burned. The building shown in this postcard was built in 1901 and then burned in 1917, the same year a devastating tornado tore through New Albany. The church's building committee cleaned brick from the local New Albany Woolen Mills that was destroyed in the tornado to use in building their new facility. The new building was completed and dedicated in 1919 and the name changed to DePauw Memorial Methodist Church.

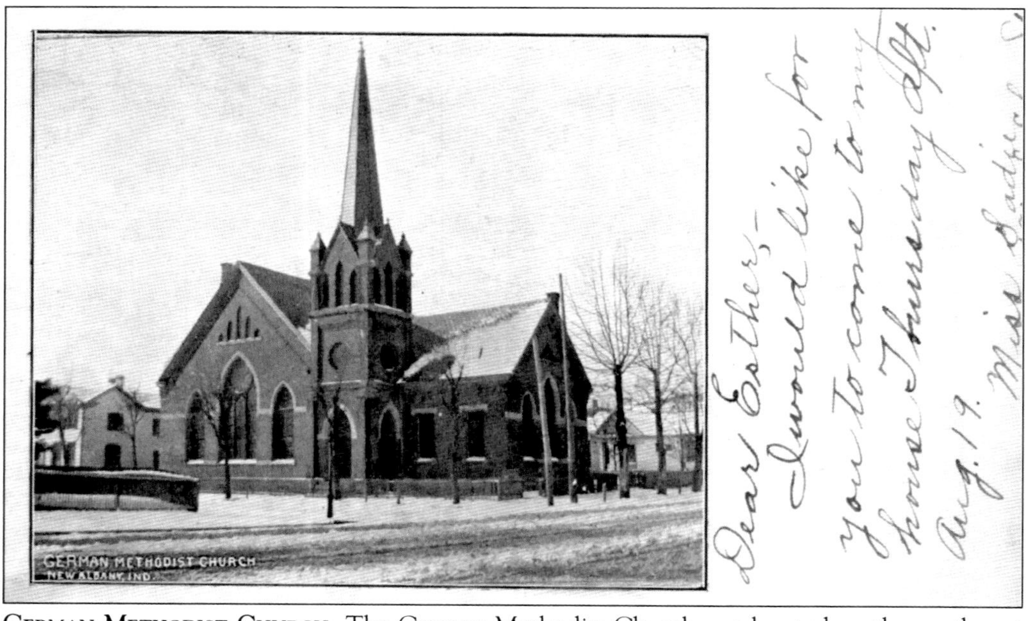

German Methodist Church. The German Methodist Church was located on the southwest corner of East Fifth and Spring Streets. The building shown here in this 1905 postcard was the church's second and built in 1889. Its name was later changed to Calvary Methodist Church. In 1955, the congregation voted to merge with Centenery Methodist, and a chapel dedicated to Calvary was created inside the Centenery building.

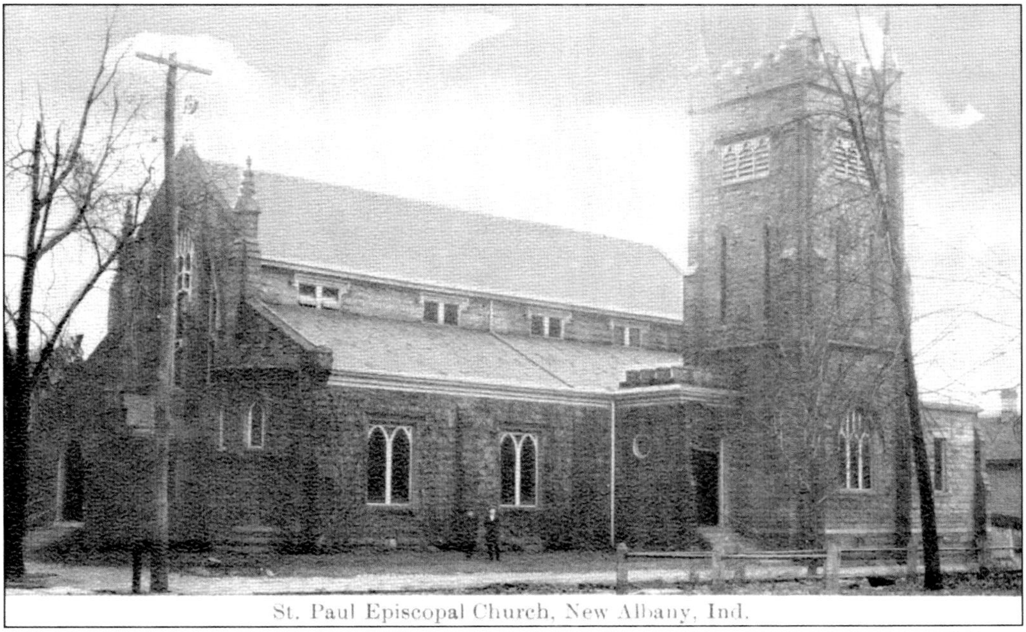

St. Paul's Episcopal Church. The first Episcopal church in Indiana was formed in New Albany in 1834, and its first building constructed in 1839 on the south side of Spring Street, just east of the alley between Bank and Third Streets. A new building project brought the church to East Main Street near Sixth Street, and the church moved into the space in 1865. It was replaced by the church building shown here at the southwest corner of East Eleventh and Market Streets, which was completed in 1896. It is still used today for the church. This postcard is from about 1910.

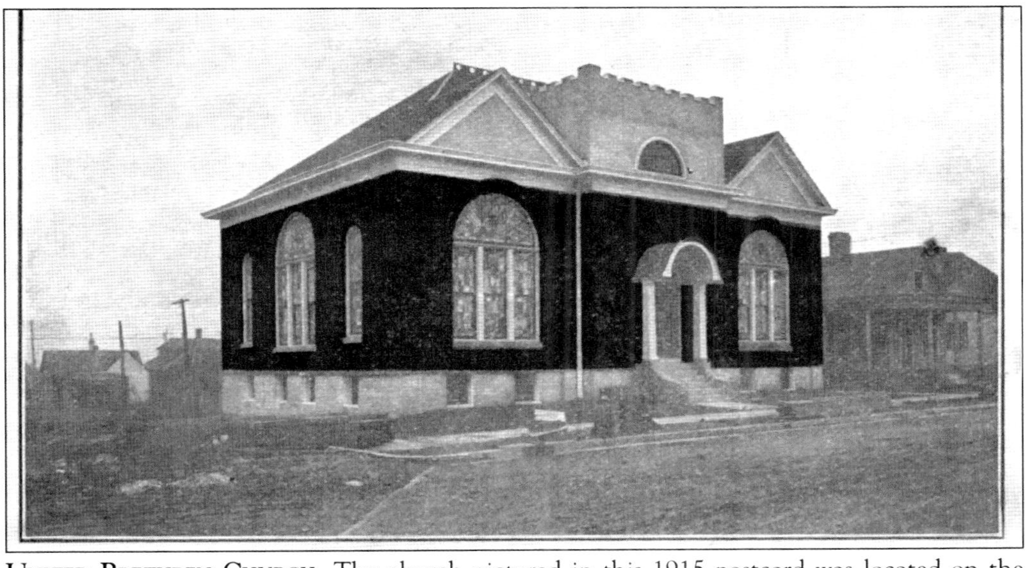

United Brethren Church. The church pictured in this 1915 postcard was located on the southwest corner of Silver and Elm Streets. It was established in 1911 and its building dedicated in 1914. In February 1949, a fire destroyed the building, and it was replaced by a new building in 1950. Today, it is home to Silver Street United Methodist Church.

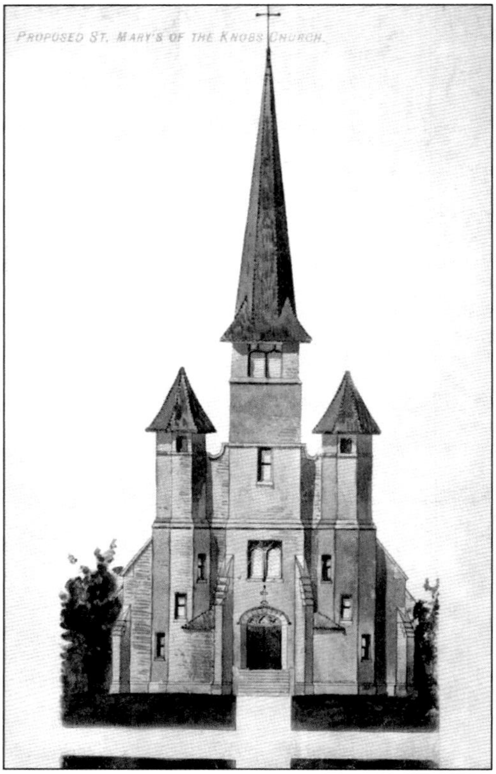

PROPOSED ST. MARY OF THE KNOBS CHURCH. Mass was celebrated for the first time in the Knobs area in 1792 in private homes. The first Catholic chapel was a log structure built in the early 1820s. In 1836, the first resident pastor, Fr. Louis Francis Neyron, came to Floyd County. The postcard shows the 1908 St. Mary, which was the congregation's third building.

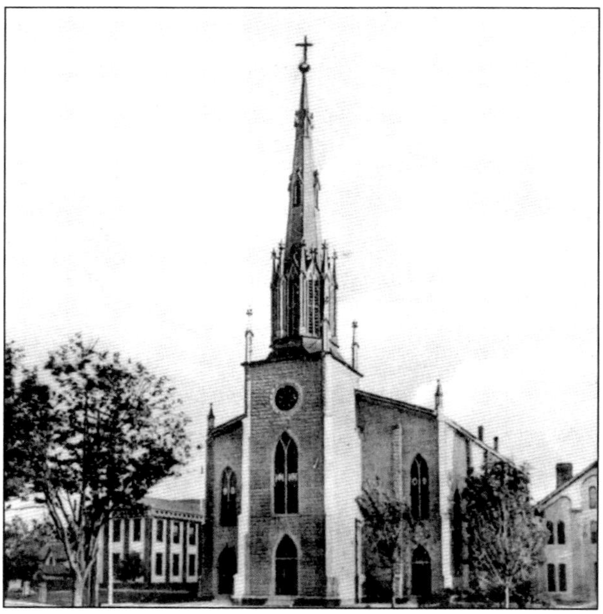

HOLY TRINITY CATHOLIC CHURCH. Founded in 1836 with the arrival of Fr. Neyron, Holy Trinity was the first Catholic parish in New Albany. The Gothic Revival structure shown in this postcard at the southeast corner of East Seventh and Market Streets was built under his leadership and opened for services in 1852. The church had only six pastors in its history. The building burned in December 1975, and its membership merged with St. Mary's of the Annunciation, one block away in New Albany. This postcard is from about 1905.

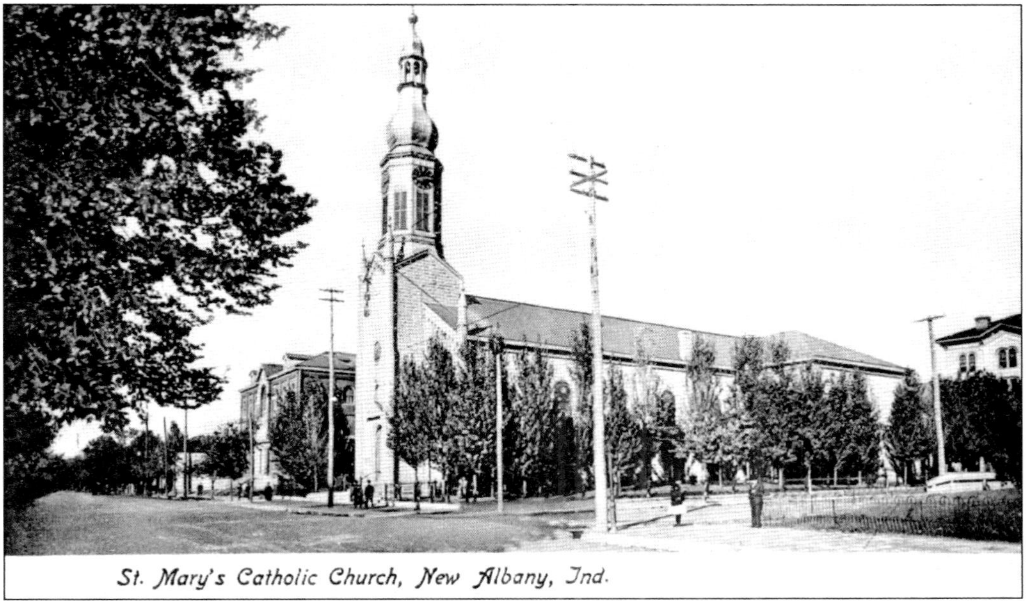

ST. MARY'S OF THE ANNUNCIATION. In 1852, the German-speaking members of Holy Trinity petitioned the bishop in Vincennes, Indiana, to organize a parish of their own. The next year, St. Mary's of the Annunciation was established. The newly formed congregation met in the frame structure formerly used by Holy Trinity until their present building was completed in 1858 at the northwest corner of East Eighth and Spring Streets. In 1886, a renovation added the transcepts which are now part of the building. This postcard is from about 1905.

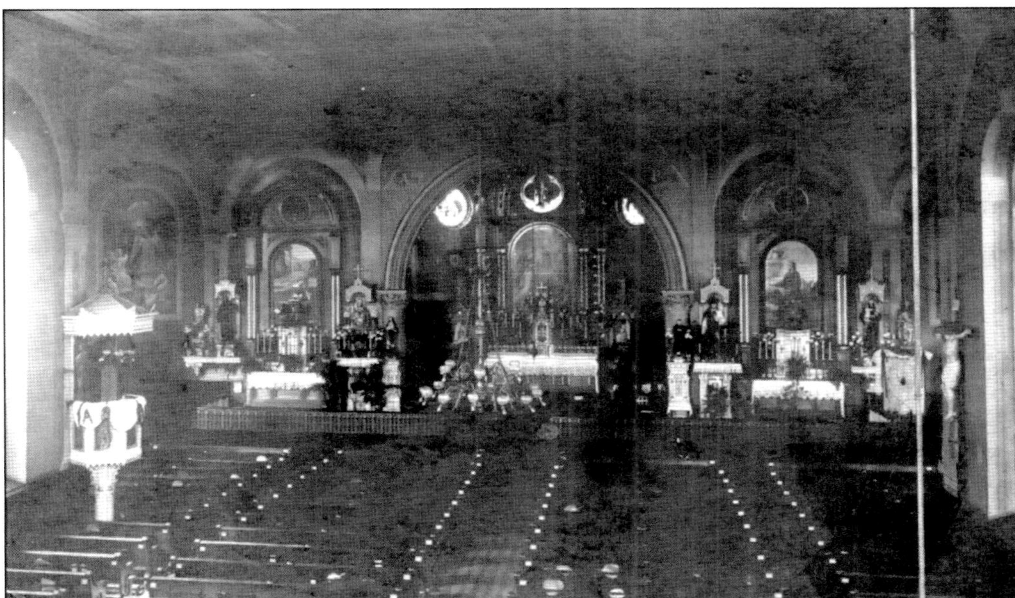

INTERIOR OF ST. MARY'S. This 1910 postcard of St. Mary's shows the 1886 interior renovation of the church. Included in the complete renovation was a new, flat ceiling, new organ, new bells, and the placement of clocks on the steeple.

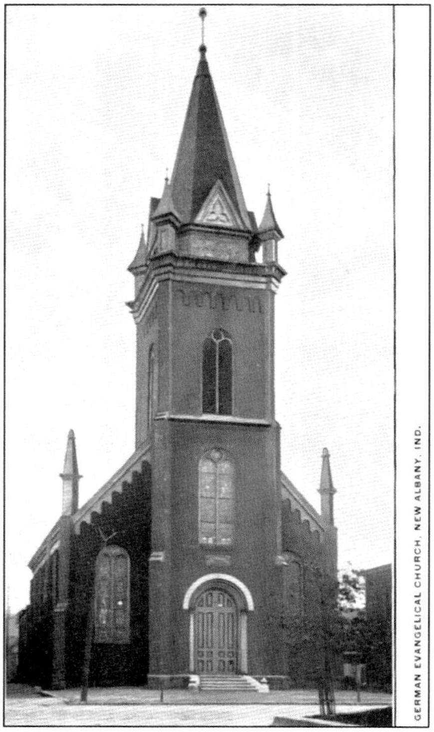

GERMAN EVANGELICAL CHURCH. This 1870 church building was the third permanent building for the German Evangelical Church, which was formed in 1837 as the German Evangelical Lutheran and Reformed Church of New Albany. Its first permanent building was constructed in 1843 on State Street north of Oak Street. The congregation next purchased the former home of St. Paul's Episcopal Church on the south side of Spring Street, just east of the alley between Bank and Third Streets. In 1870, a new church was built on the other side of the alley. The church eventually became known as St. Marks United Church of Christ, and the congregation tore down the 1870 structure in 1957. The former Episcopal Church building was moved to Vincennes Street, where it was known as the Kingsley Mission until it burned. This postcard is from about 1910.

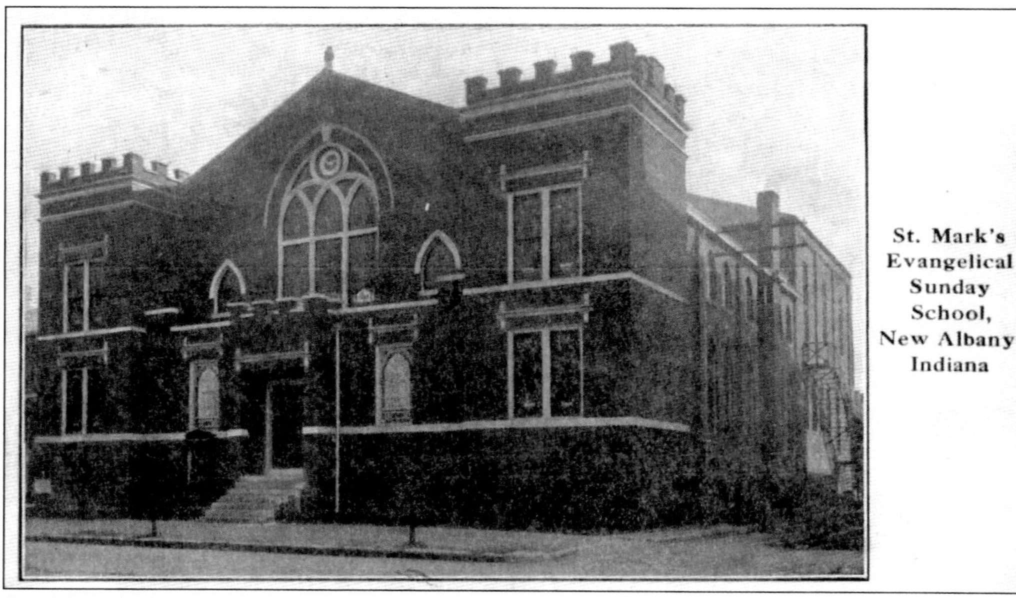

ST. MARK'S EVANGELICAL SUNDAY SCHOOL. After the former St. Paul's Episcopal Church building was moved to Vincennes Street, St. Mark's built a parsonage on this lot and later built the Sunday School building on this same site in 1899. The structure was extensively renovated in 1923. This postcard is from 1924, shortly after the remodeling. St. Marks razed the building in 1968 for a more modern educational building.

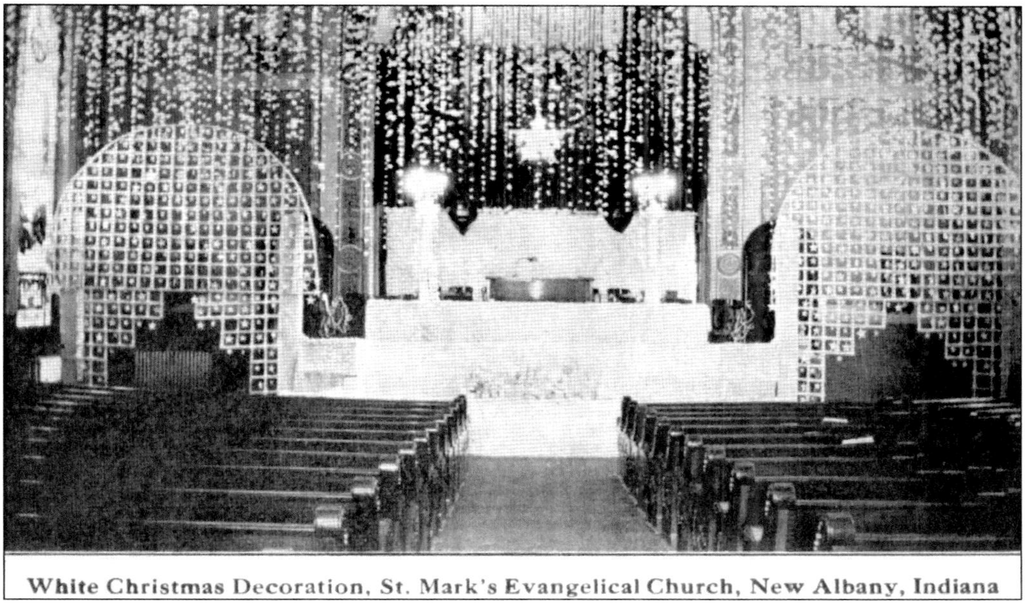

WHITE CHRISTMAS DECORATIONS. The Sunday School of St. Mark's conducted a "white gifts for the king" service for several Christmas seasons. The money and items collected were divided among the Cornelia Memorial Orphans' Home, Elmhurst College, Eden Seminary, and the Hoyleton Orphans' Home. This postcard is from about 1920.

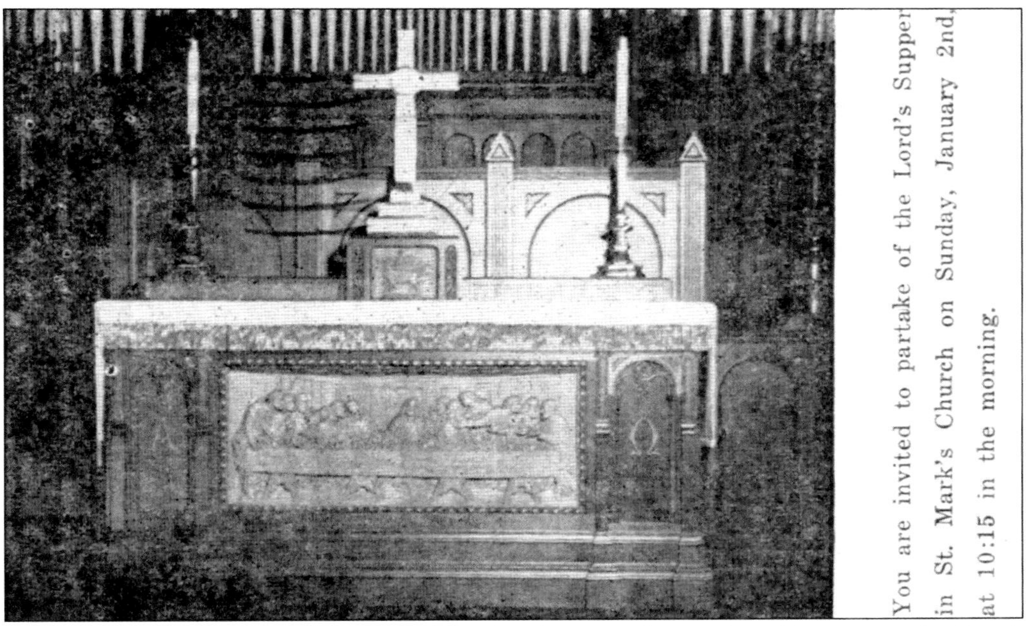

CHURCH ALTAR. George Korb presented this hand-carved altar made in Germany to St. Mark's in 1938. It features an inset panel of the Lord's Supper. It is still used in the chapel of the church's educational building. This postcard is from about 1940.

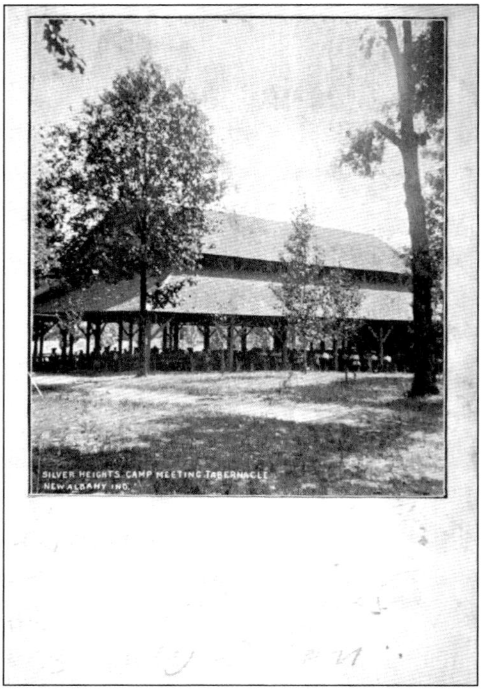

CAMP MEETING TABERNACLE. James Harvey Conner founded the facility in 1888 at 501 Camp Avenue in Silver Hills. The tabernacle, shown in this 1905 postcard, was built in 1892. It is possibly the oldest continuously operated religious campground in Indiana. The first Silver Heights Camp meeting was held at the facility in 1888, and the first National Holiness Association Camp meeting in 1894. The first Ohio Falls Holiness Association camp meeting was held at the facility in 1898. Several sections of barrack-style housing were moved from Camp Taylor in Kentucky after World War I to accommodate larger groups.

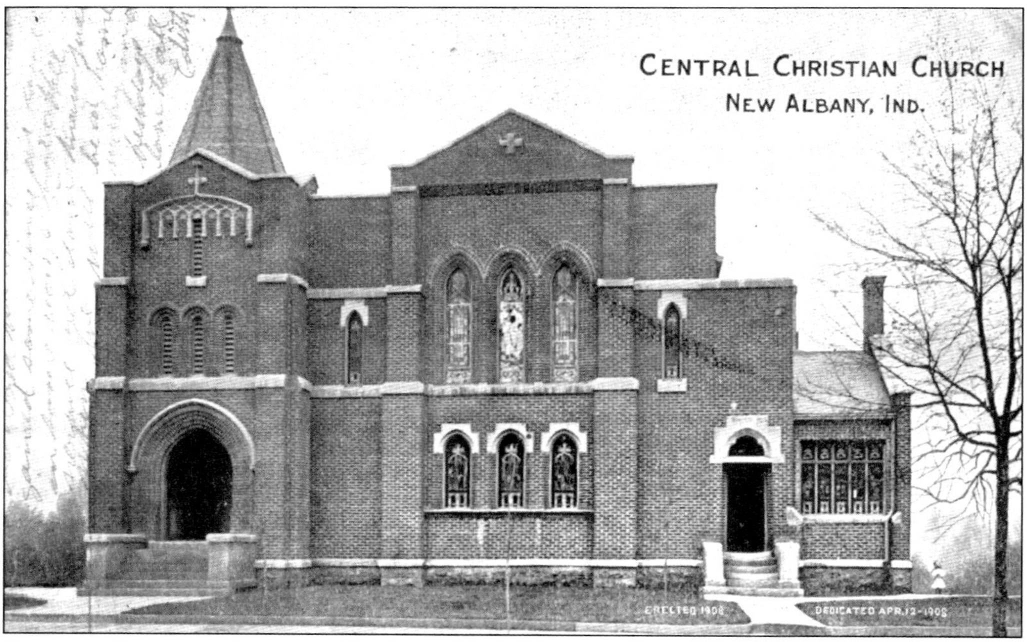

CENTRAL CHRISTIAN CHURCH. Members of Park Christian Church formed this new congregation in 1874. Initially, the group rented the edifice of the Universalist Church, later known as Maennerchor Hall, and then built a frame structure in the Gothic Revival style on East Spring Street between Fourth and Fifth Streets. The present church, shown here, was completed in 1908 at 1315 East Spring Street. This postcard is from 1908.

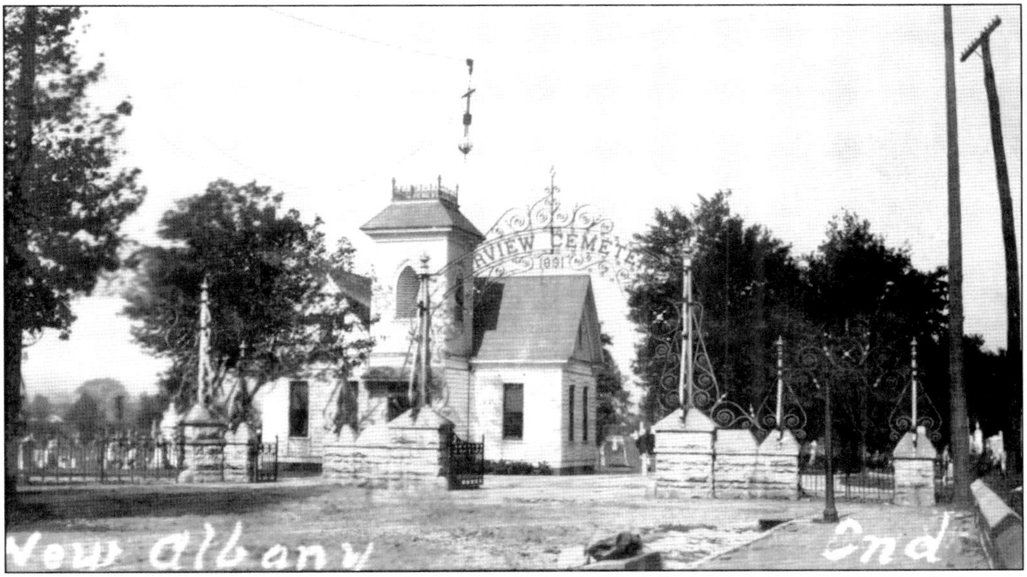

FAIRVIEW CEMETERY. Founded in 1841 as the Northern Burial Ground at 800 East Sixth Street, Fairview Cemetery is the resting place of some of the city's most notable former residents, including a governor, members of congress, founding fathers, and veterans. The City of New Albany cared for the cemetery until 1891, when a board of regents was authorized to oversee its operation. The name was changed to Fairview in 1896. In 1974, the property was re-conveyed to the city. These two postcards are from about 1910.

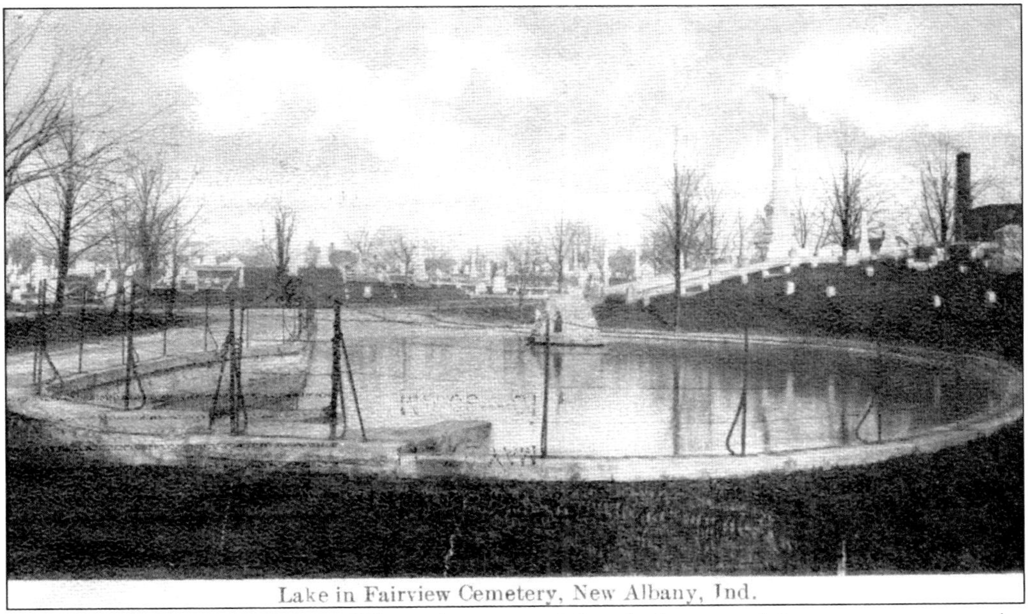

LAKE IN FAIRVIEW CEMETERY. When the national Rural Cemetery Movement came to the attention of the caretakers of Fairview, they decided to beautify the property by adding a lake, a grotto, and a heart-shaped plot for the burial of infants known as "Baby Land."

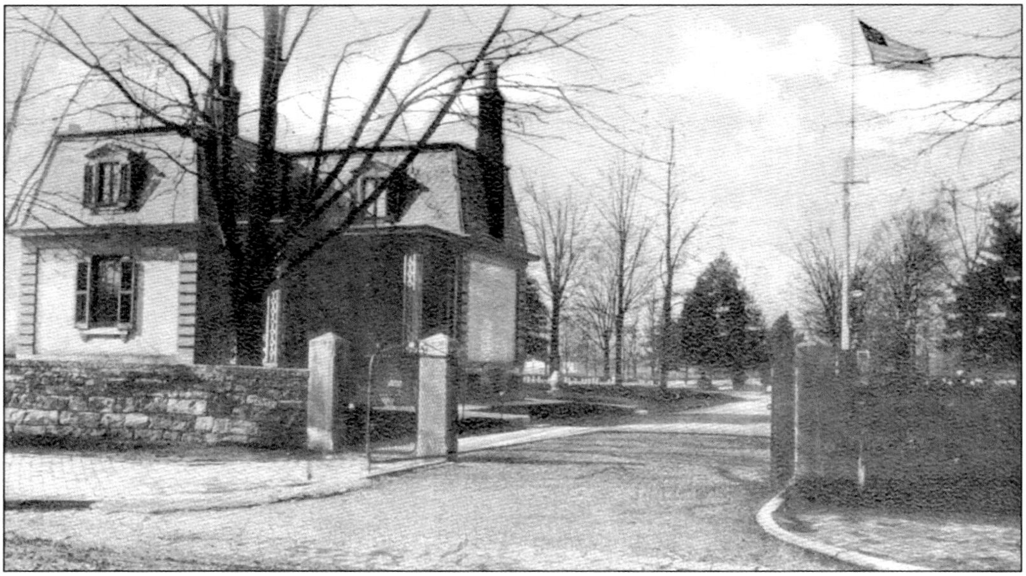

ENTRANCE TO NATIONAL CEMETERY. New Albany National Cemetery at 1943 Poplar Street was one of seven such places authorized by Congress in 1862. (Poplar Street was later renamed Ekin Avenue.) The cemetery is comprised of 5.46 acres purchased from Dr. Charles Bowman. This postcard is from about 1910.

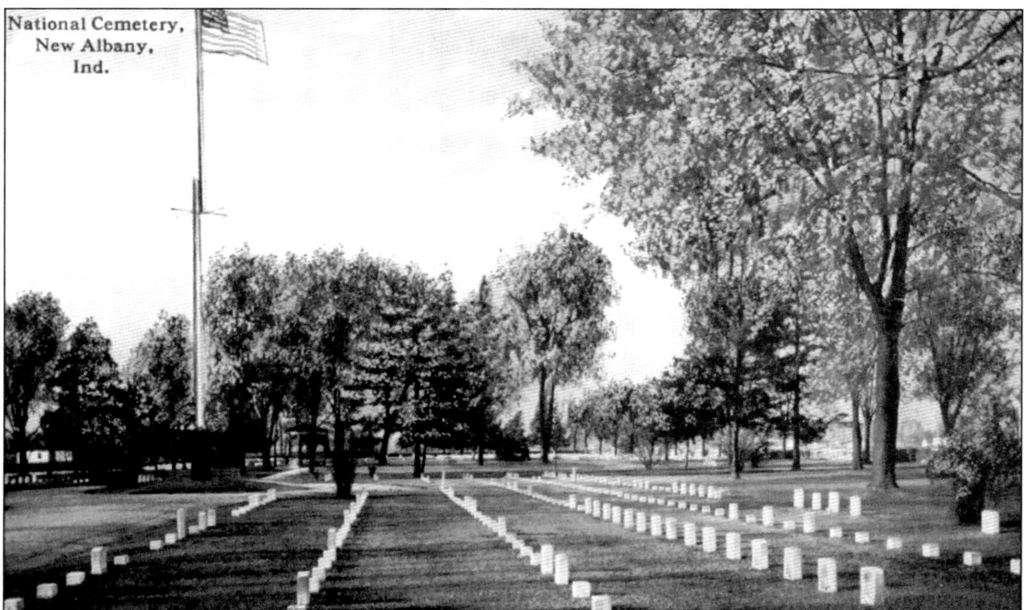

NATIONAL CEMETERY. Originally, the cemetery was used for burial of Union and Confederate Civil War dead. Veterans of seven wars and military conflicts now are buried in the cemetery.

Four

HOUSES AND SILVER HILLS

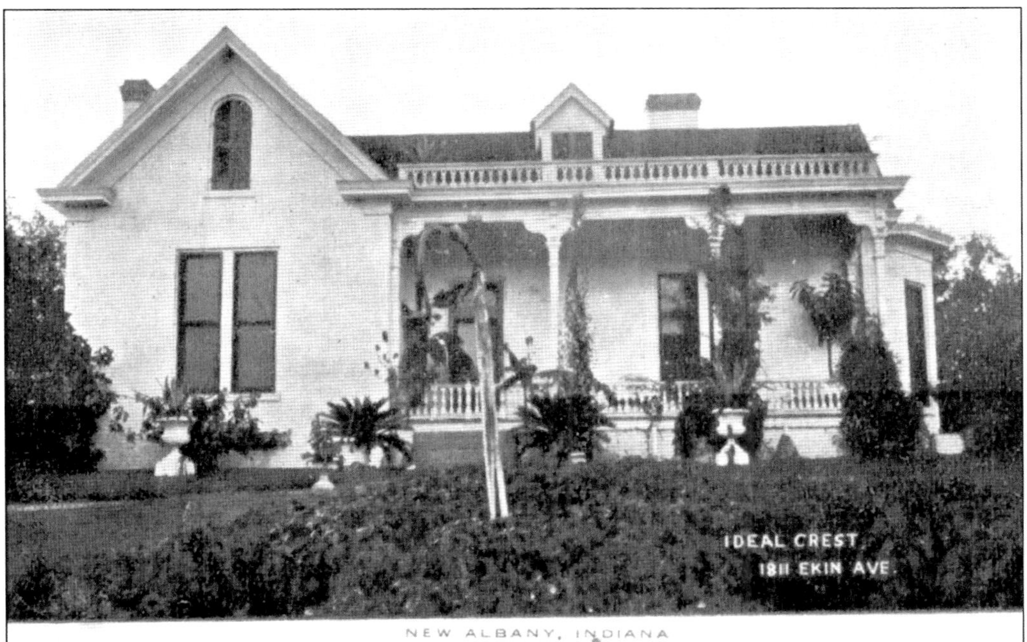

IDEAL CREST. Herman Rockenbach built this Italianate cottage at 1811 Ekin Avenue in 1883 for his family. Mr. Rockenbach operated the Eagle Tannery in New Albany. His daughters occupied the house until the late 1970s. Etelka Rockenbach, daughter of Herman, taught German and Latin at nearby New Albany High School for several decades. Home to co-author Robyn Sekula and her husband Greg, the residence recently had its front porch reconstructed to resemble this 1905 image.

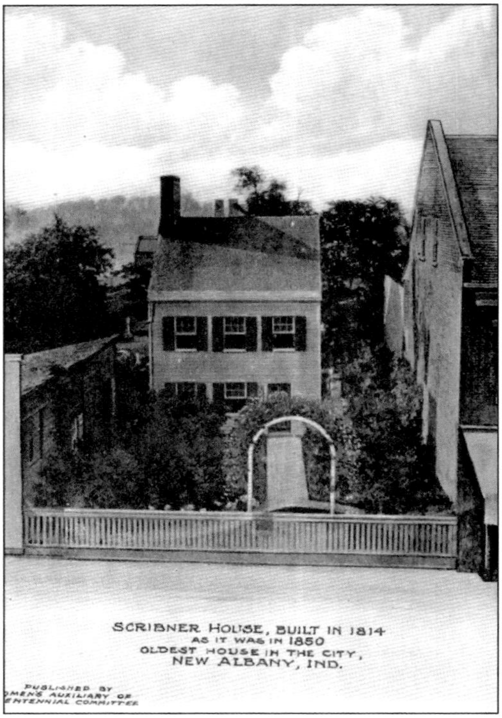

SCRIBNER HOME. Joel Scribner, one of the founders of New Albany, built this home at the southeast corner of State and Main Streets in 1814. Joel Scribner and his two brothers, Nathaniel and Abner, founded New Albany in 1813. The Federal-style house is now a house museum, but also serves as the home of the Piankeshaw Chapter of the Daughters of the American Revolution, established in 1898. This postcard was created in 1913 to commemorate the centennial.

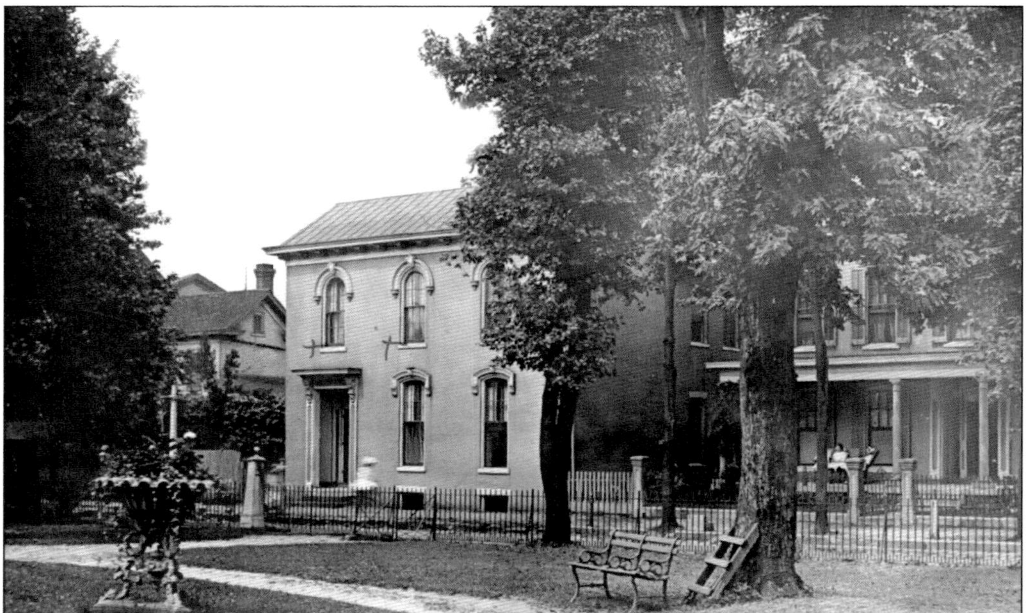

DASH RESIDENCE. The residence of Dr. and Mrs. George E. Dash was at 224 Washington Street, opposite Scribner Park. The Italianate-style house, in the center of the card, was torn down for bridge construction in the 1960s. This postcard is from about 1910.

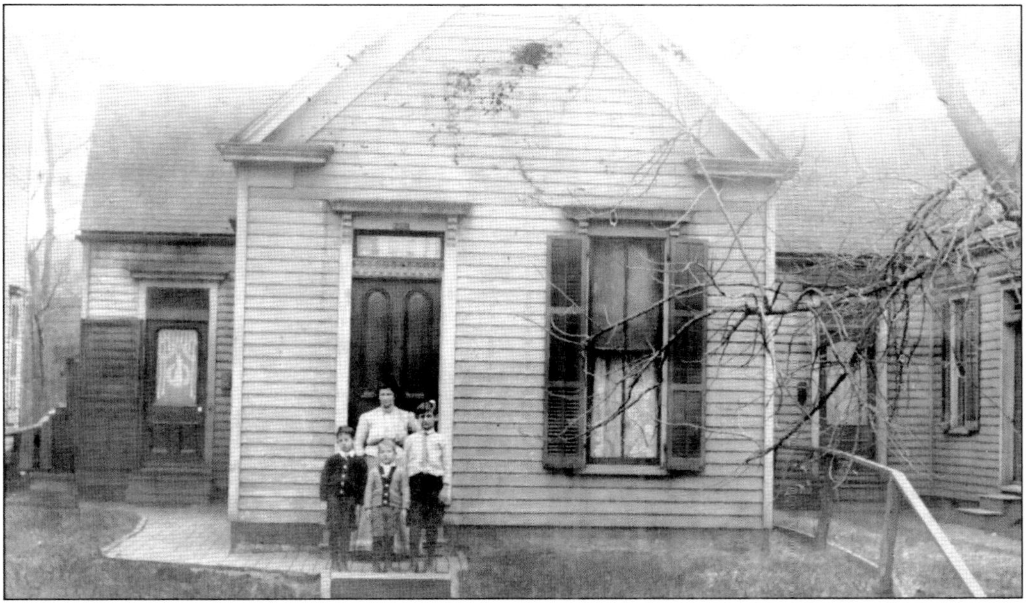

FAMILY PORTRAIT. The writing on the back of this card indicates that the family pictured on the front has suffered a recent tragedy: their only girl child died. The deceased child is not pictured in the card, which is postmarked 1911. The house shown is 602 East Oak Street and was the home of Mr. and Mrs. Joseph Stemle, according to records. The narrative on the back of the card does not indicate how the child died.

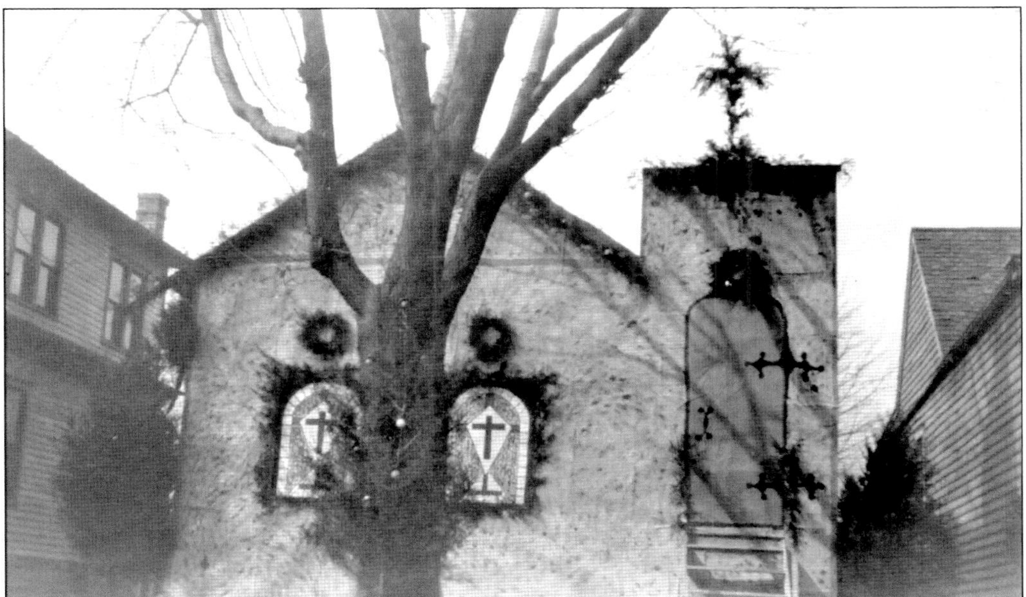

HOLIDAY SETTING. A Christmas scene reminiscent of Israel was created at this home on Chartres Street. A hand-written notation on the back indicates that Ken Miller possibly designed the scene, which appears to be a home shrouded with fabric to make it appear Middle Eastern. It is from about 1910.

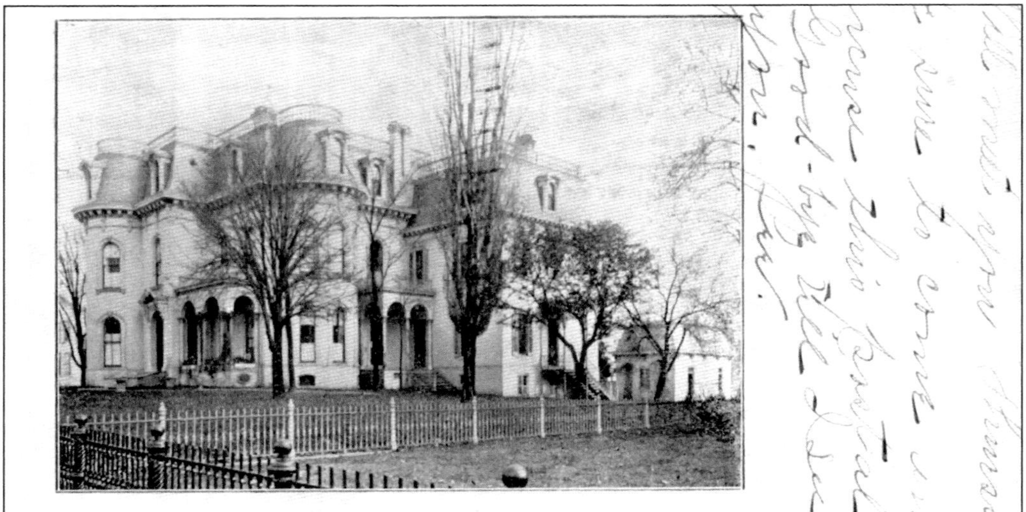

Home of John S McDonald, New Albany, Ind.
On Line of Louisville and Southern Indiana Traction Co.

HOME OF JOHN S. MCDONALD. At the time this postcard was created in 1905, this was the home of John S. McDonald. Today it is the Culbertson Mansion State Historic Site and is open to the public as a house museum. Mr. McDonald purchased the Second Empire style mansion for the bargain price of $7,100 from the Culbertson family at auction in 1899; the house had been constructed in 1869 for $120,000. Mr. McDonald intended to turn the house into a hospital, but never did, and instead moved his family into the home. Mr. McDonald was the owner of the McDonald Grain Co.

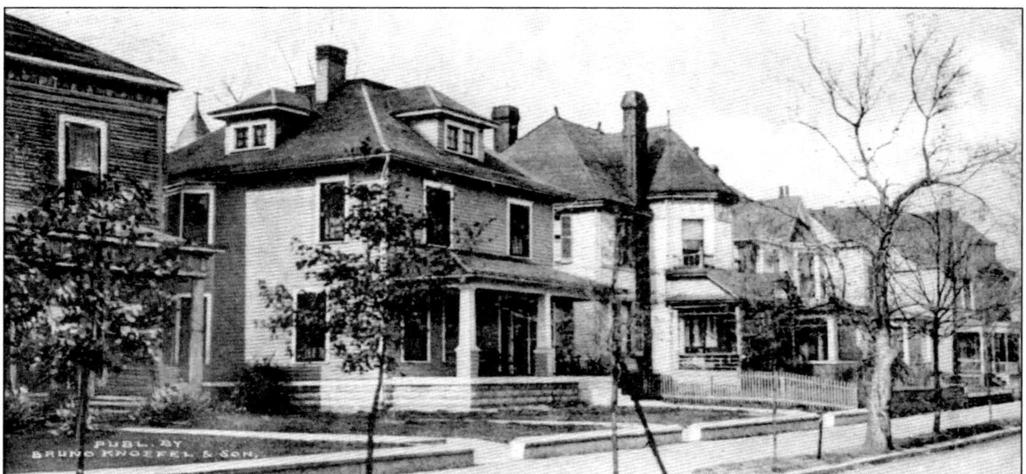

EAST MAIN STREET.

EAST MAIN STREET. New Albany's Mansion Row Historic District appears today much as it is seen here in this 1913 centennial postcard. Mansion Row is listed on the National Register of Historic Places. The oldest homes on Mansion Row are of the Federal period, dating to about 1820. Most of the other homes are Victorian or early 20th century, including the homes shown in this postcard of East Main Street, looking east toward Sixth Street. East Main Street was considered the most fashionable address in town in the late 19th century.

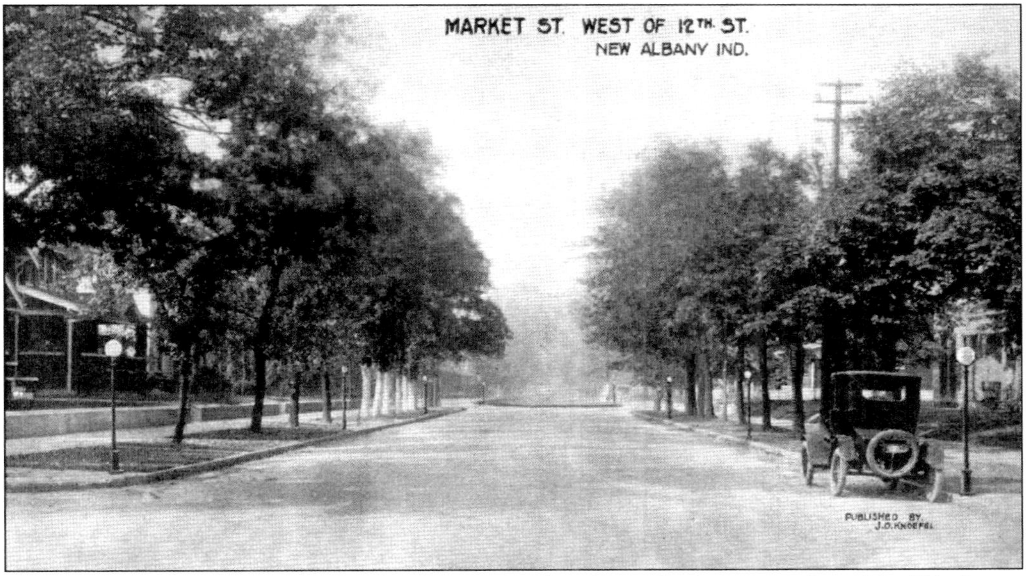

MARKET STREET WEST OF TWELFTH STREET. Market Street looking west from Twelfth Street was tree-lined when this card was created in about 1920. The center island of the street, which divides it and provides a small green space, was once home to the Upper Market House, also known as the Little Market House. Today it is a war memorial, established in 1919 to honor Floyd County military personnel who have died defending the United States.

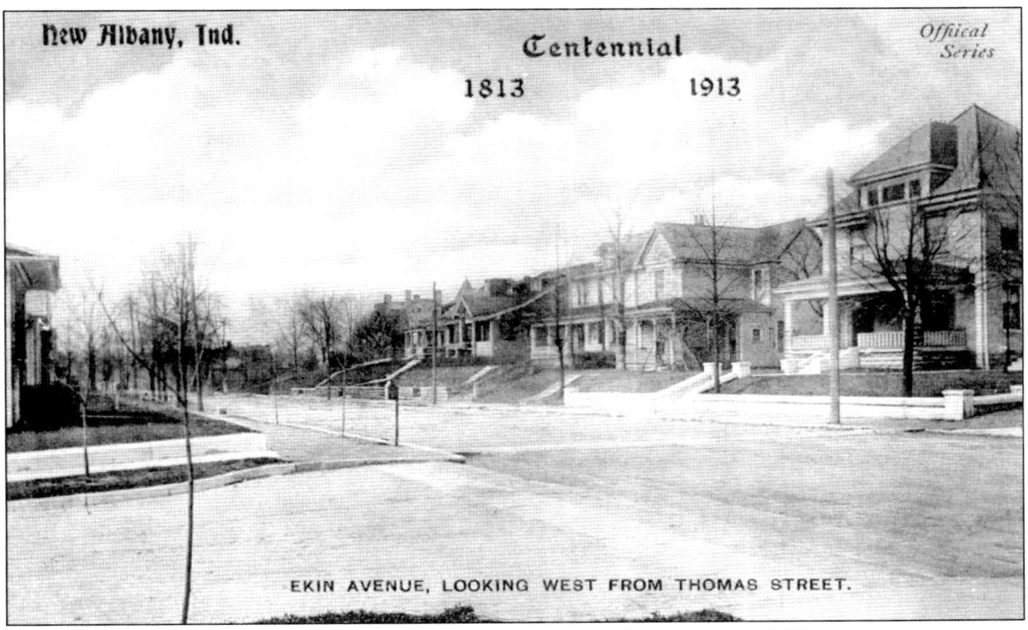

EKIN AVENUE LOOKING WEST FROM THOMAS STREET. This section of Ekin Avenue was just being developed as a residential street when this postcard was created for the 1913 centennial. This card looks west from Thomas Street and shows a house that is virtually new on the right-hand side of the card.

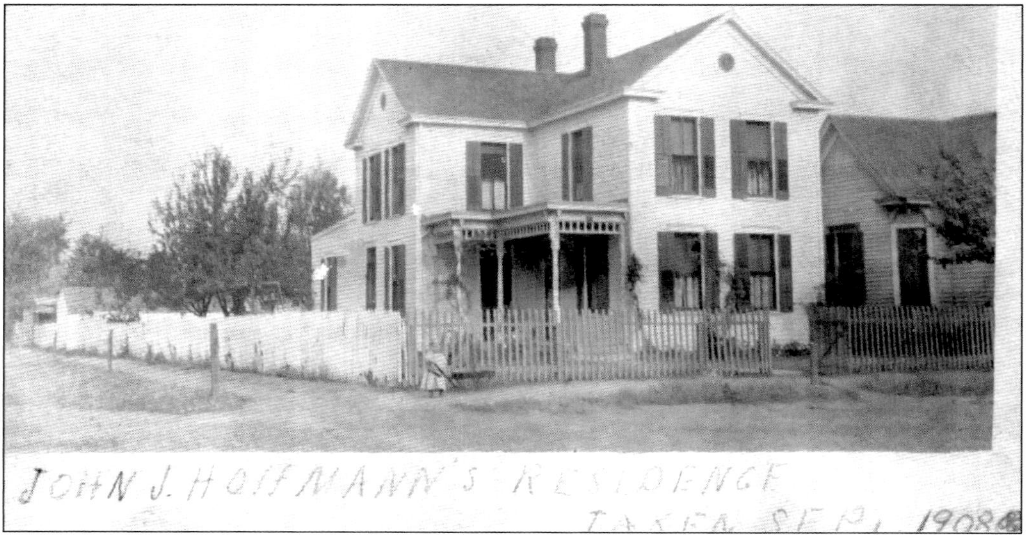

John J. Hoffmann Residence. This postcard image, taken in September 1908, shows the family residence of John J. and Mary Anna (Renn) Hoffmann at 1309 Locust Street. Henry J. Graf, son-in-law of the Hoffmanns, added a grocery to the front of the residence in 1922. The store continued until 1999. The house is still in the Graf family.

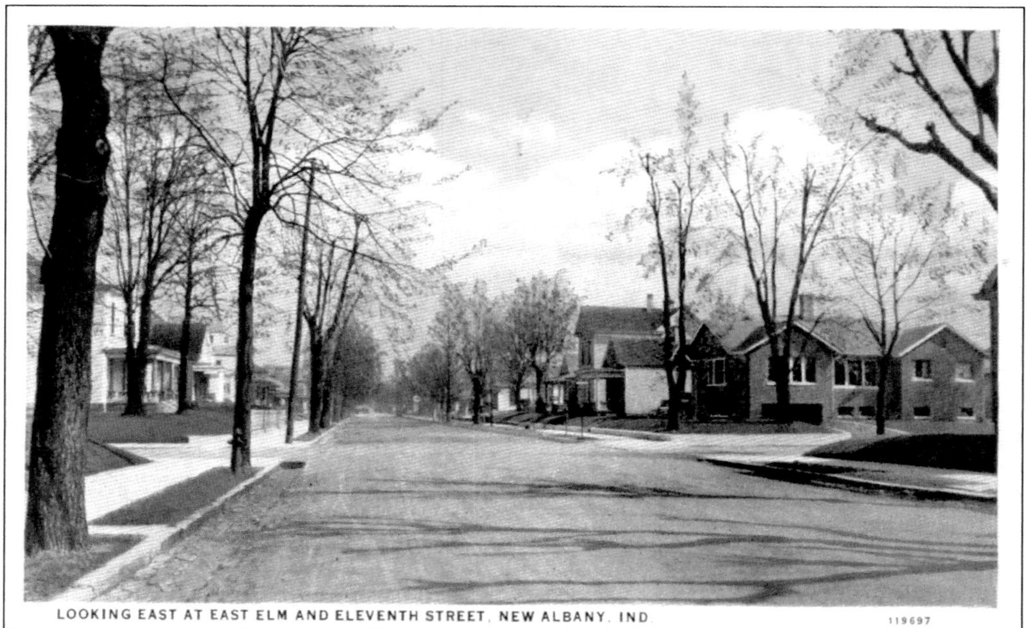

Elm Street. Looking east from Elm and East Eleventh Streets shows a scenic residential community that was blossoming around the time this card was created in 1925. Elm, Spring, Oak, and Culbertson Streets have a peculiar bend that was created when the towns of Providence and New Albany merged at East Tenth Street. Epaphras Jones, the founder of Providence, laid out his town's streets to be perpendicular to Vincennes Street, while the Scribners oriented New Albany's streets to be perpendicular to State Street.

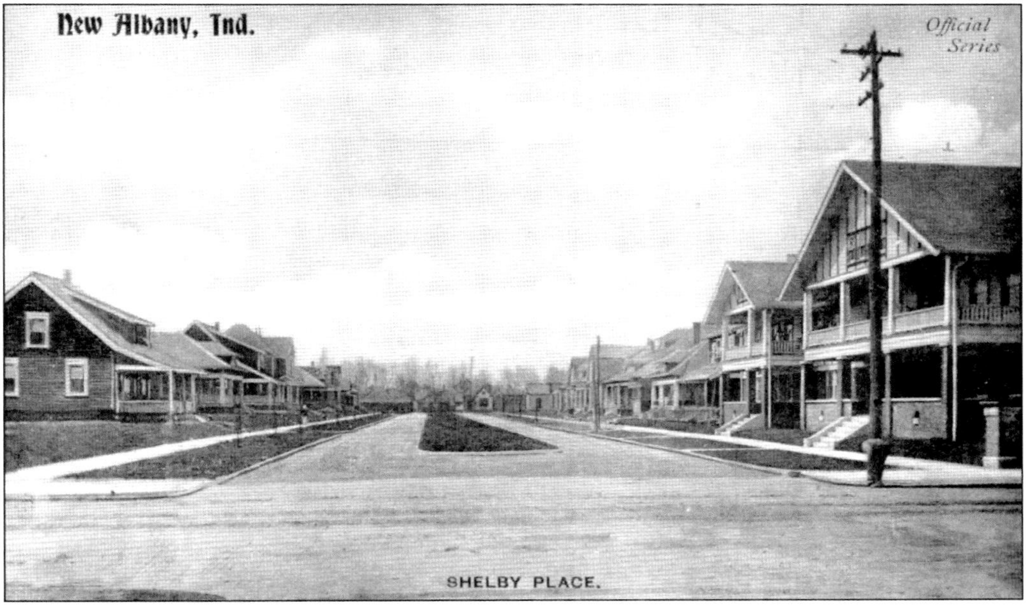

Shelby Place. Just two blocks long, Shelby Place extends between East 15th and Vincennes Streets and has a generous esplanade separating the two sides of the street, shown in this 1913 postcard. The houses on this short street were all built around the same time period and today are still a lovely collection of Craftsman, Colonial Revival, and American Foursquare architectural styles.

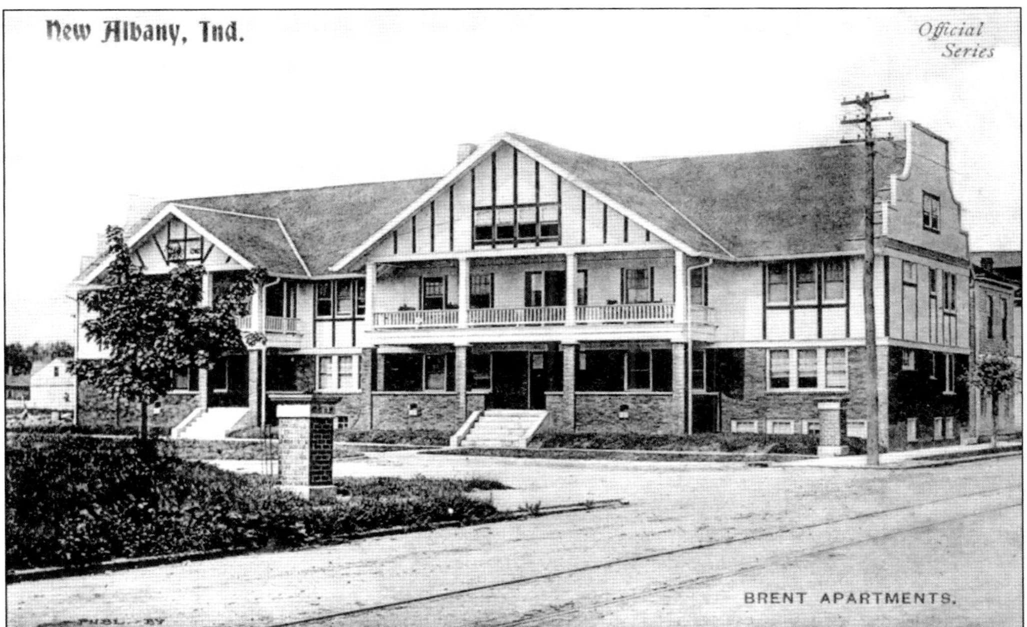

Brent Apartments. Located at the northwest corner of Vincennes Street and Shelby Place, "The Brent" was commemorated in this 1913 centennial postcard. The apartments were destroyed by fire in January 1984.

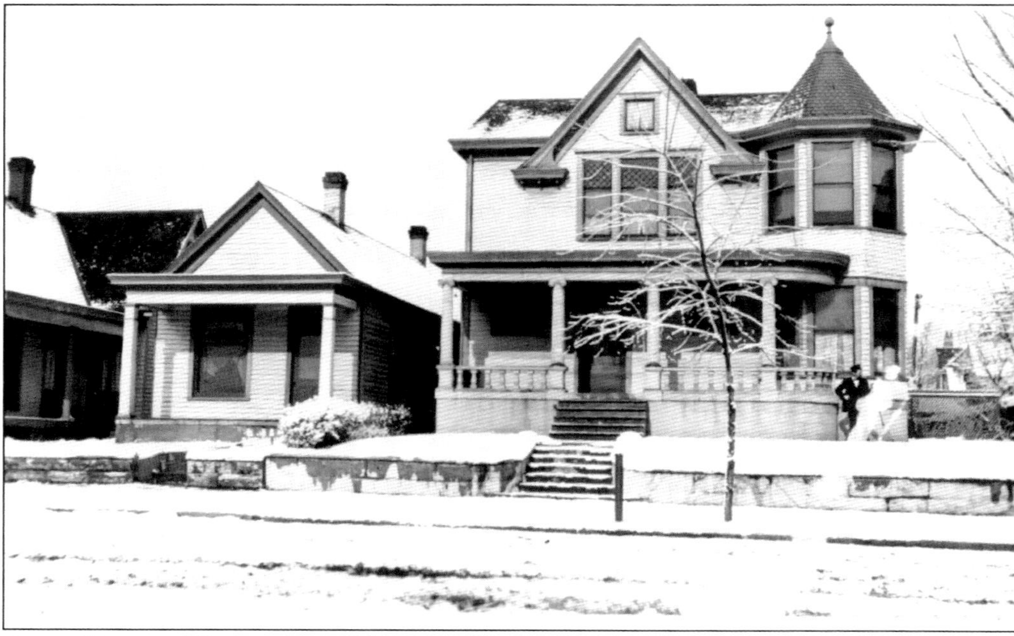

SOWLE HOME IN WINTER. Mr. and Mrs. William D. Sowle lived in this late Victorian home at 1819 East Spring Street. The card is postmarked 1908. According to records, Mr. Sowle ran a machine shop at the rear of this property. On the left side of the postcard is a simple frame shotgun home, which is 1815 East Spring Street.

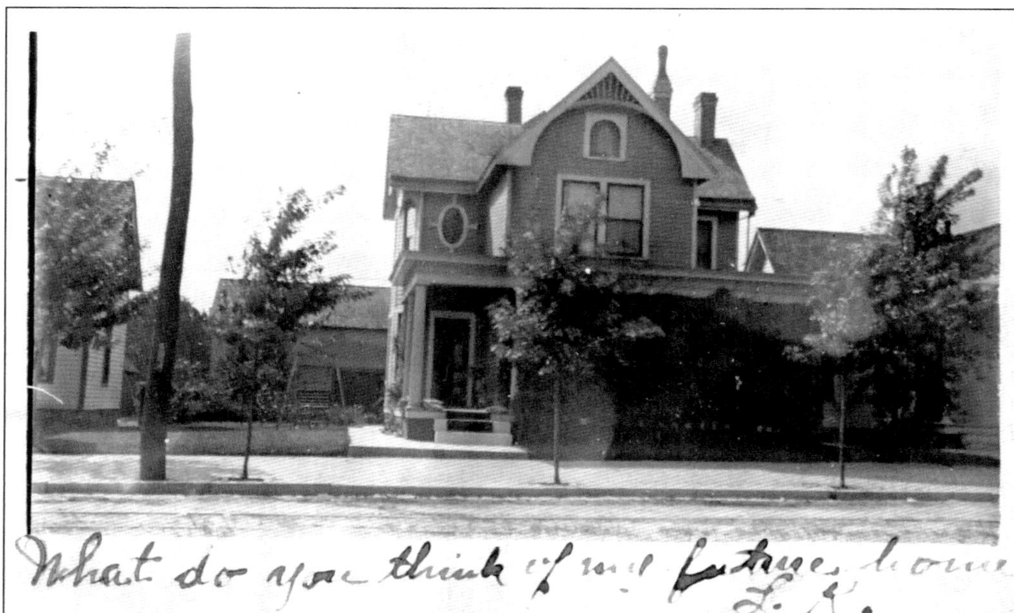

KELLER RESIDENCE. This late Victorian residence is located at 1910 East Spring Street. The postcard is postmarked 1908, and on the bottom is written, "What do you think of my future house?" In 1910, it was the residence of Mr. and Mrs. Frank H. Keller.

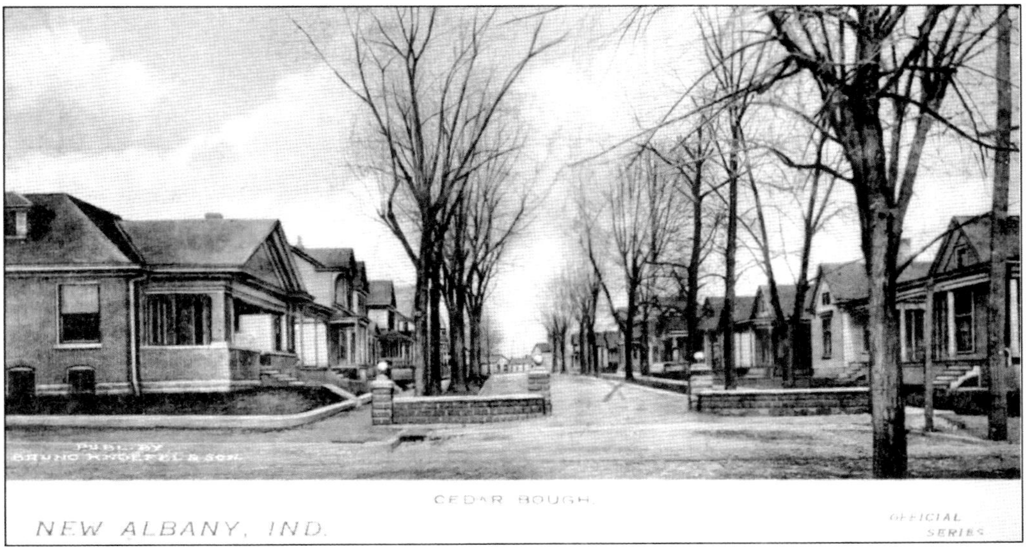

Cedar Bough Place. One of only a handful of private streets within the City of New Albany, Cedar Bough Place runs between Ekin Avenue and Beeler Street. All of the houses on the street were built between 1890 and 1910 and are primarily Queen Anne style homes or cottages with some Queen Anne detailing. At the time of its development, "living on the Bough" was considered to be a prestigious address, as it still is today. This postcard is from 1913.

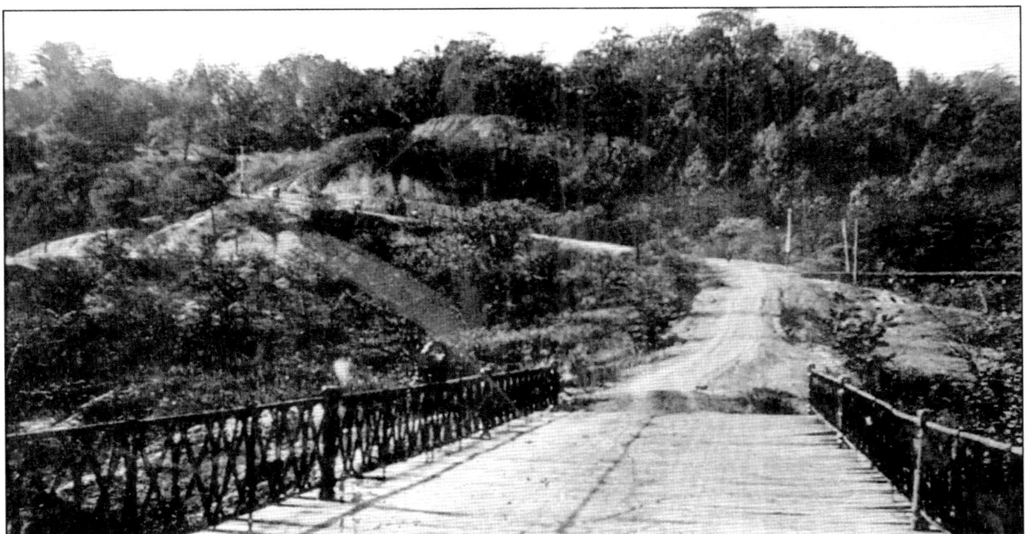

Approach to Silver Hills. One of the earliest and most prestigious suburbs of New Albany was Silver Hills. The Tuley family owned the land, and several of the original Tuley homes are still standing. Silver Hills was annexed in 1853 and removed in 1876. It was annexed again in 1956. Beginning in 1890, the New Albany Highland Railroad Company began providing streetcar service to Silver Hills, greatly increasing its popularity. Its development included homes in the Queen Anne, Victorian Shingle, Colonial Revival, Bungalow, and other architectural styles.

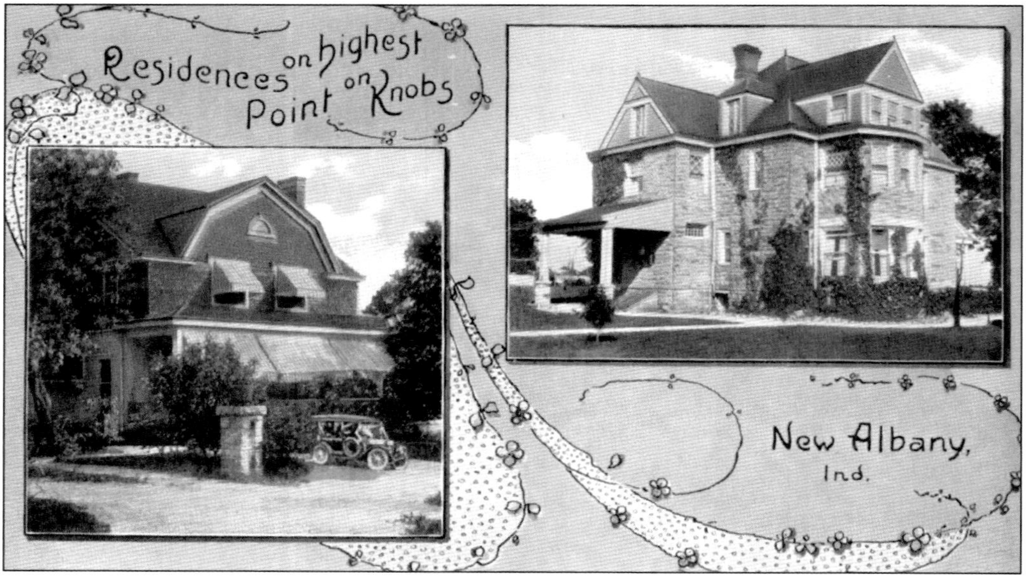

Residences on Highest Point of the Knobs. This card was made in about 1920 to show off homes on the highest point of Knobs, which today is actually known as Silver Hills. Included on the card is a Shingle-style Victorian home on the left, which is located at 1325 Ridgeway Avenue. The home shown on the right is located at 1301 Riddle Road and is Queen Anne in style. Riddle Road was named for Charlotte Riddle Tuley, wife of William Tuley.

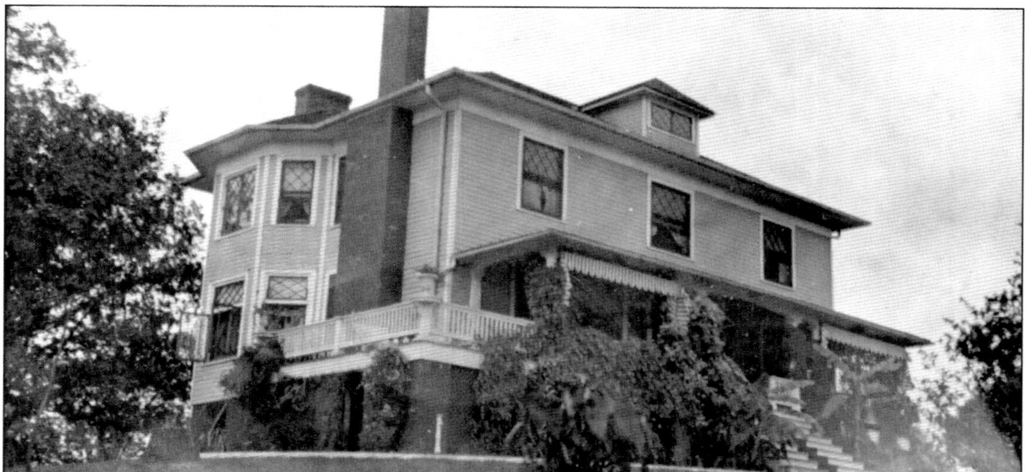

Creedmont. Walter B. Creed built this home which combines Classical Revival and American Foursquare styles in 1904 on Riddle Road overlooking the Ohio River in Silver Hills. Mr. Creed's hardware company was located at 315 State Street. Mr. Creed was involved in the New Albany Chamber of Commerce and appointed to the War Board during World War I to assist in making purchases for the U.S. Department of Defense. On May 21, 1919, a fire that originated in the attic destroyed the home. Neighbors saved a considerable part of the home's furnishings. The home was rebuilt after the fire using its original footprint and a few other details, but mostly taking on the Arts and Crafts style that was popular around 1920.

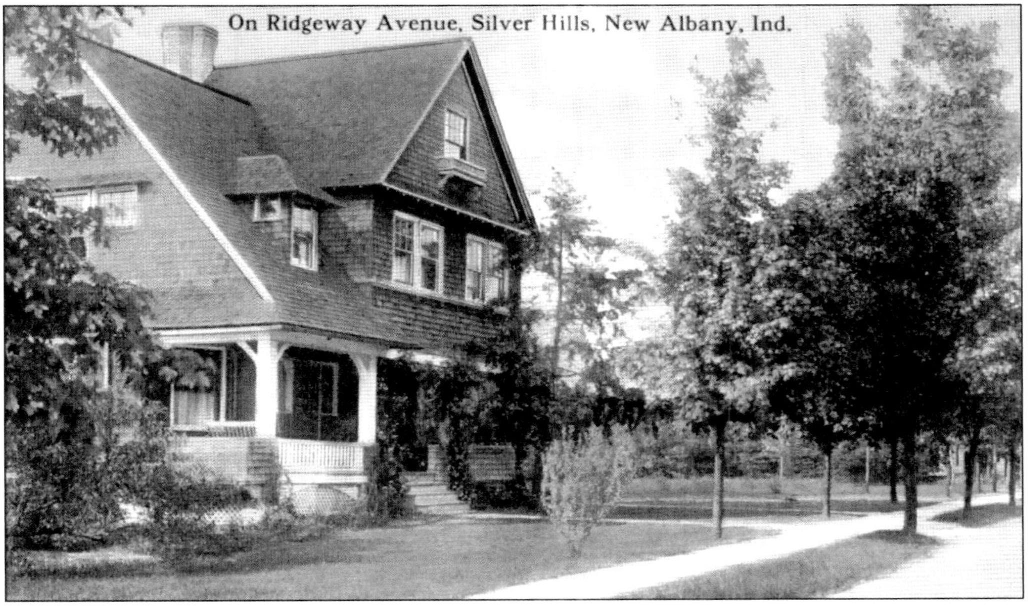

ON RIDGEWAY AVENUE, SILVER HILLS. Ridgeway Avenue was created when a parcel of land was sold to the Silver Hills Land Company in 1892 for $3,000. This 1903 Shingle-style Victorian home was one of the fashionable homes of Silver Hills. The postcard was made in about 1920. This home at 1318 Ridgeway was severely damaged in a fire on April 13, 1933, and was drastically altered during the repairs. It is now more of a Craftsman or Bungalow style home.

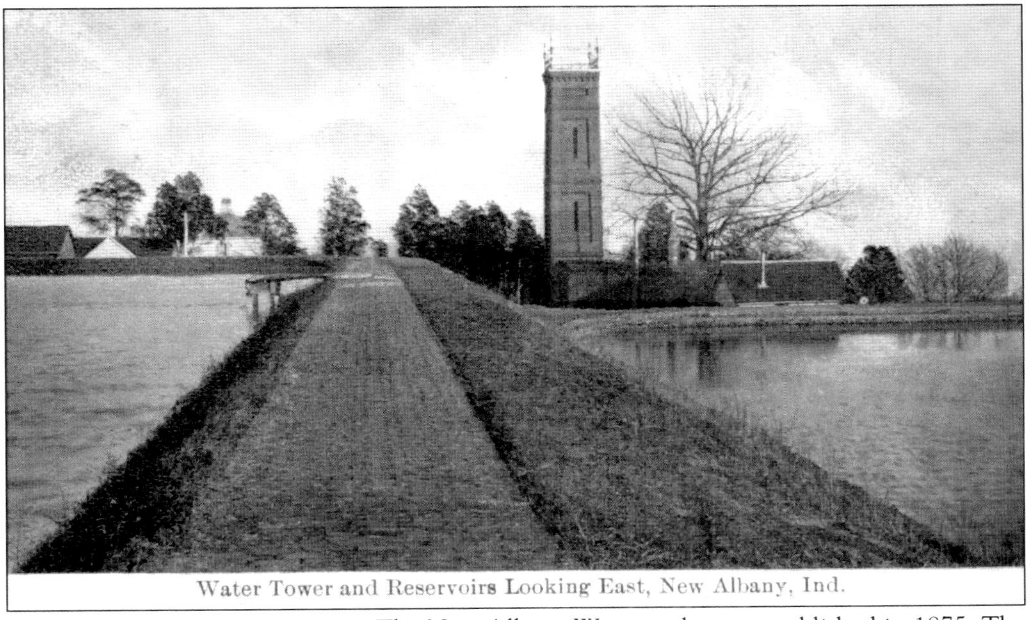

WATER TOWER AND RESERVOIRS. The New Albany Waterworks was established in 1875. The tower and new reservoir were built in 1880 in Silver Hills, but this card was created in about 1910. The water service was used in New Albany. The structures are no longer standing.

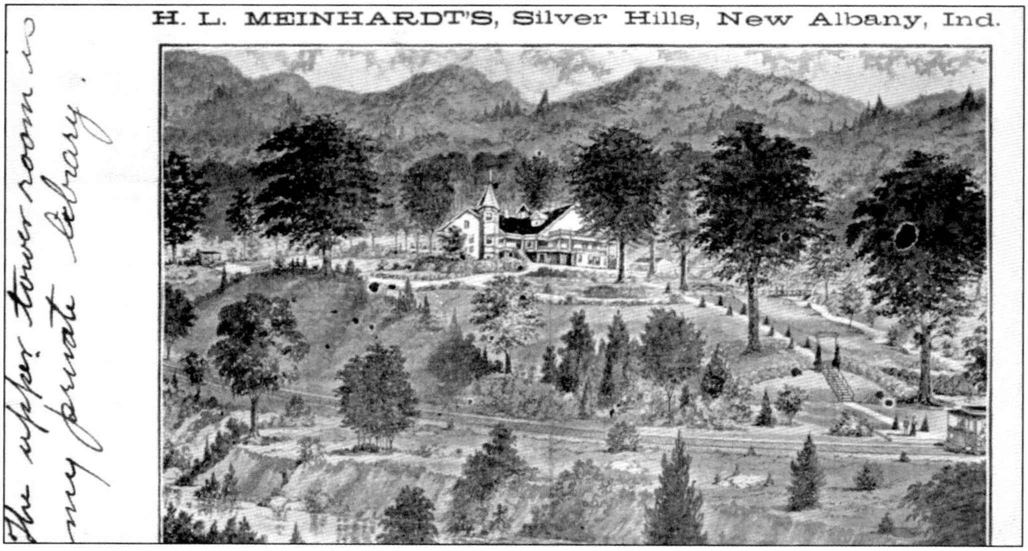

H.L. MEINHARDT RESIDENCE. H.L. Meinhardt built his summer home in Silver Hills while he was president of the Paul Reising Brewery, located at West Fourth and Spring Streets. The brewery operated from 1861 to 1915. Meinhardt wrote on the back of the postcard, "I suppose you are getting enough postals from me of late. Just had these printed. Our house is higher on the hill than it seems." The tower contained his library. This postcard is from about 1910. In June 1925, the house was destroyed by fire. Mr. Meinhardt had died by that time. The house was occupied by Mrs. Elizabeth Toggweiller and her daughter at the time of the fire, and they escaped without harm.

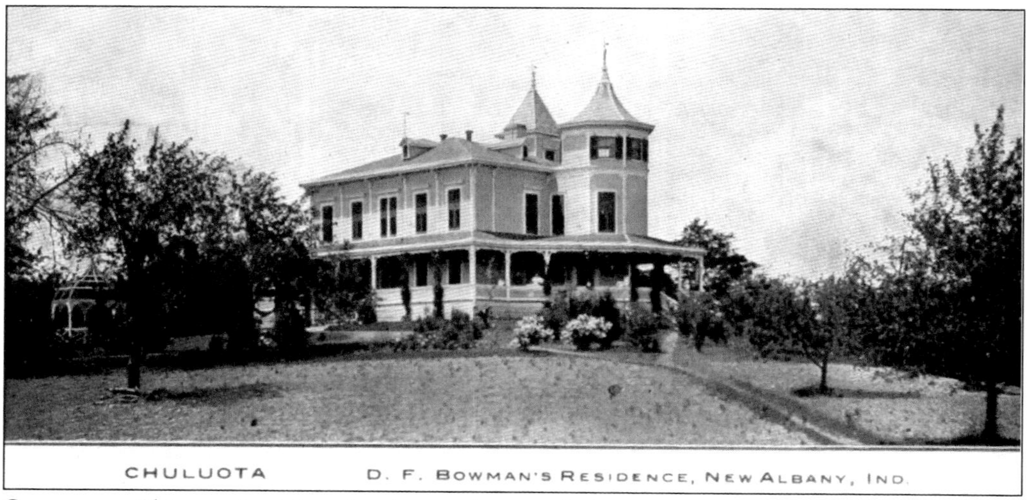

CHULUOTA. This massive Victorian Queen Anne-style home was named Chuluota and was D.F. Bowman's residence in an area now known as Crestview. The card is from about 1905. David F. Bowman was a manufacturer and distributor of cotton and woolen railroad waste; his business was one of a handful of such companies in the United States. The plant was located on the southeast corner of West Fourth and Main Streets. He was connected with the old Woolen Mills before establishing his waste factory. He died January 19, 1916. The house is no longer standing.

Five

Parks

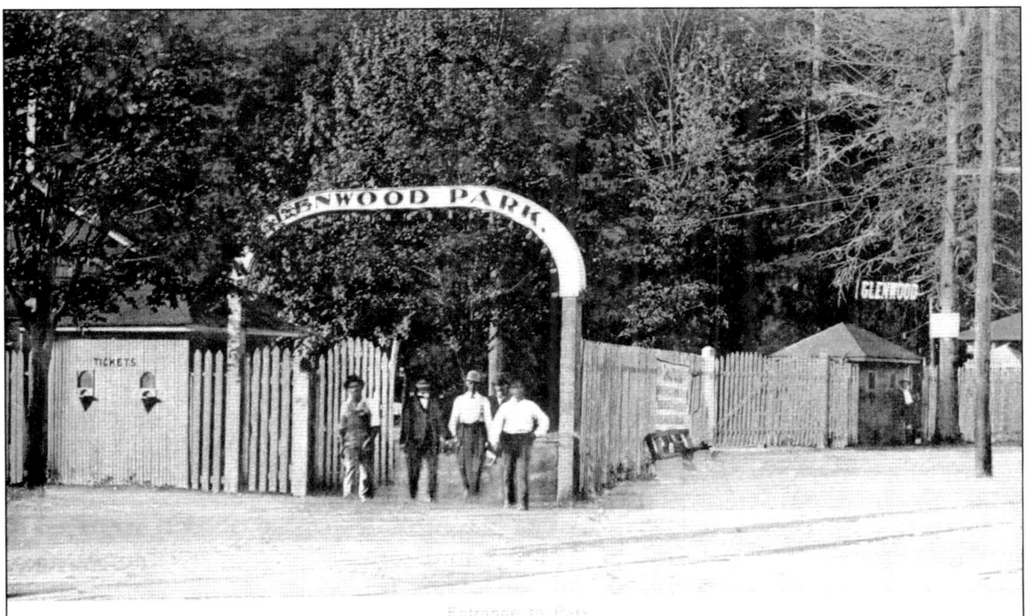

Glenwood Park. One of the city's most popular parks was Glenwood, located at the northeast corner of Spring Street and Beharrell Avenue. Glenwood opened in 1903. It was used for picnics, summer opera, entertainment, recreation, political speeches, and a Chautauqua event. In 1935, the park property was sold for residential development. This postcard, which shows Glenwood's entrance, is from about 1908.

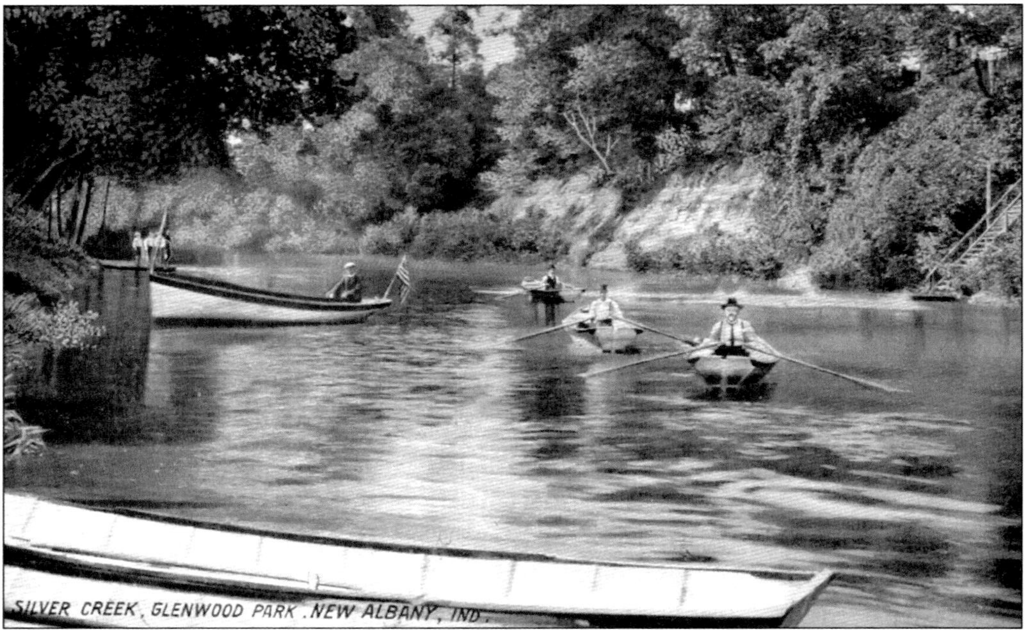

SILVER CREEK. This 1909 postcard shows the area of Silver Creek that was dammed for recreational uses. The dam was installed just below the bridge that carried the Interurban street cars.

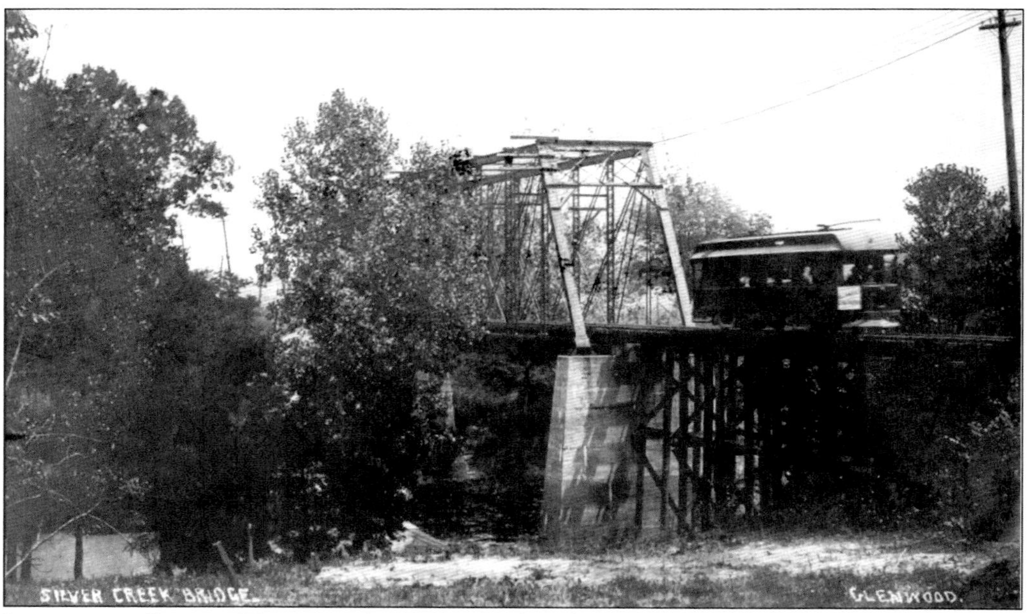

INTERURBAN BRIDGE. The Interurban street car line from Jeffersonville to New Albany opened in 1903, the same year as Glenwood Park. This 1907 image shows the bridge that carried it over Silver Creek along side the park.

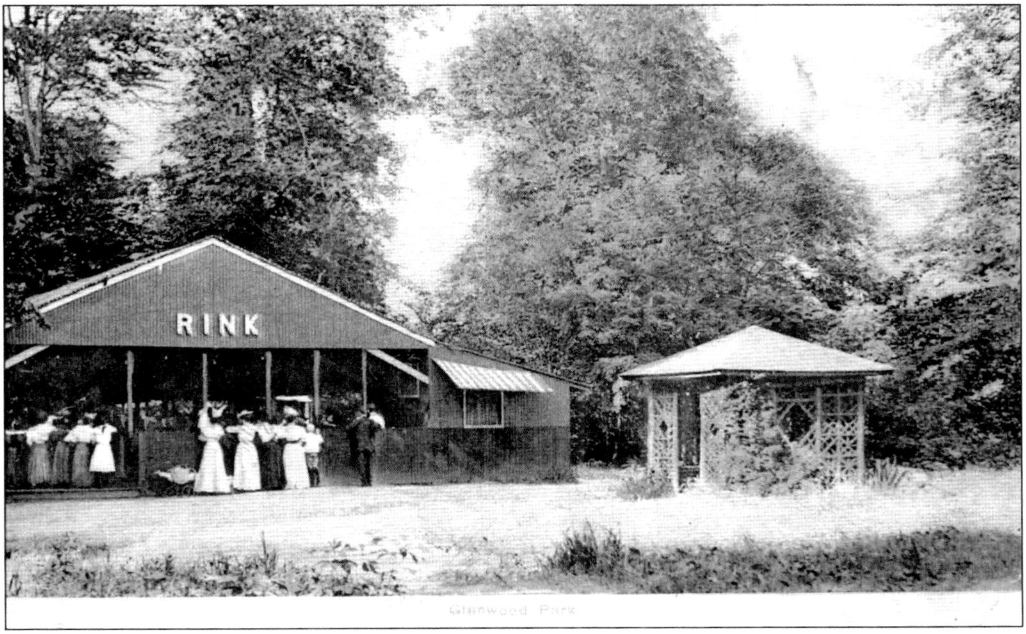

SKATING RINK. The roller-skating rink in Glenwood Park was one of many amusements found in the park in 1908.

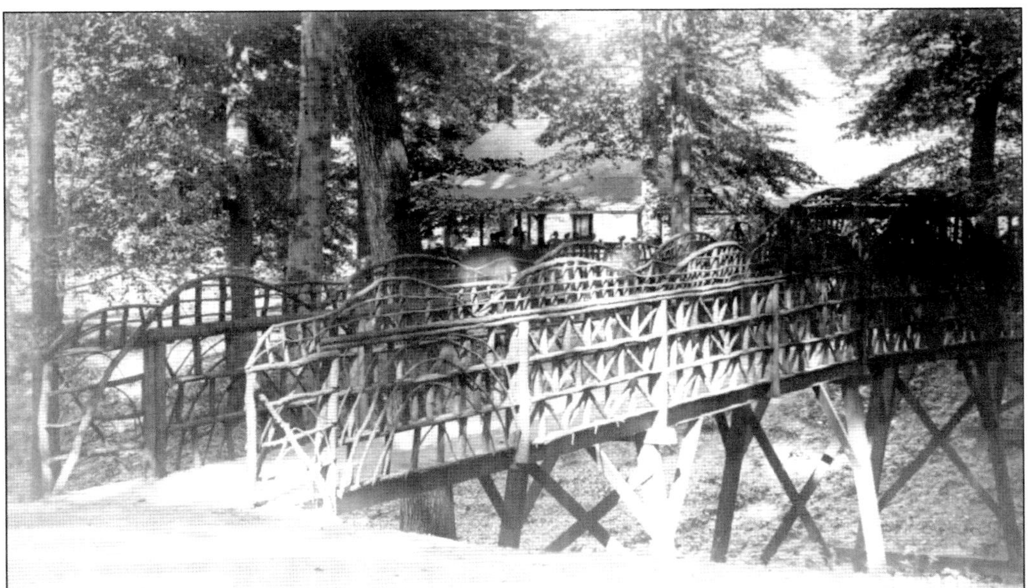

RUSTIC BRIDGE. This image is from about 1907. It shows one of several rustic bridges in Glenwood Park to carry park visitors across its many ravines.

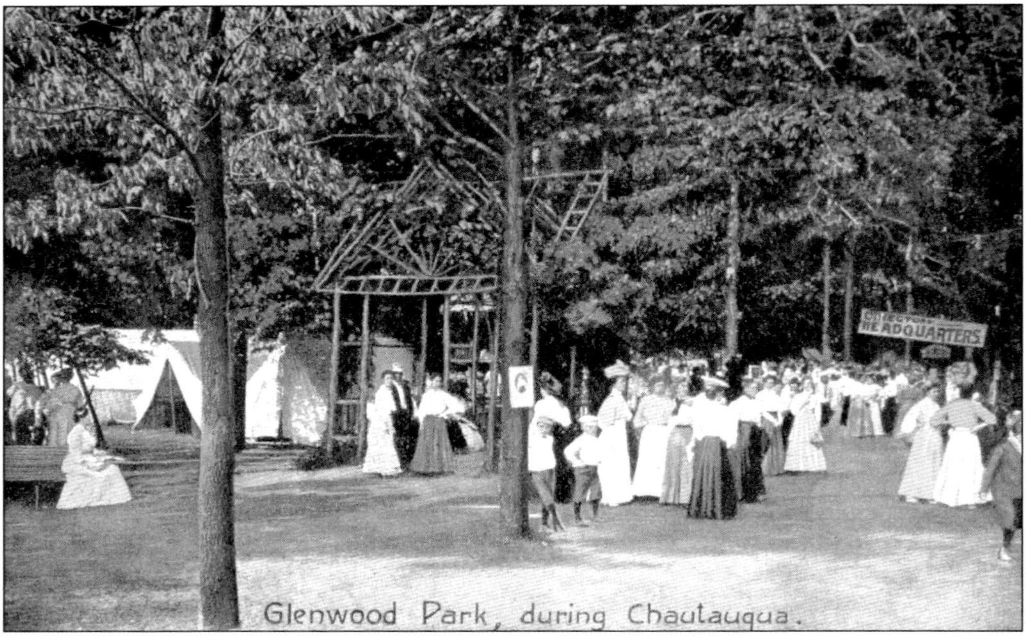

CHAUTAUQUA. An educational outdoor event modeled on a similar one in Chautauqua, New York, this event came to Glenwood Park in 1904 and lasted through 1916. In 1922, there was one last attempt to revive the festival, but it failed. This postcard is from about 1909.

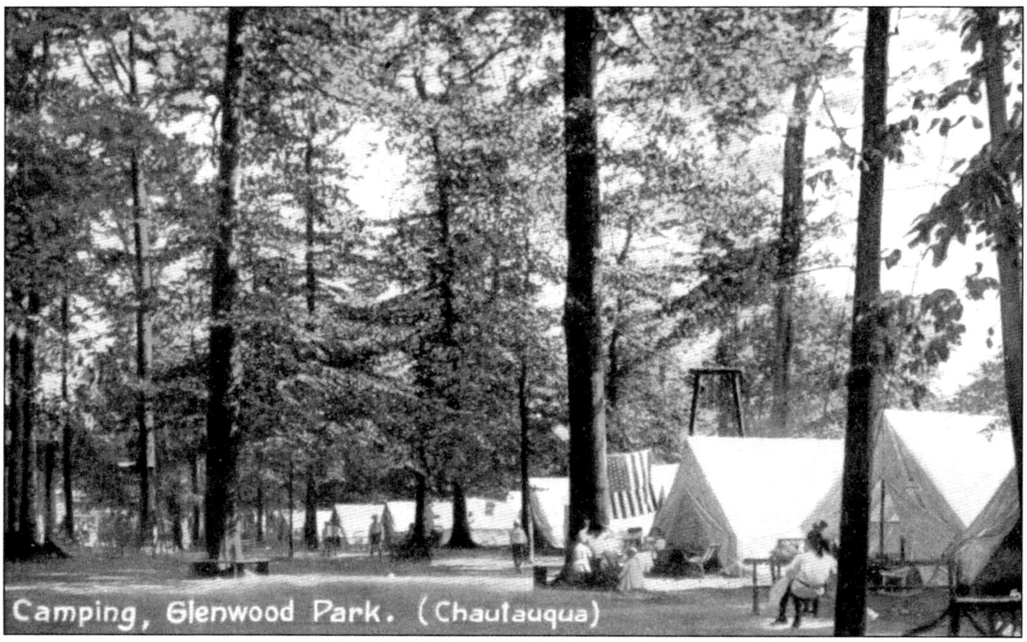

CAMPING. Families would rent tents and camp out during the Chautauqua assembly in Glenwood Park. This image is from about 1909.

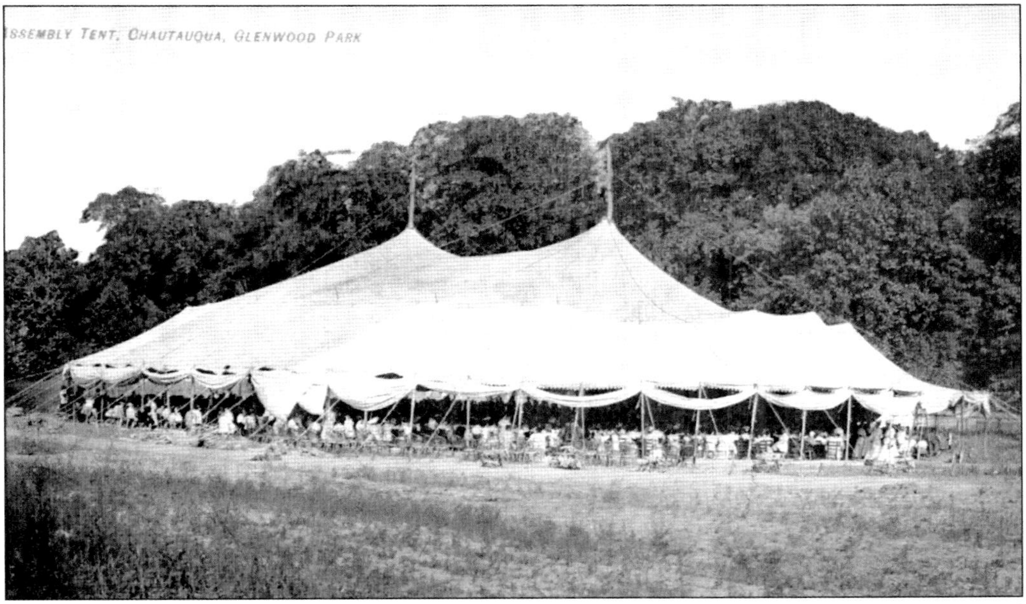

ASSEMBLY TENT. This large tent seated 3,000 people at Chautauqua and was even equipped with electric fans to keep the crowd cool. The tent was erected in the athletic field of the park beyond the baseball diamond and near the creek. This postcard is from about 1908.

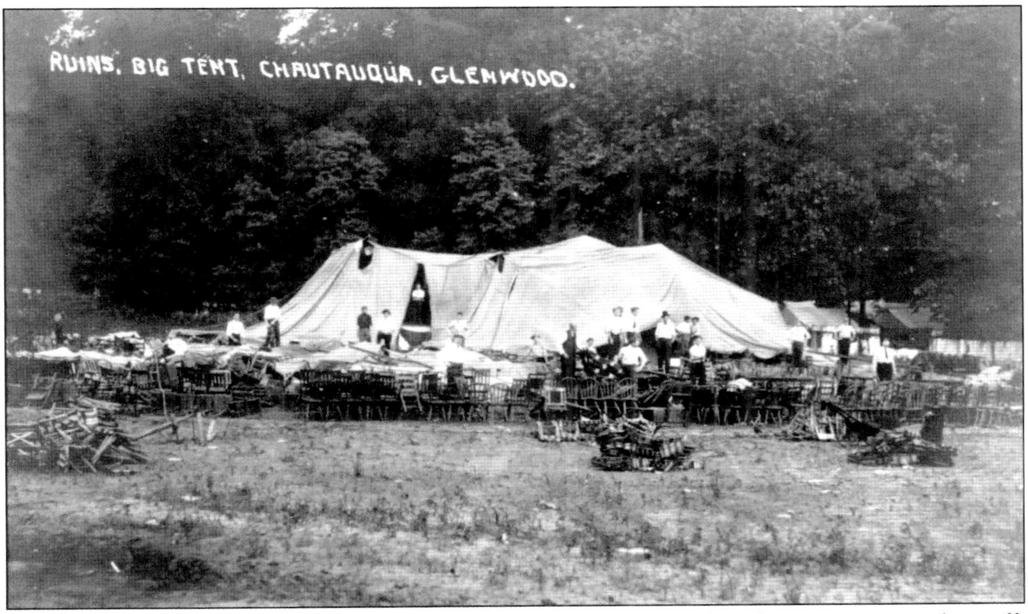

RUINS OF ASSEMBLY TENT. A sudden severe thunderstorm caught Chautauqua attendees off-guard and ripped the main assembly tent to shreds. The 2,000 people attending were drenched and some were slightly injured. Earl Hedden and his fellow musicians were performing in the tent when the storm hit. Hedden later enjoyed bragging that he "had brought down the house" at Chautauqua. This postcard is from 1908.

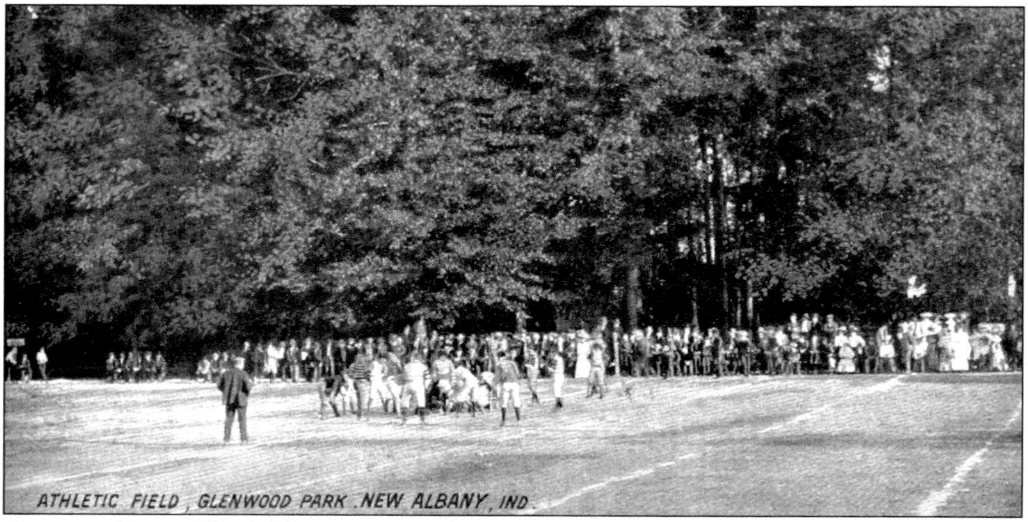

Athletic Field. The field was contained in a separate section of Glenwood and leased to the park by its owner, Nora Duffy. Most area teams played at the athletic field, as it was the only one in the area. New Albany High School used the field for its fall football games until Buerk Field was established. The Calumet Club made use of the field for competition. This is the present day Glenwood Court. This postcard is from about 1909.

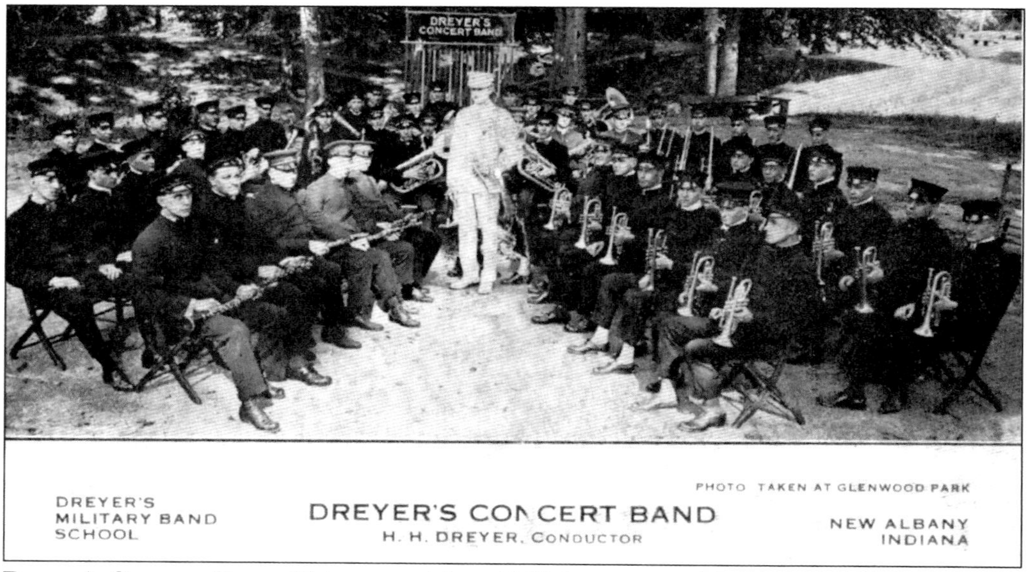

Dreyer's Concert Band. This postcard from 1915 depicts one of the most popular bands at the time, that of Professor H. H. Dreyer. He often performed at Glenwood Park. Professor Dreyer was a native of Indiana who began work for the Indiana State Reformatory directing the band and teaching music at age 21. In 1912, Professor Dreyer and his wife purchased the Packard Music Hall at the northwest corner of East Ninth and Main Streets and the band moved to New Albany. The professor's bands played classical music and standards rather than the popular tunes of the day. He died August 9, 1927, and his son, Henry H. Dreyer Jr., took over the direction of the band. The new leadership was short-lived; Dreyer Jr. died in 1932 at the age of 22.

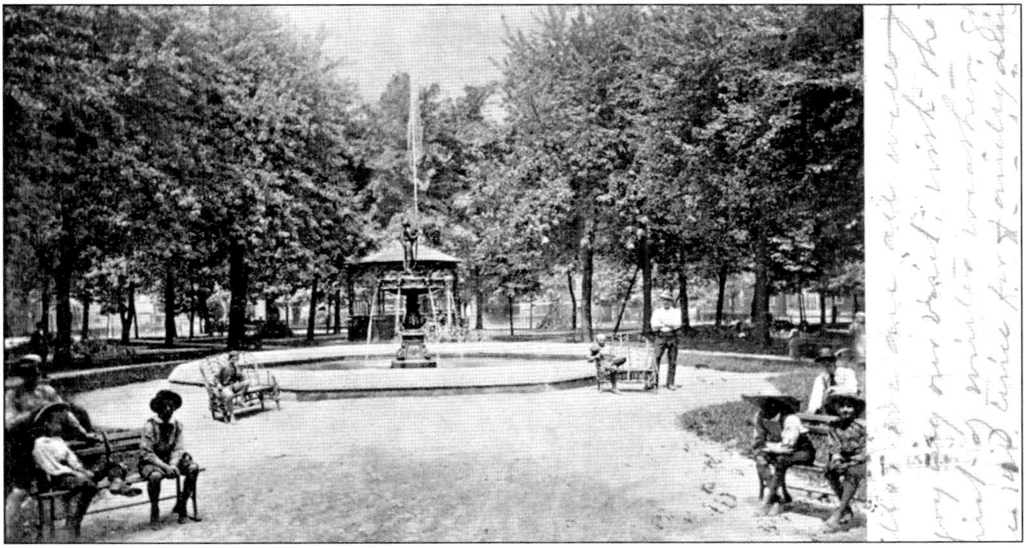

SCRIBNER PARK. This scenic park, named for New Albany's founding family, was located between Lafayette and Washington Streets and Lower Market and Lower Main Streets. The land was donated by the Scribner brothers to the city for the creation of its first park. It is referred to by several different names throughout the city's history, including the Public Square, the Public Promenade, the Public Park, and finally Scribner Park. It was enclosed by an iron fence with four gates, and included benches and meandering walkways. The fountain, shown in this 1905 postcard, featured a fireman shooting water from a nozzle. In 1961, the park was cleared of its 100-year-old trees for the construction of the Sherman Minton Bridge on Interstate 64.

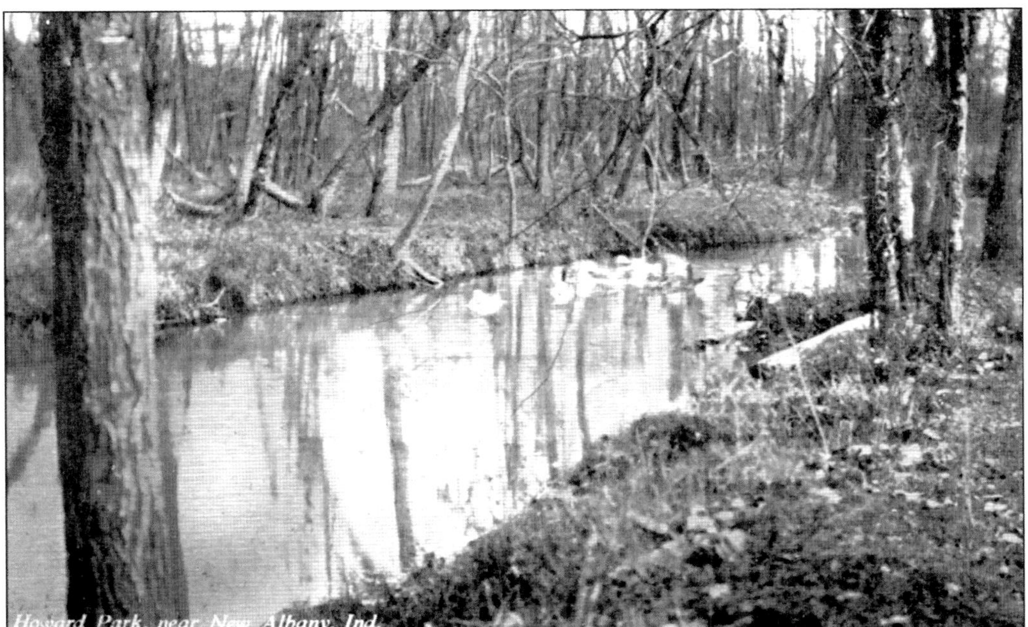

HOWARD PARK. This park was located near New Albany. This postcard is from 1909.

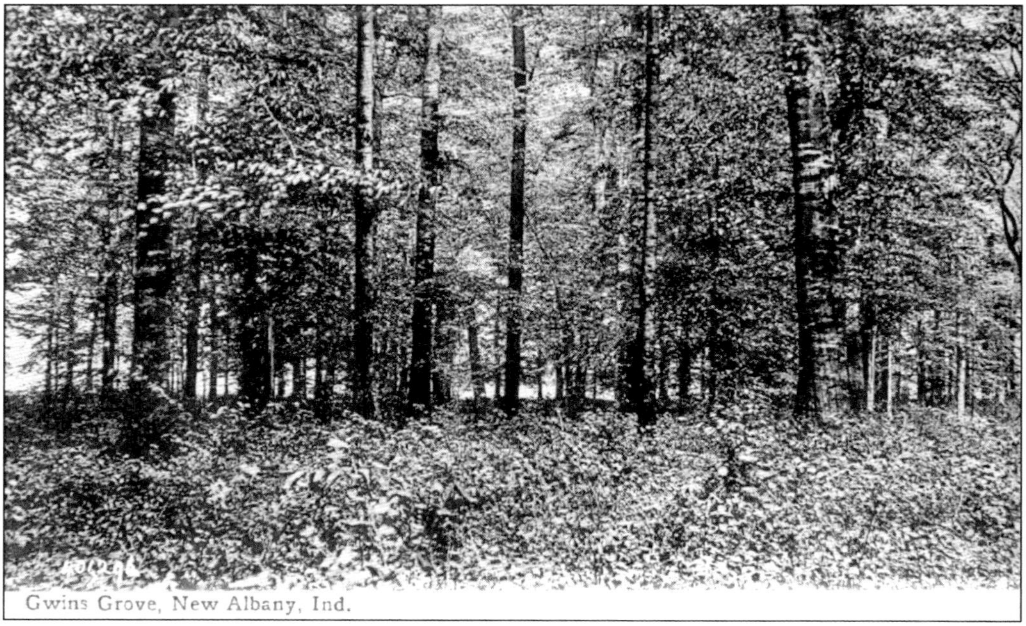

Gwins Grove. This 1910 postcard shows Gwins Grove, located near Dead Man's Hollow.

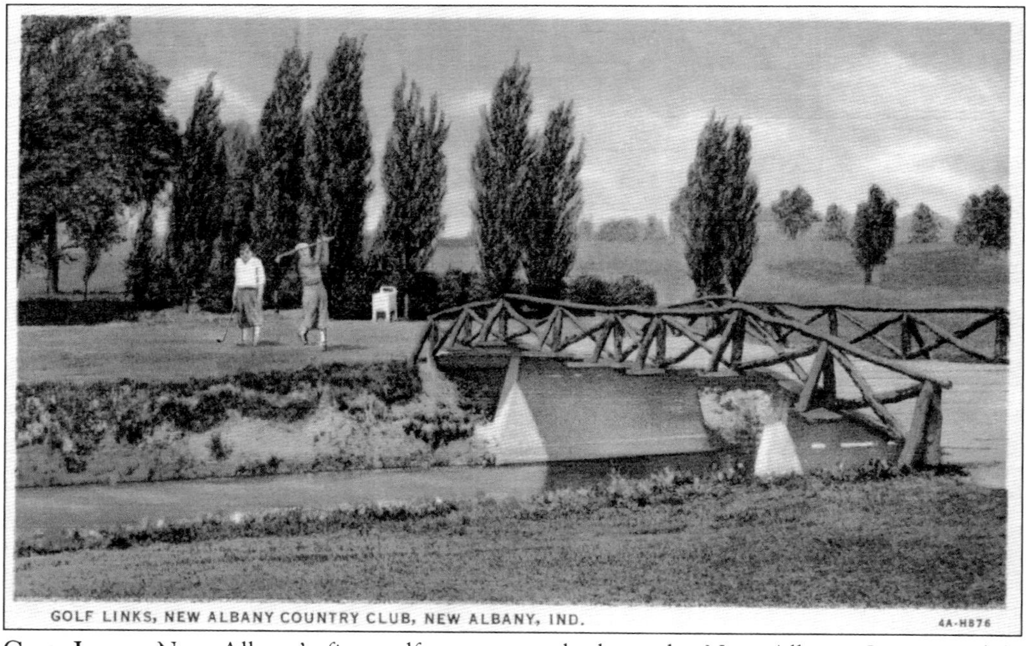

Golf Links. New Albany's first golf course was built at the New Albany Country Club. Chartered May 11, 1922, the club is located at 1702 Graybrook Lane. The building of a country club was a project of the Young Business Men's Club of New Albany. It was built on land owned by Charles McCulloch. The club leased the land for the golf course for $900 annually, with a five-year option to buy the property for $15,000.

Six

Centennial of 1913

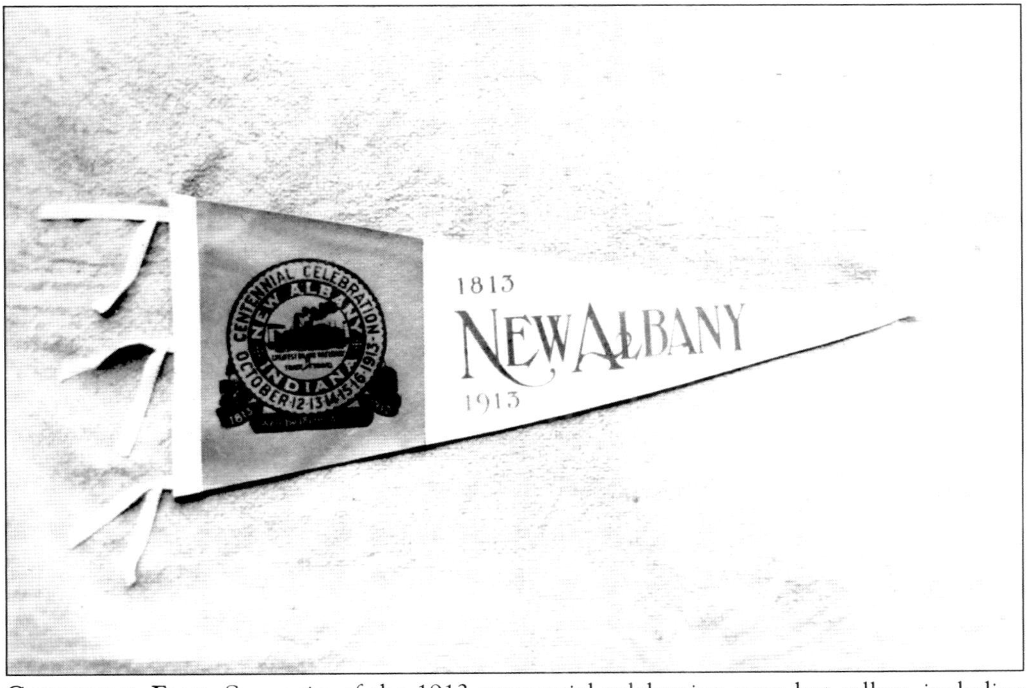

Centennial Flag. Souvenirs of the 1913 centennial celebration were hot sellers, including this 36-inch pennant decorated with the official New Albany Centennial seal. Pins sold for 25 cents, and watch fobs for $1 each. A collapsible drinking cup decorated with a picture of the Scribner house was 10 cents. The sales of souvenirs raised $400, which was given to Miss Hattie Scribner to reimburse her for damage to her home during the centennial open house.

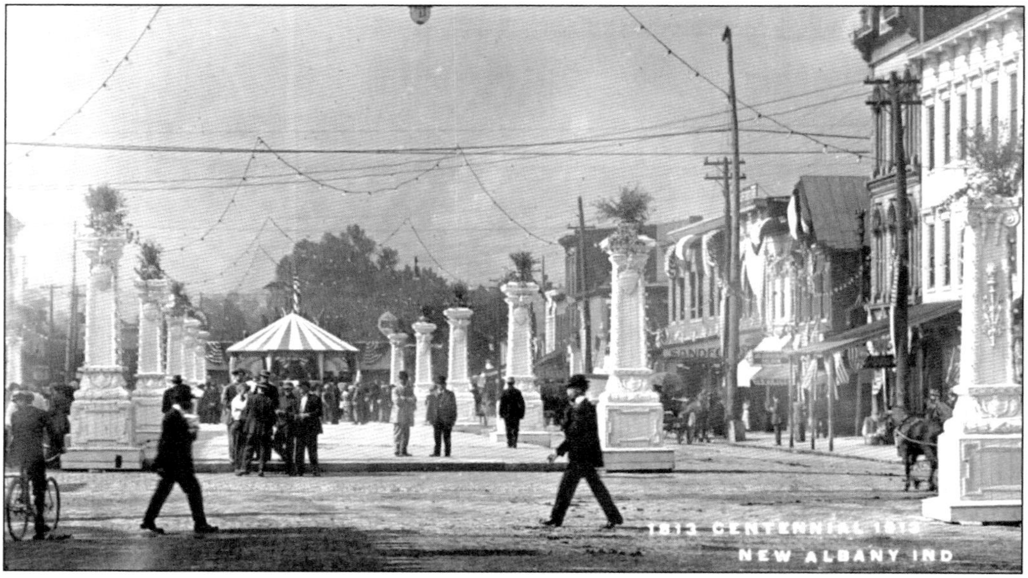

Centennial Plaza. Much of downtown New Albany was decorated for the centennial, as shown in this postcard image of Market Street looking west from Pearl Street. Electric light festoons formed a canopy over the open space, and an immense decoration with an eagle and wreaths bearing the dates 1813–1913 topped the front of Lower Market House at the State Street end.

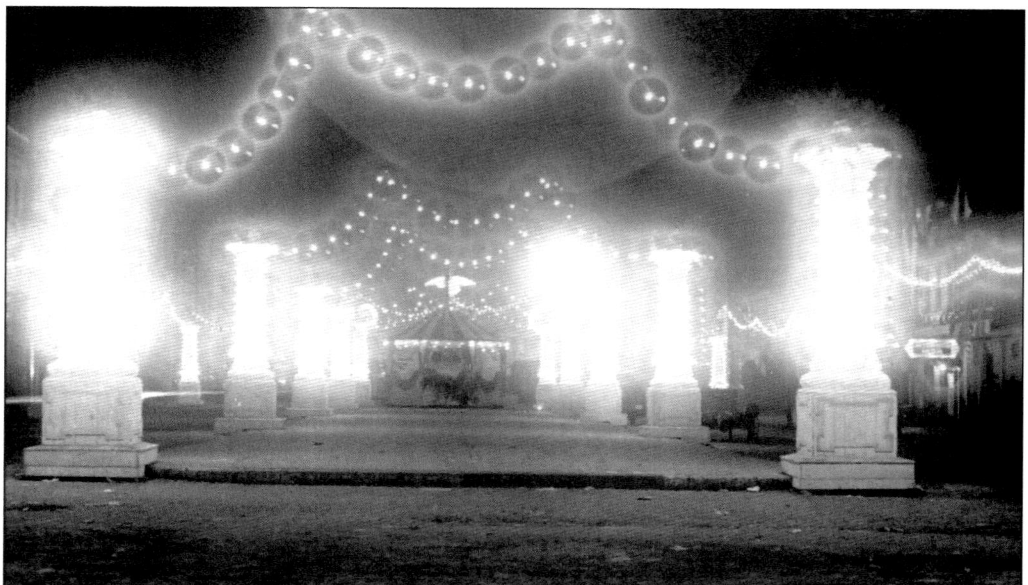

Plaza at Night. This view shows the same area lit with the canopy of electric lights at night. Similar electric light canopies were placed on Main Street from Bank Street to Scribner Park, State Street from Main Street to Spring Street and up Spring Street to Vincennes Street, and on Pearl Street from Main to Spring Streets.

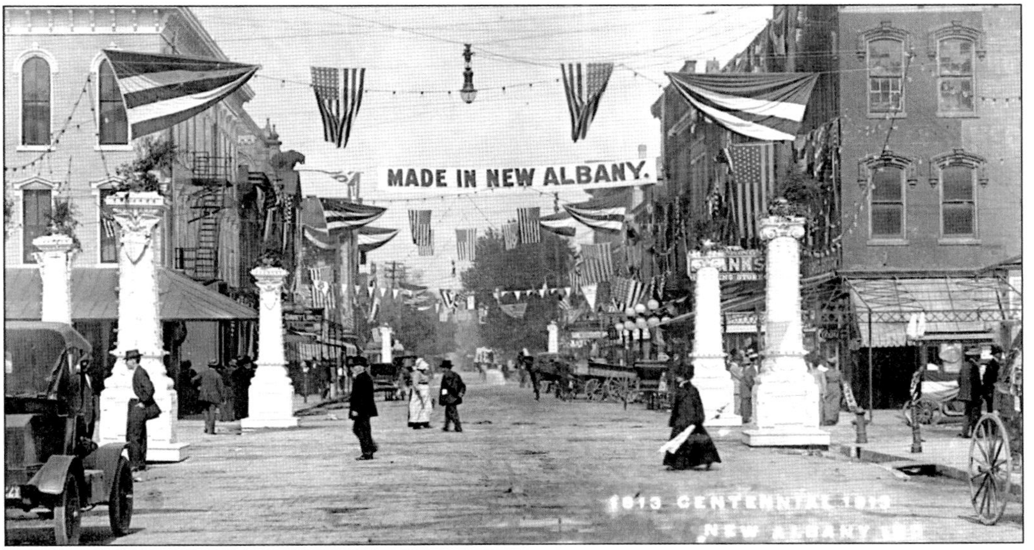

Made in New Albany. One of the central parts of the centennial celebration was an exhibit that showed all of the various wares manufactured in New Albany. Some 90 companies were represented in the exhibit, including at least four that still exist today: Kaiser's, Vernia's, the New Albany Ledger and the New Albany Tribune. The centennial was celebrated from October 12 to October 16, 1913.

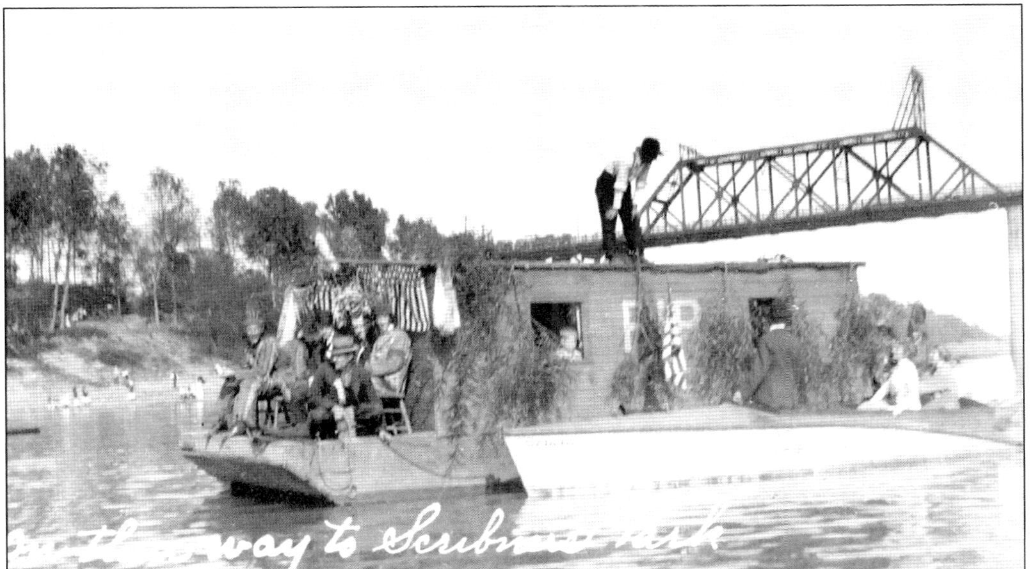

On Their Way to Scribner Park. New Albany's civic leaders invited the descendants of the city's founding fathers to come to New Albany and join them in the centennial celebrations. George Scribner, a great-grandson of Abner Scribner, and his three sons rode a replica of an early houseboat about a mile down the Ohio River to commemorate their forefathers historic landing in the city 100 years before them. All of the men lived in Indianapolis and came to New Albany for the centennial celebration.

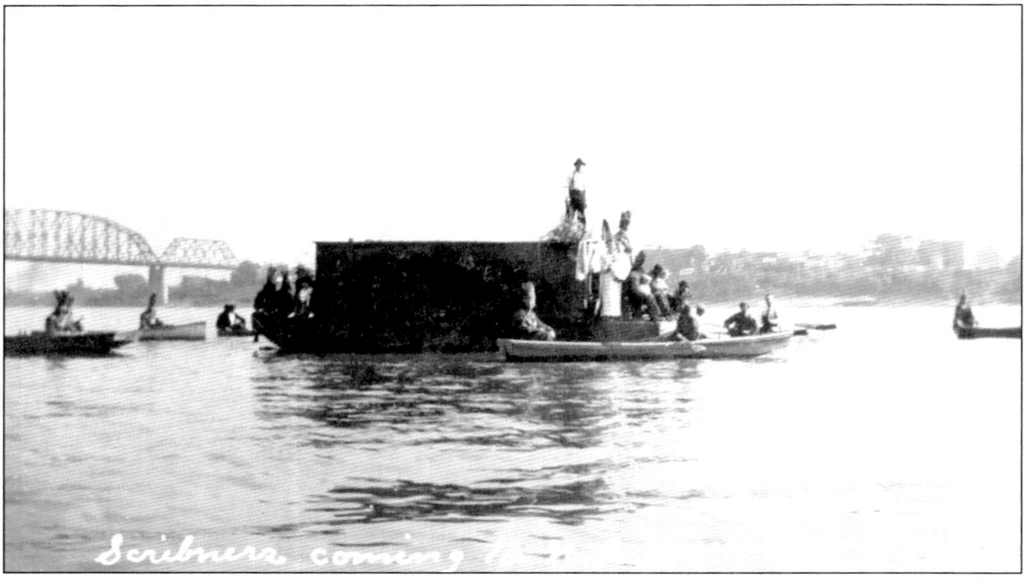

Scribners Coming to New Albany. The Scribner descendants began their journey near the Kentucky and Indiana Railroad Bridge, escorted by three men dressed in what was then believed to be Native American garb. Their journey down the river on October 13, 1913, was about a mile long.

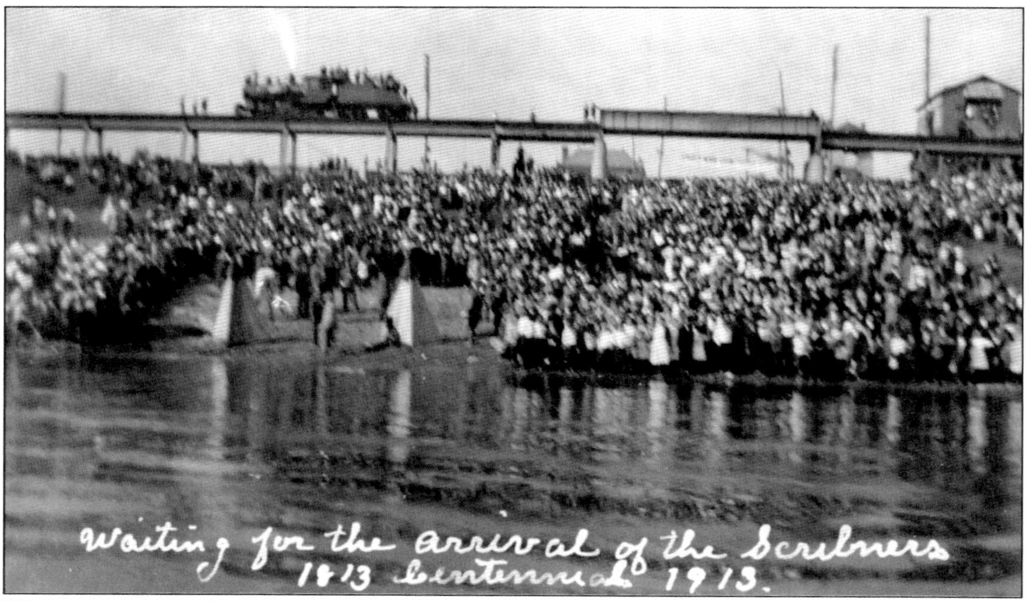

Waiting for the Scribners. Thousands gathered on the banks of the Ohio River to watch as descendants of the town's founders, the Scribners, made their way down the river to replicate the journey of their forefathers.

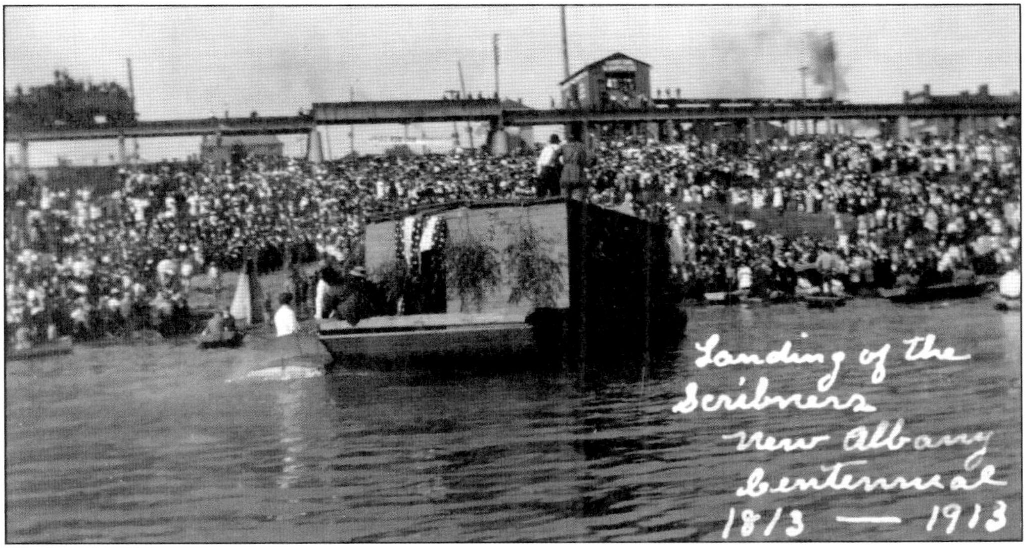

Landing of the Scribners. The Scribner descendants landed at the riverfront en route to the park named for their forefathers. They were greeted by members of the local group of the Improved Order of Red Men Manzanita Tribe No. 276 fraternal organization, who donned Native American costumes for the ceremony.

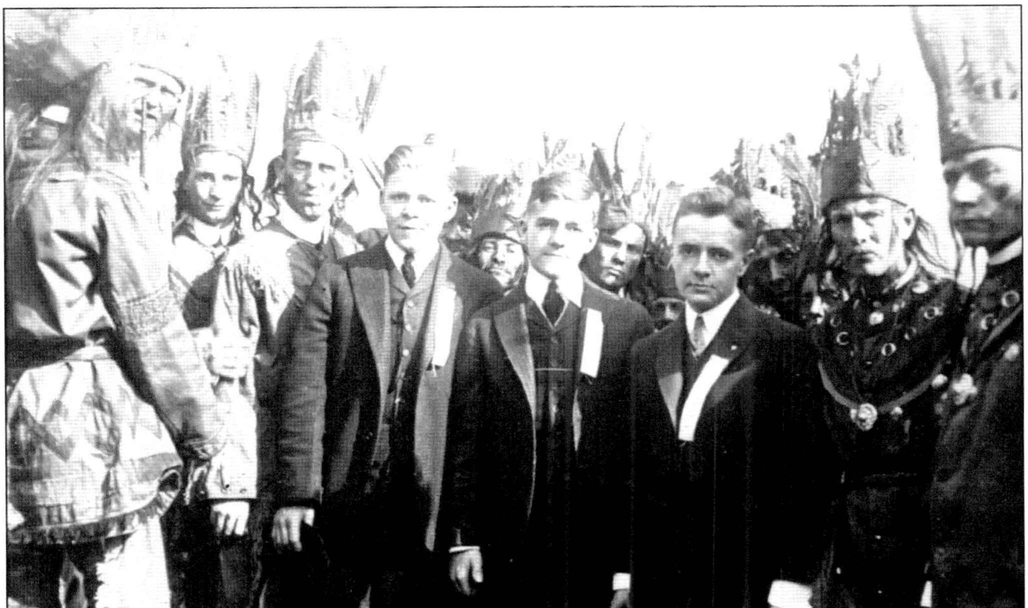

Scribners Arrive. The three Scribner great-great-grandsons pose for a photograph with the members of the Improved Order of Red Men Manzanita Tribe No. 276 fraternal organization. The Scribners were also greeted by New Albany Mayor Newton Green. George Scribner, the father of the three Scribner great-great-grandsons, gave a speech at the park.

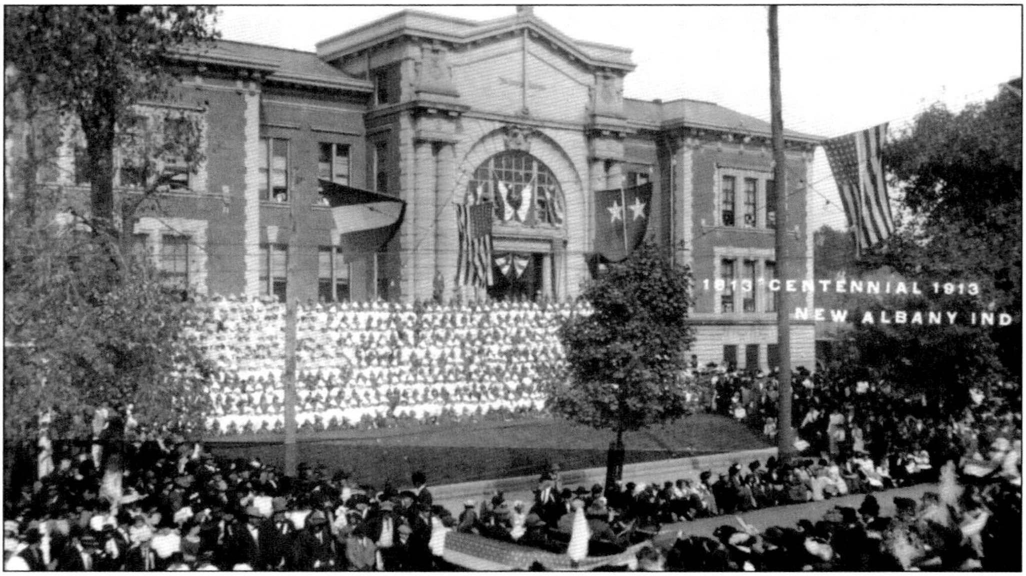

LIVING FLAG. To commemorate the centennial, 700 school children formed a human flag at the People's College, East Sixth and Spring Streets, for the centennial parade. The students formed 13 red and white stripes and a blue field of 130 students holding 48 stars for the number of states at that time. The parade was held on October 14, 1913.

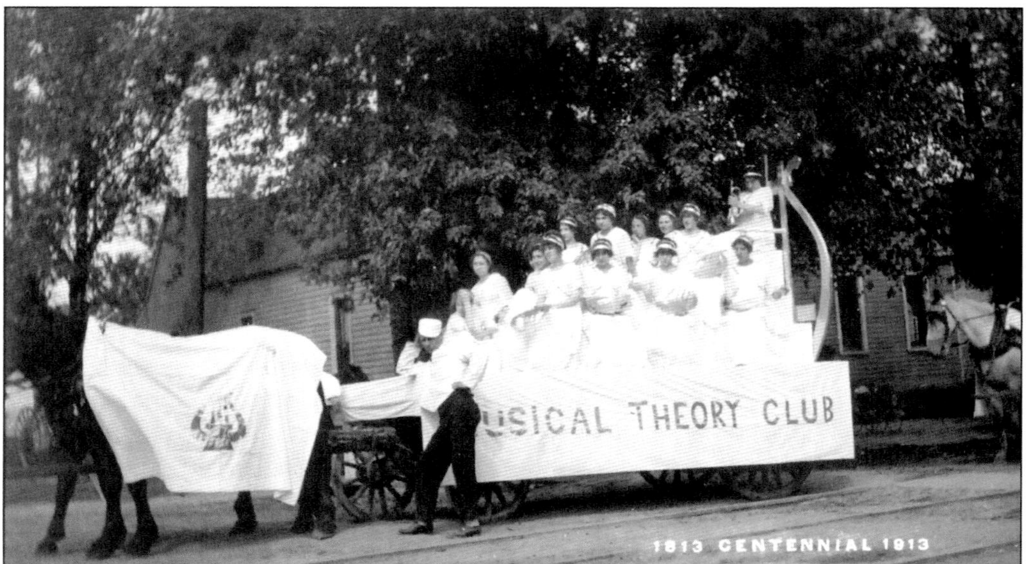

MUSICAL THEORY FLOAT. Among the 108 floats in the centennial parade was one by the Musical Theory Club.

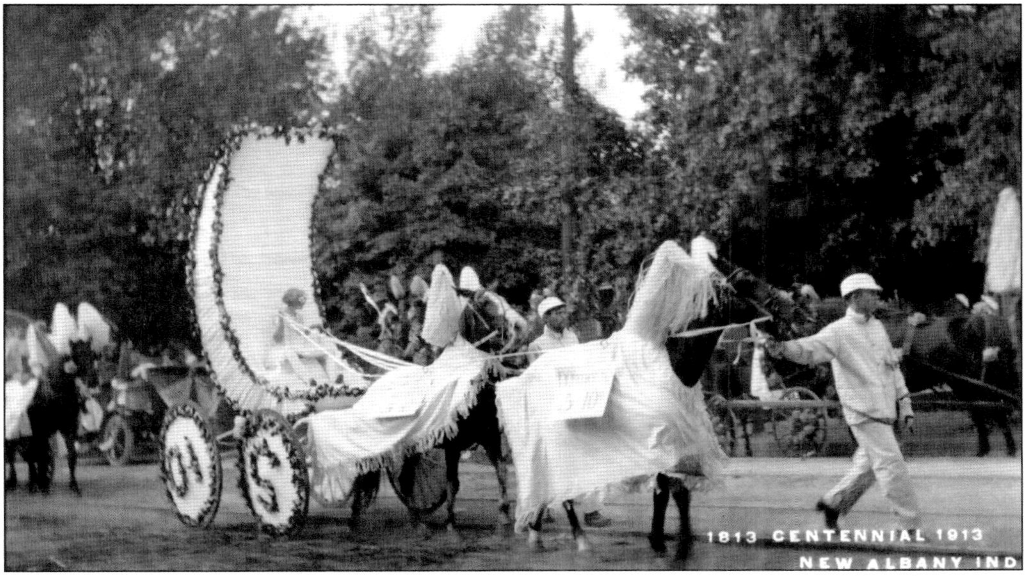

WOOLWORTH FLOAT. Dimestore retailer F.W. Woolworth created a whimsical float featuring a girl in a crescent moon-shaped carriage pulled by festively dressed horses. Note the numbers "5" and "10" on the wheels of the carriage.

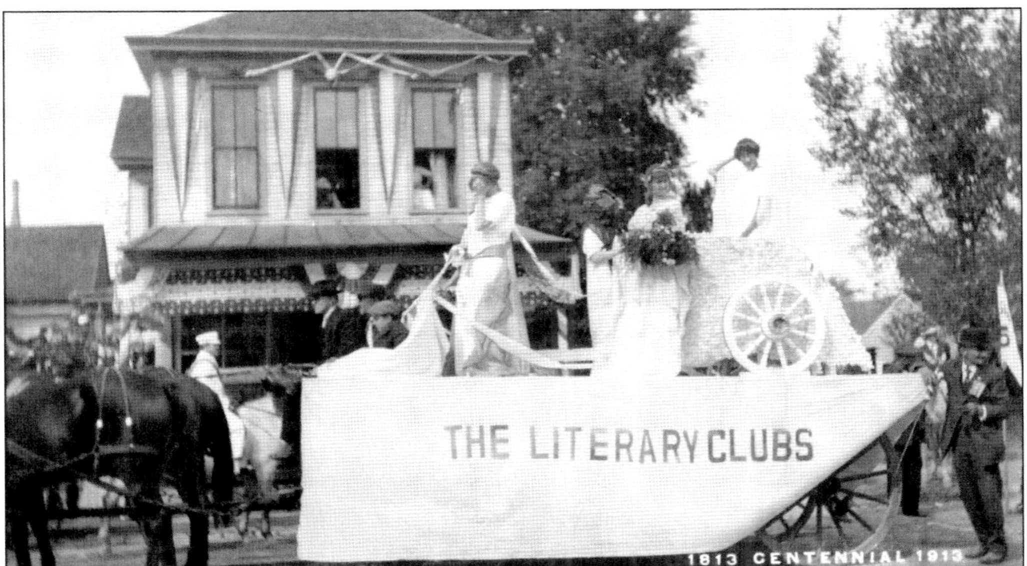

LITERARY CLUBS FLOAT. Betty Crecelius is one of the women on the Literary Clubs float. This float was photographed in front of 1747 East Spring Street.

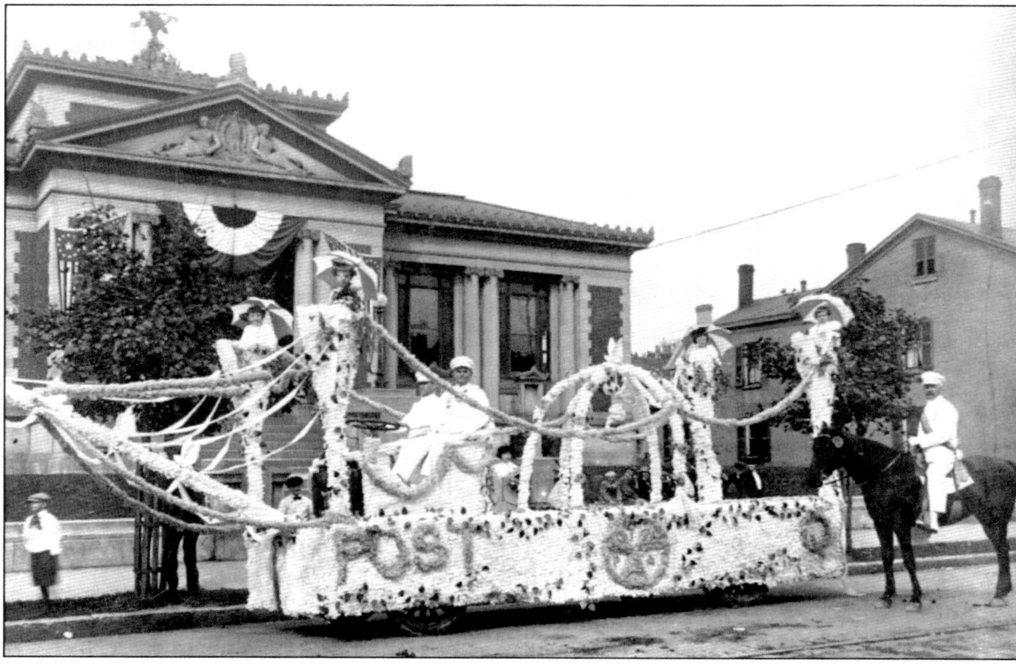

TRAVELERS' ASSOCIATION FLOAT. This fanciful, flower-covered float was created by the Travelers' Protective Association of America New Albany Post Q. The float was photographed in front of the Carnegie Library on East Spring Street.

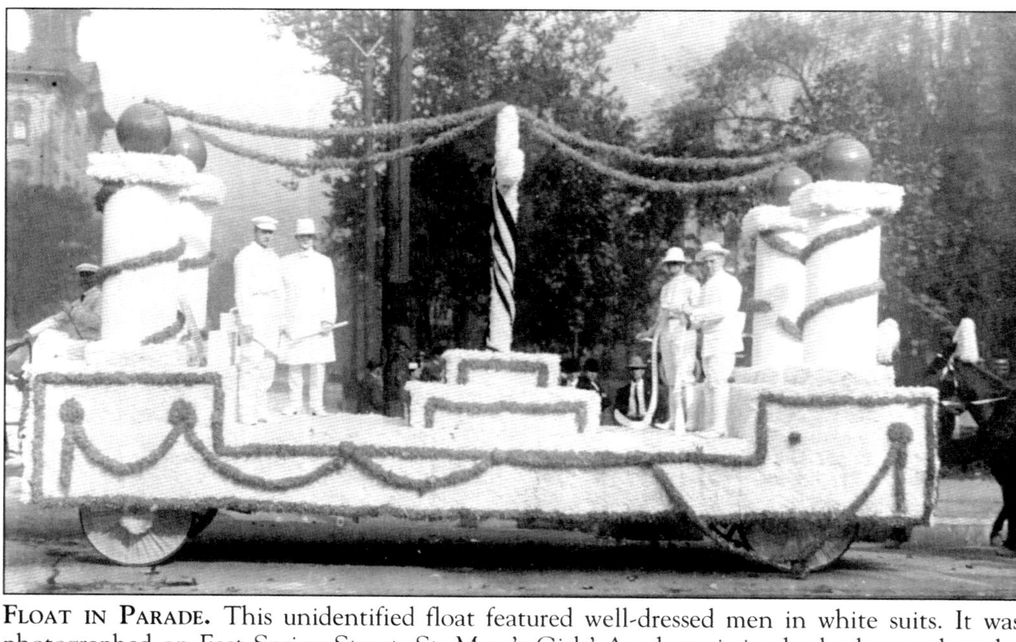

FLOAT IN PARADE. This unidentified float featured well-dressed men in white suits. It was photographed on East Spring Street. St. Mary's Girls' Academy is in the background to the left.

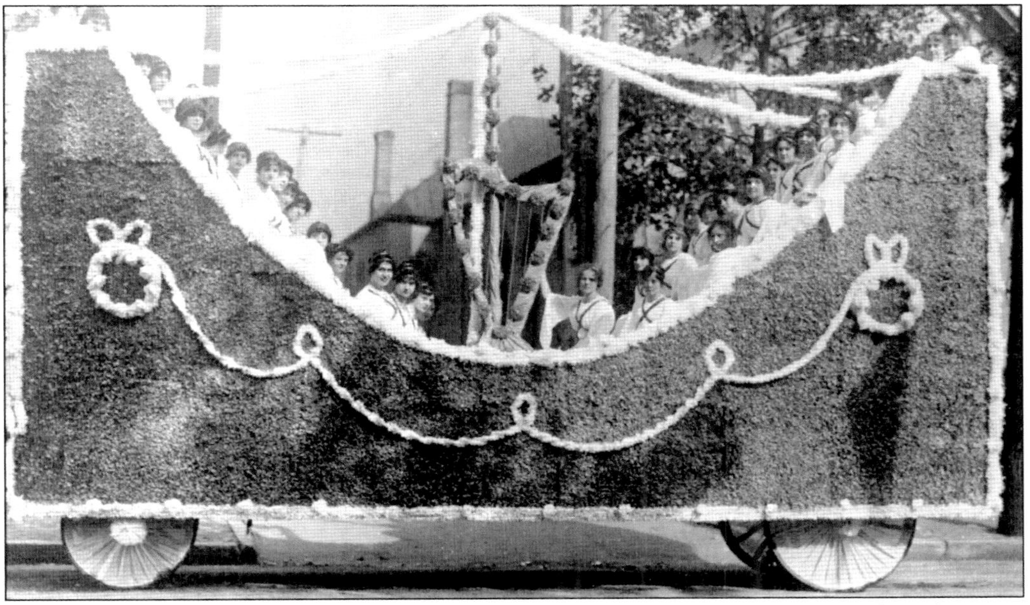

Float in Parade. This float was photographed in front of what was then the Third Presbyterian Sunday School building, 813 East Spring Street.

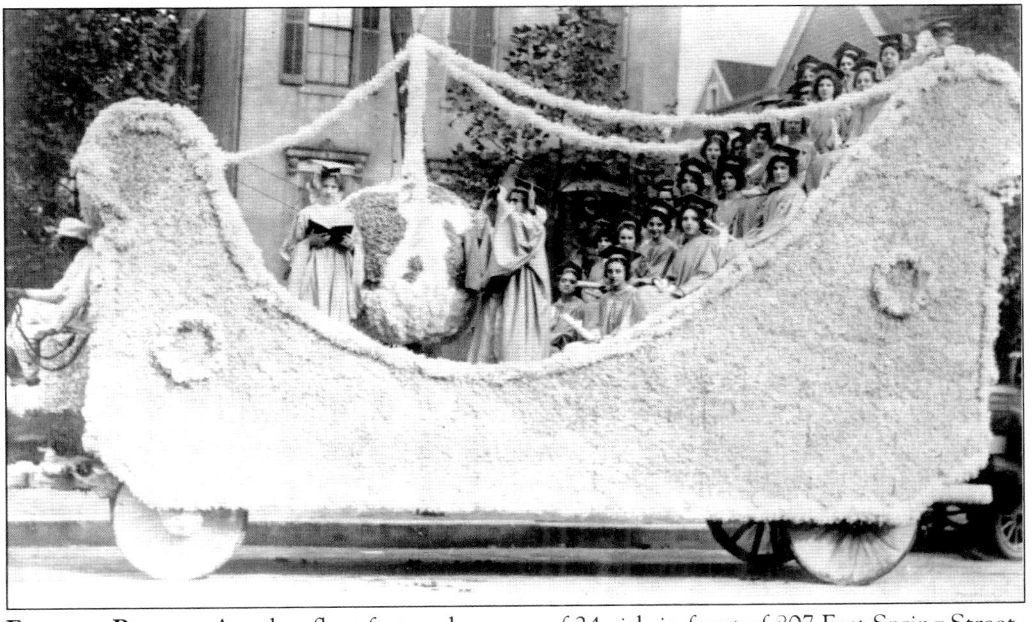

Float in Parade. Another float featured a group of 24 girls in front of 307 East Spring Street.

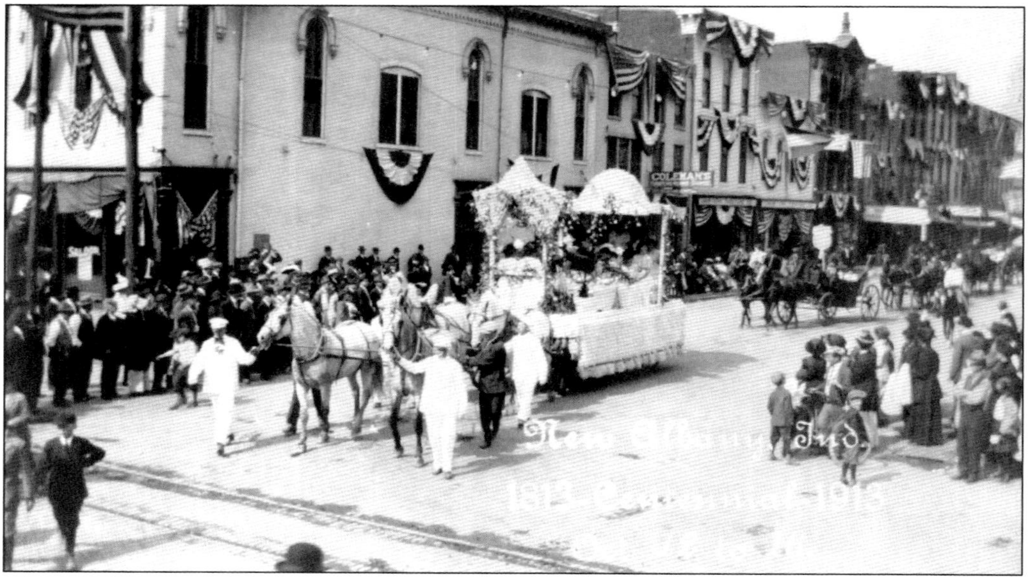

VIEW OF PARADE. The centennial parade wound through downtown streets. This view shows the parade at the corner of State and Main Streets looking northwest.

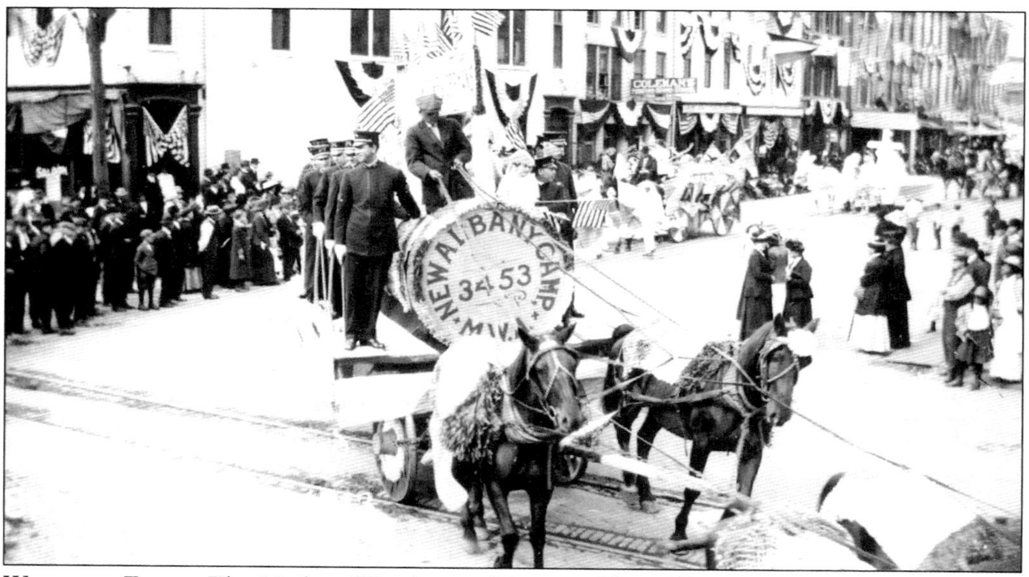

WOODMEN FLOAT. The Modern Woodmen of America New Albany Camp No. 3453 created a float that looked like a large log and was pulled by horses. The float is shown at the intersection of State and Main Streets looking northwest.

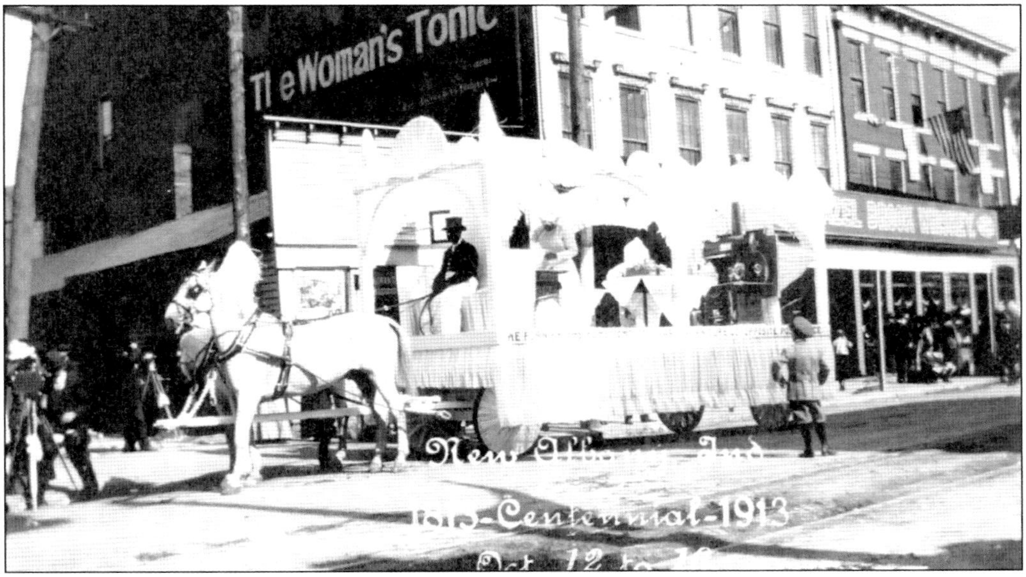

Gable Furniture Float. Along with various civic and fraternal organizations, businesses also had floats in the centennial parade. Gable Furniture Co., which sponsored this float, was located at 334 Pearl Street in 1913. The float was parked in front of 108 West Main Street in this postcard image.

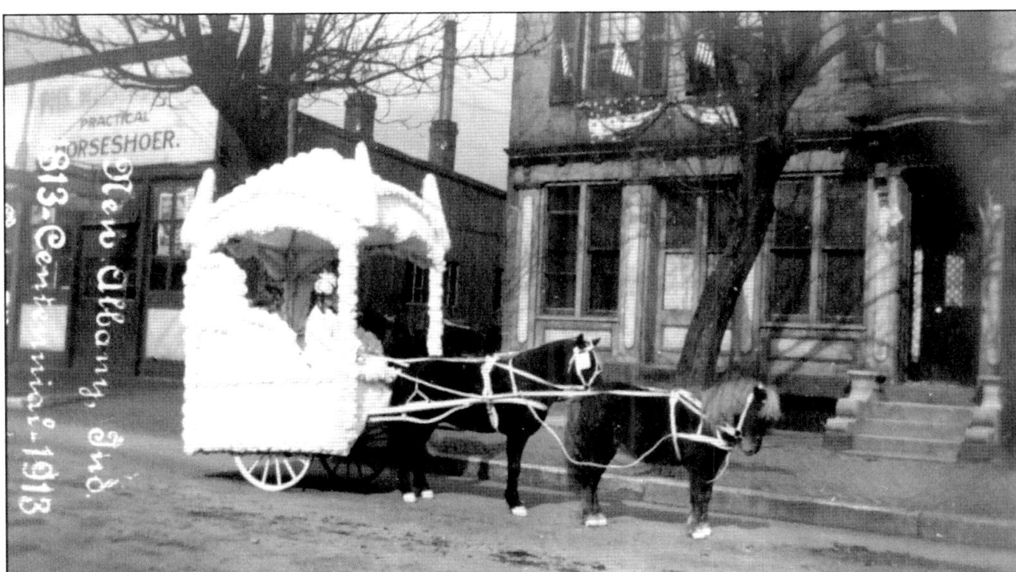

Float in Parade. This centennial float was photographed at the corner of Pearl and Elm Streets.

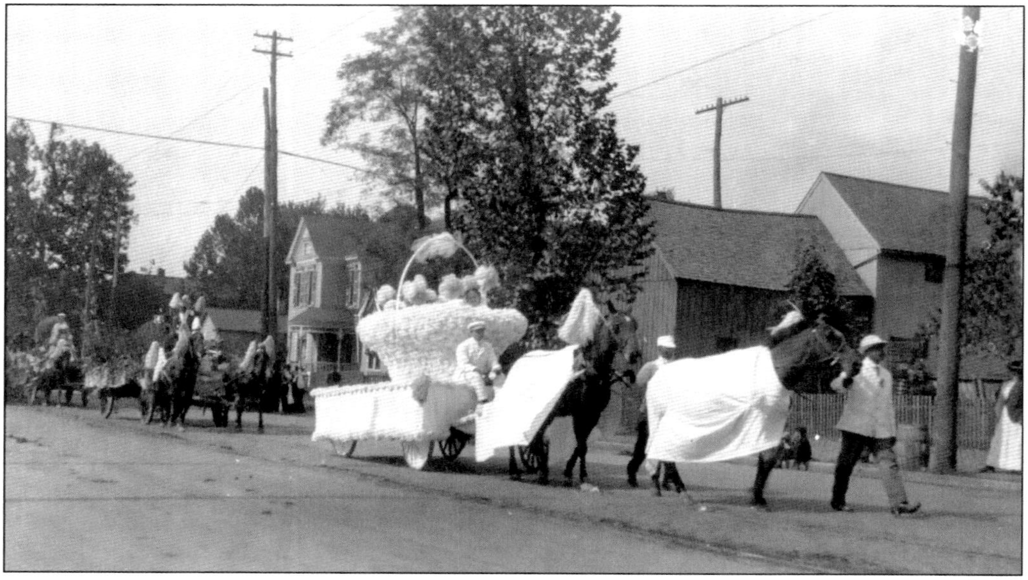

Float in Parade. This float, designed to look like a basket, was photographed in front of 146 West Spring Street.

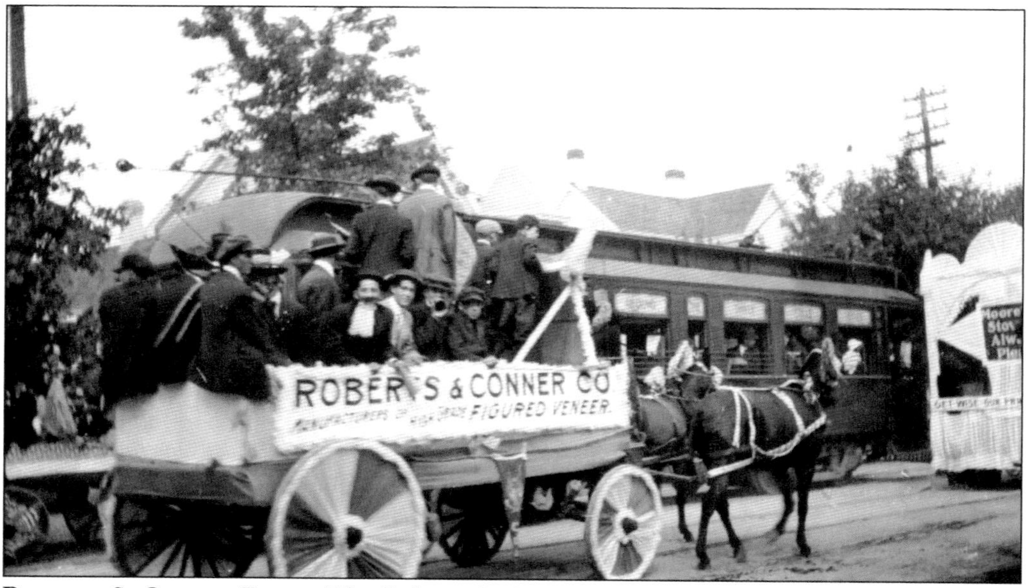

Roberts & Conner Float. The Roberts & Conner Co. was a New Albany manufacturing business that created wood veneer. Its float was photographed at 1819 East Spring Street. Its factory was located along the Ohio River at Woodruff Street and its office at 510 Pearl Street.

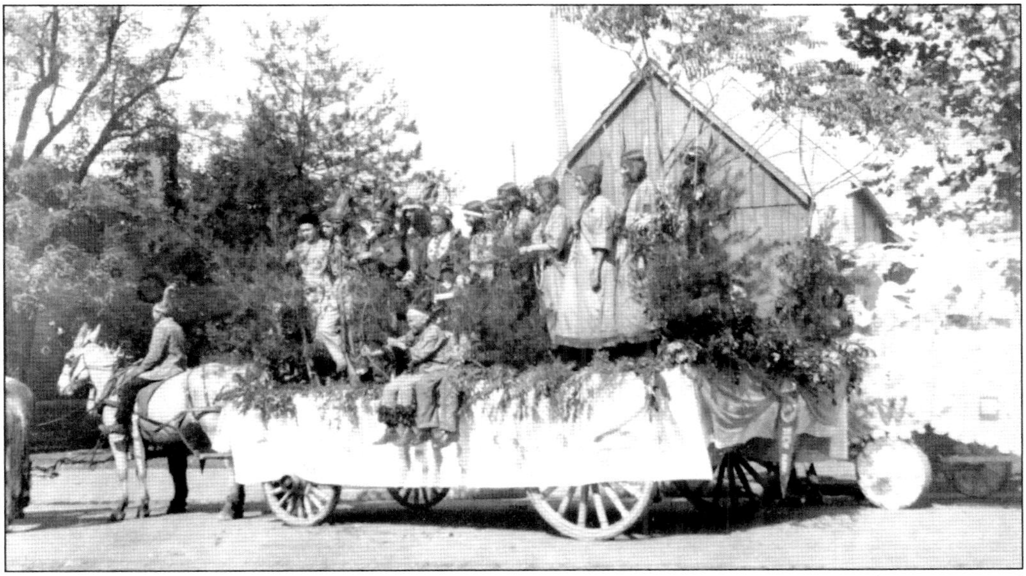

DAR Float. The Piankeshaw Chapter of the Daughters of the American Revolution created a float for the parade. Members of the group dressed in Native American costumes for the occasion.

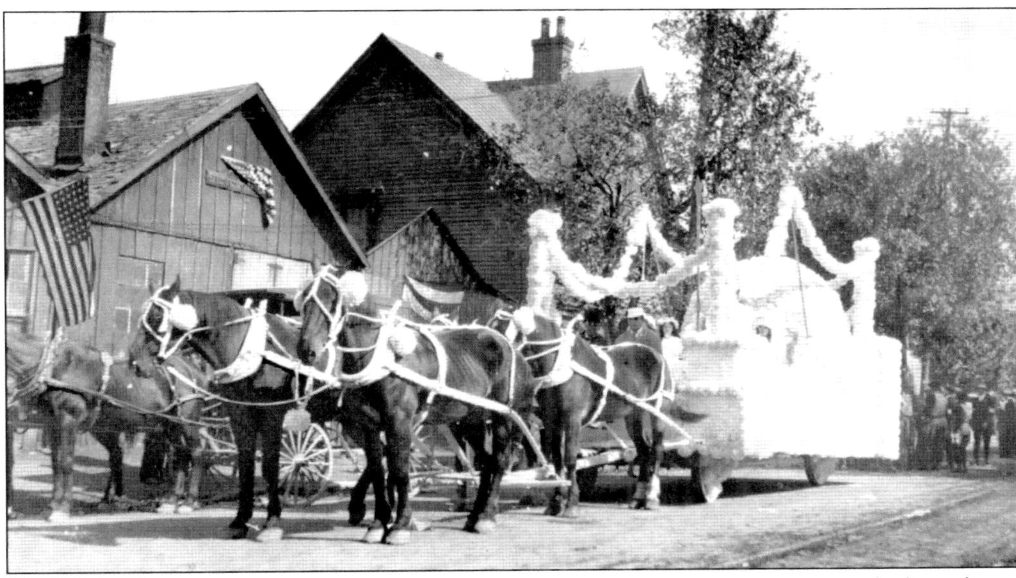

Float in Parade. This float was photographed in front of the old Fred Sievers Blacksmith and Horseshoer at 120–130 West Spring Street looking north.

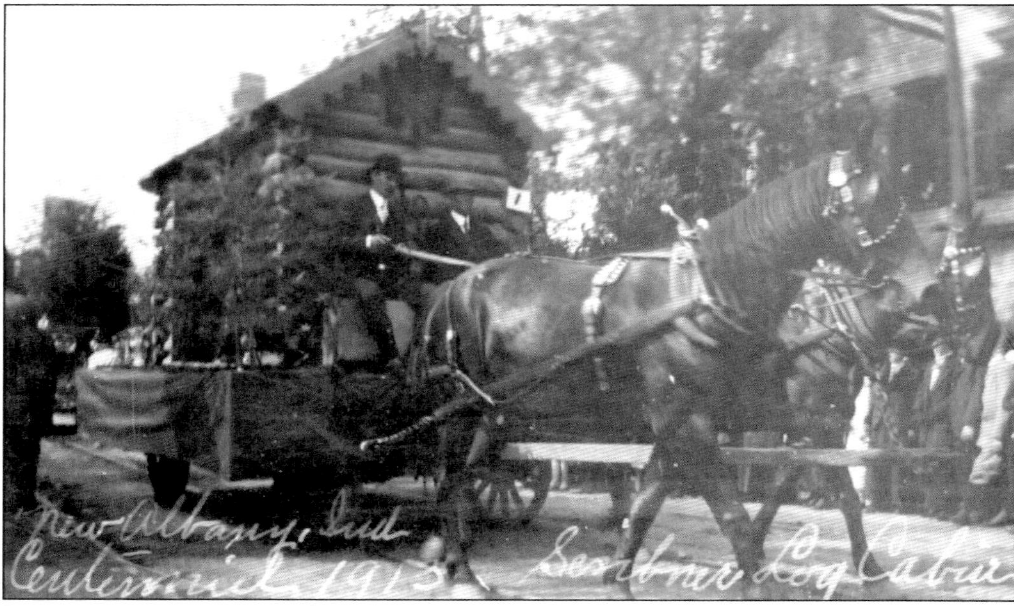

SCRIBNER DESCENDANTS. A log cabin reminiscent of the home the Scribners first used in New Albany was part of a centennial parade float. The Scribner descendants rode that float during the parade.

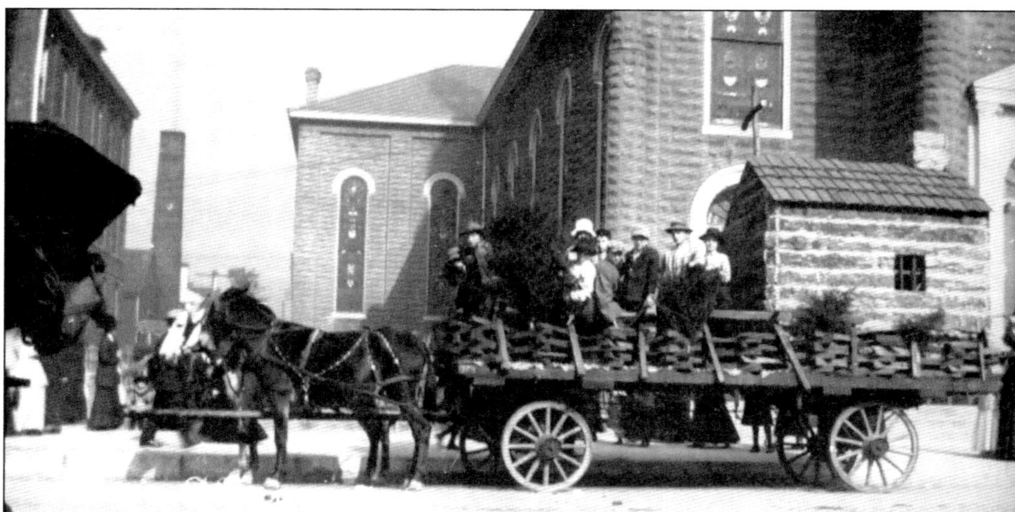

FLOAT IN PARADE. A second float with a log structure was used in the centennial parade, this one appearing to represent a church. This float was photographed in front of St. Mary's of the Annunciation on Spring Street.

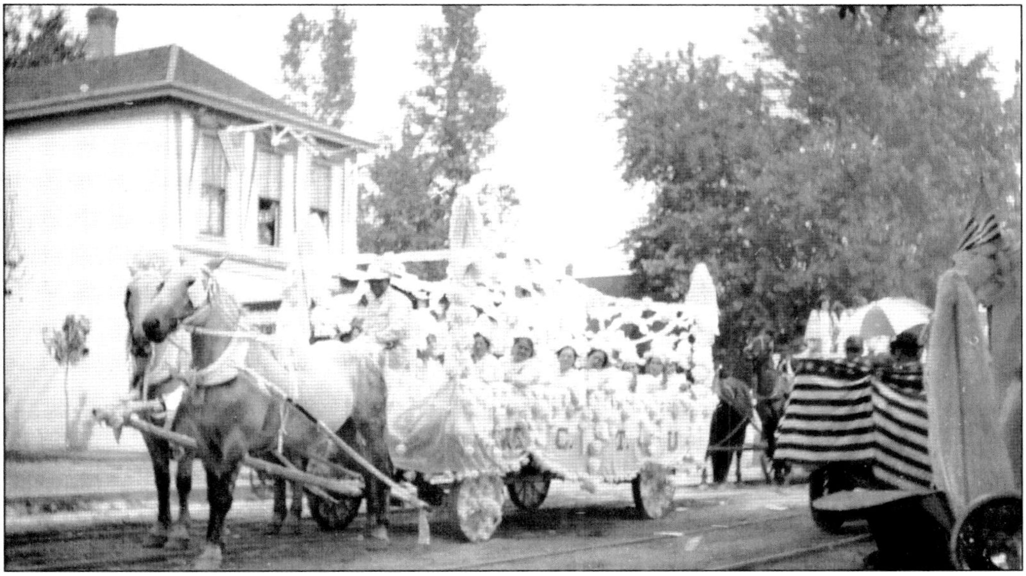

Temperance Float. The Women's Christian Temperance Union float held a large group of women wearing white uniforms. They were photographed in front of 1747 East Spring Street.

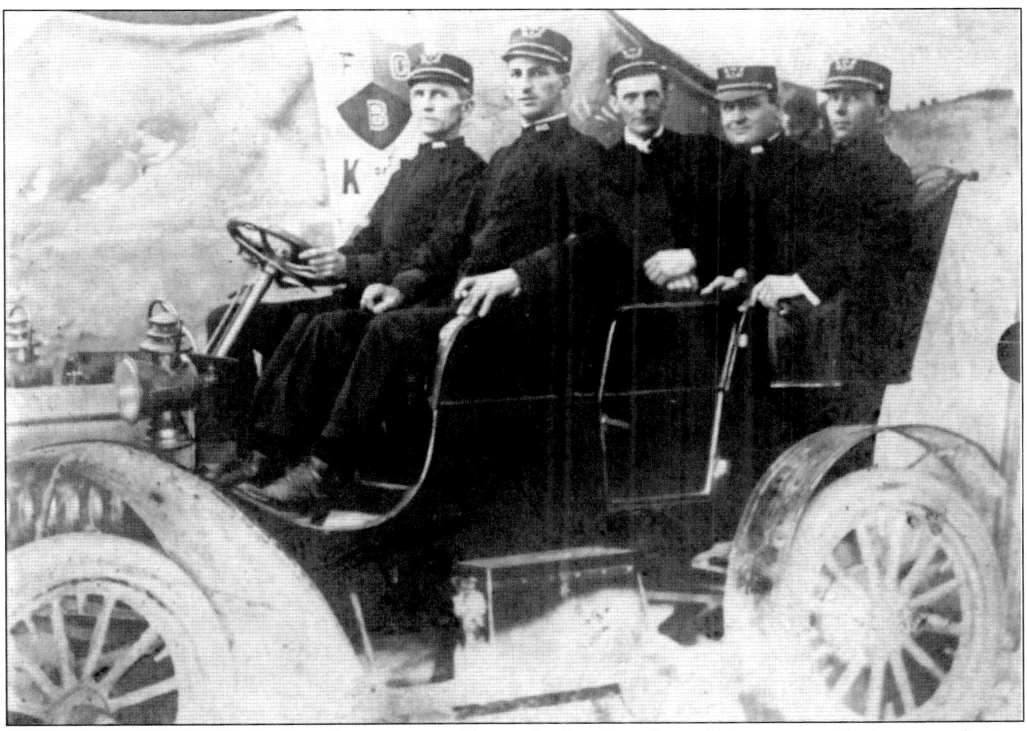

Car in Parade. This group of men, possibly with the Knights of Pythias, rode in a car during the parade.

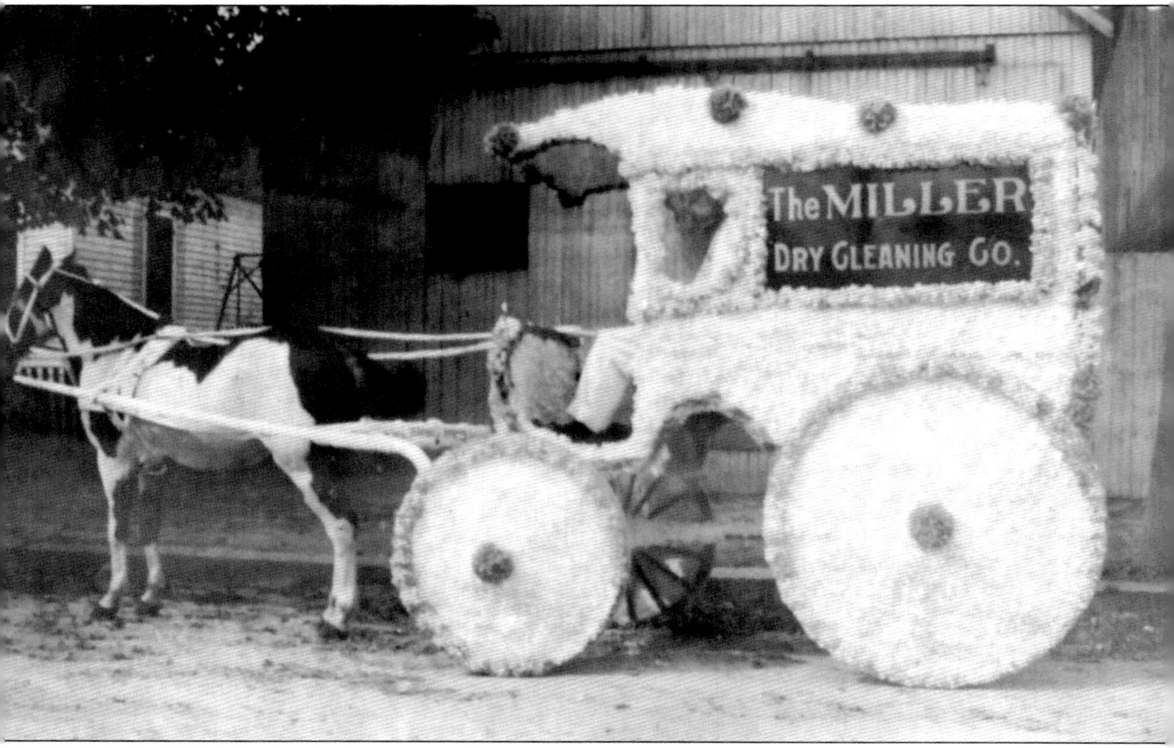

Miller Dry Cleaning. This business was new to New Albany when it put its decorated horse and buggy in the centennial parade. The business was established in Louisville in 1906 by John H. Miller and moved to New Albany in 1910. It was located at 330 Vincennes Street in 1913. Miller is believed to have been the first man in New Albany to install a modern steam-pressing machine. The company was advertised in the centennial book as being "complaint proof." The business offered pick up and delivery.

Seven

Floods

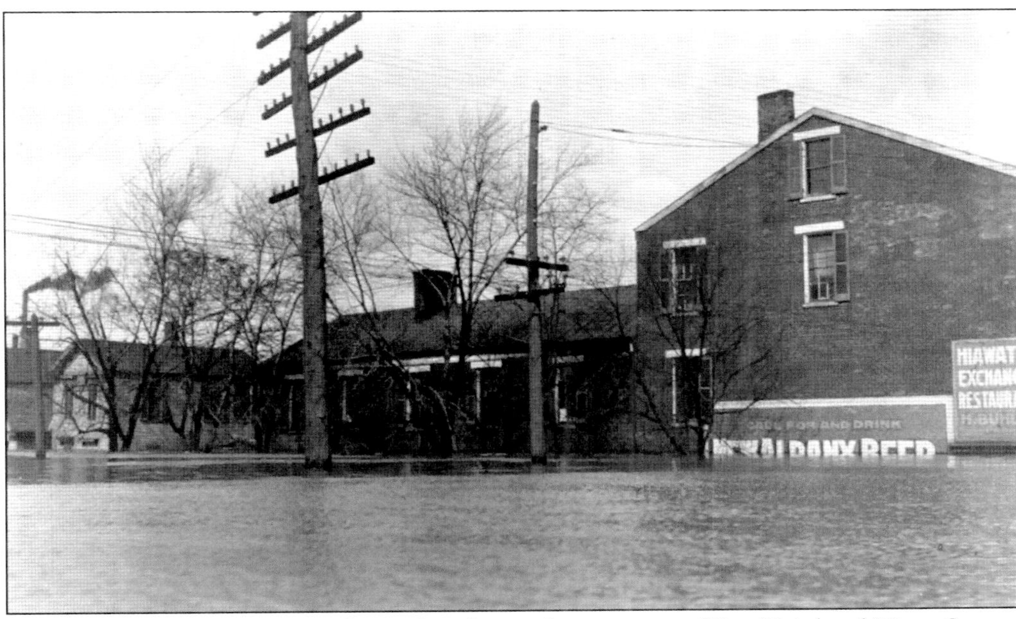

1907 Flood. This building was located on the northeast corner of East Third and Water Streets. For years, the building housed the John E. Meyer Saloon. In 1907, when this area flooded, the building was vacant. The 1907 flood recorded a crest of 69.1 feet above flood stage on the Ohio River on January 22 and 23.

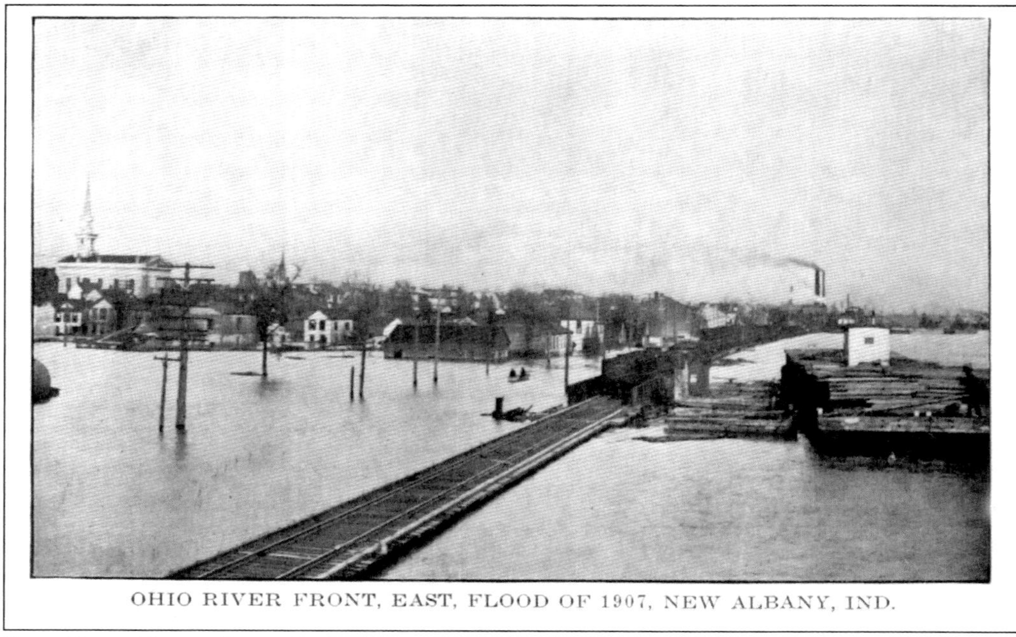

Ohio River Front East. Second Baptist Church, built in 1852, is shown on the left-hand side of this postcard image. Its original steeple can be seen. The steeple was struck by lightning and destroyed in 1914. This image is from the 1907 flood.

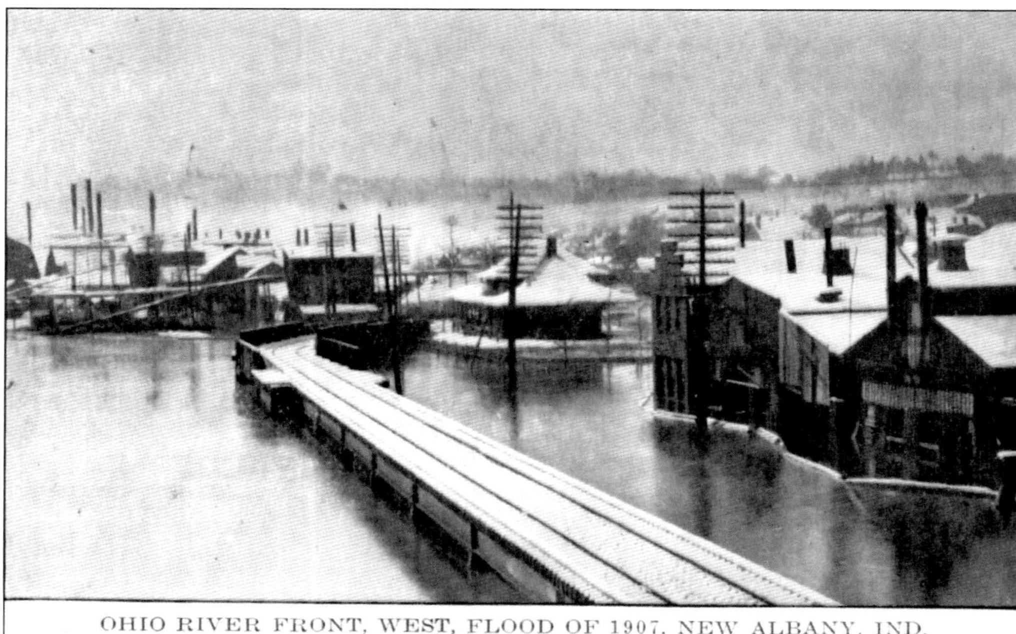

Ohio River Front West. The Southern Railroad Depot, located on the northwest corner of West First and Water Streets, is shown in the middle of this postcard image from the 1907 flood.

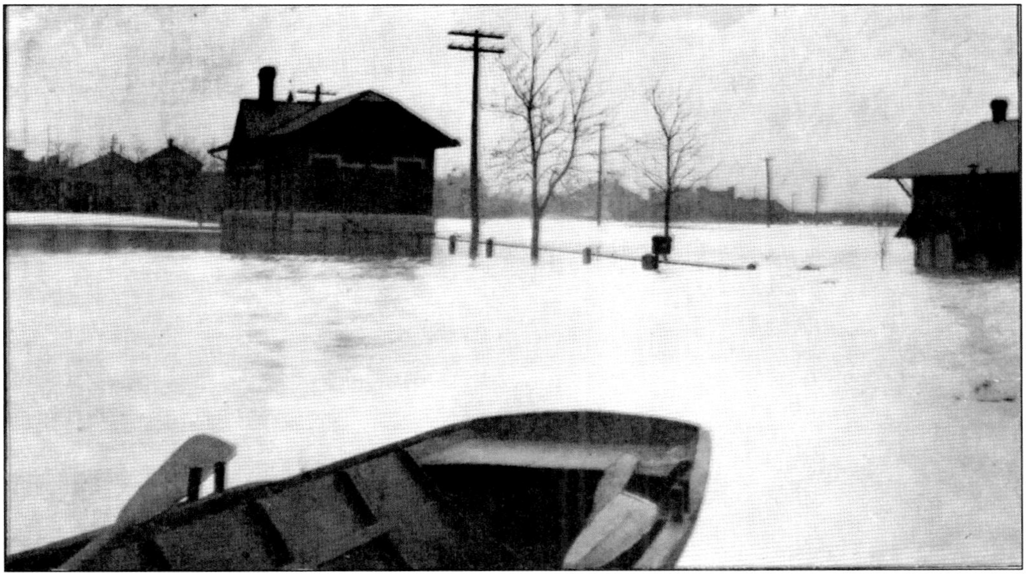

Freight and Passenger Station. The Pennsylvania Railroad Passenger Depot, built in 1883, was located one block south of Main Street between State and Pearl Streets. In this 1907 postcard, it is in the center, and the Pennsylvania Railroad Freight Station can barely be seen to the right. Though extensively modified, this structure still stands today at the foot of State Street on the east side.

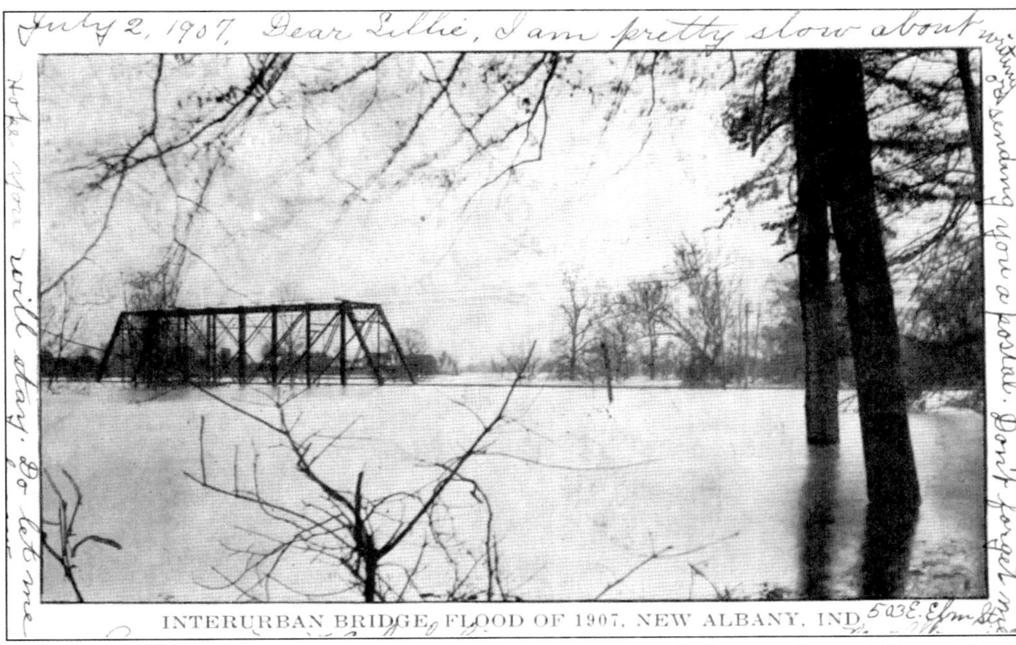

Interurban Bridge. Interurban street car service between Jeffersonville and New Albany began in 1903, and this image is from the flood of 1907. The bridge was over Silver Creek, just south of Glenwood Park.

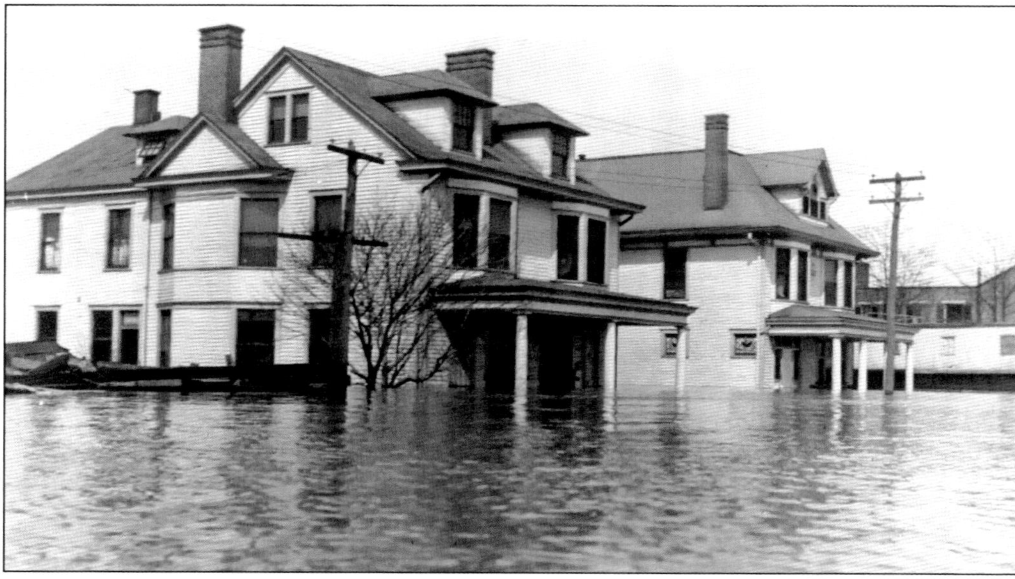

Water Street Homes. During the 1913 flood, these homes in the 400-block of East Water Street were flooded. The homes shown here are 415, 417, and 419, which was the home of E.T. Slider. Water Street fronted the Ohio River and often flooded. The 1913 flood was actually two separate floods. The first recorded a crest on January 15 of 67.2 feet above flood stage. The second came after torrential rains in the spring. That crest was recorded on April 2 at 72.7 feet above flood stage.

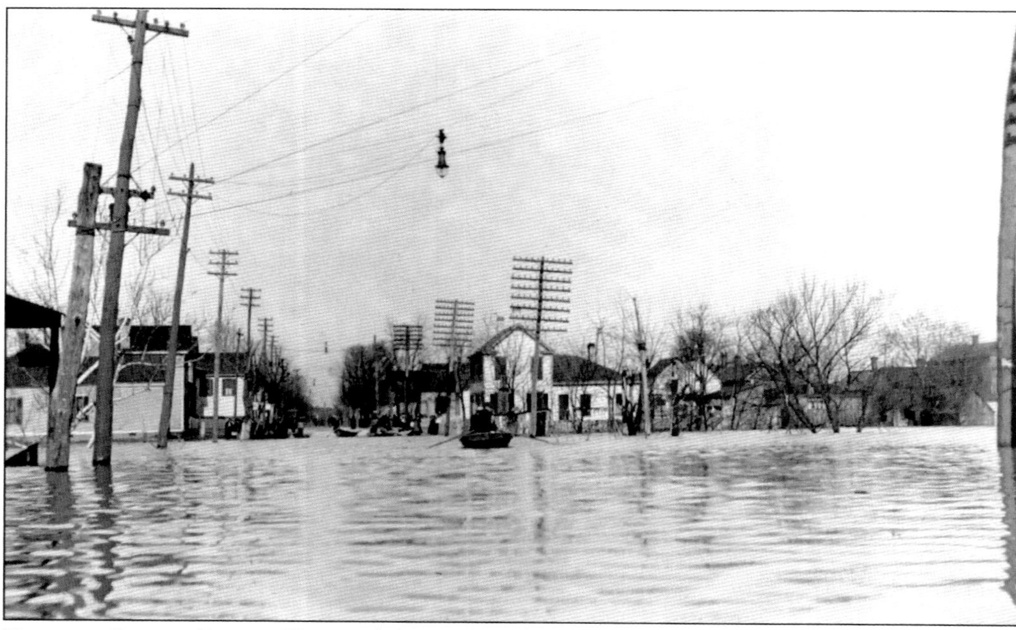

Flooded Street Scene. This card depicts another flooded street scene from the 1913 floods. News accounts from the time noted that New Albany was situated better than many cities along the river and did not need much outside assistance in its recovery efforts.

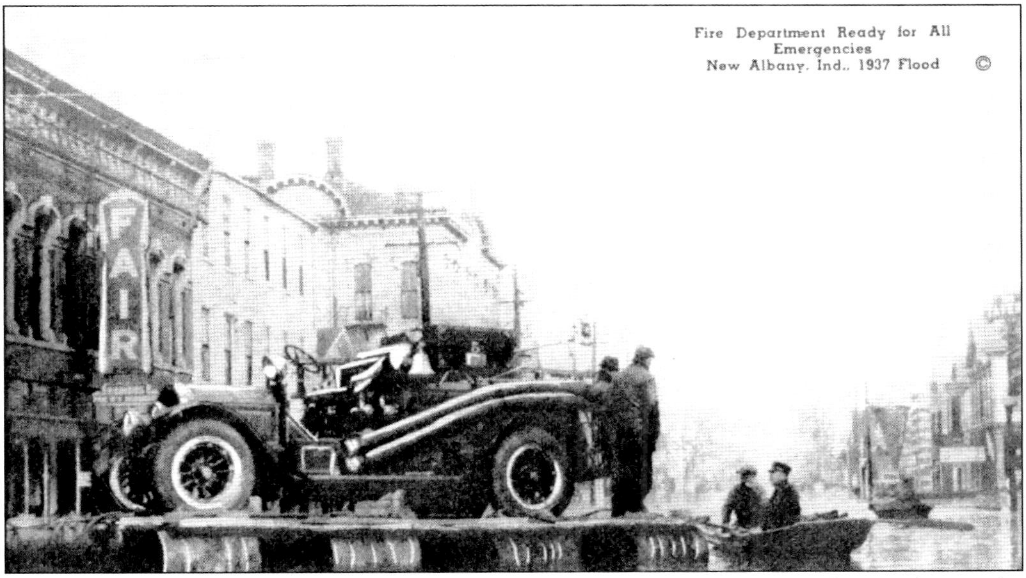

FIRE TRUCK. The New Albany Fire Department put its truck on pontoons to float to fires in the flooded areas of downtown during the 1937 flood, which was the worst in the city's history. The Ohio River crested at 85.48 feet above flood stage on January 27. This scene was captured in front of the Fair Store on Market Street between Pearl and Bank Streets.

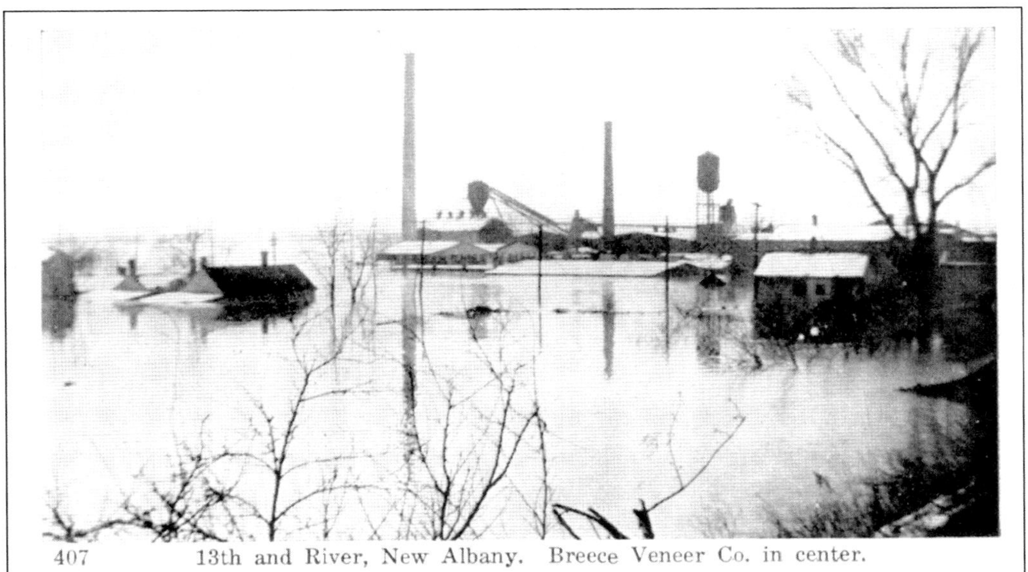

VENEER PLANT. Shortly after the 1937 flood, John T. Breece leased the former New Albany Veneer Co. plant seen in this photo and started his custom plywood factory. The Breece Veneer and Panel Co. produced plywood for furniture and custom cabinet manufacturers throughout the country. It closed in September 1969.

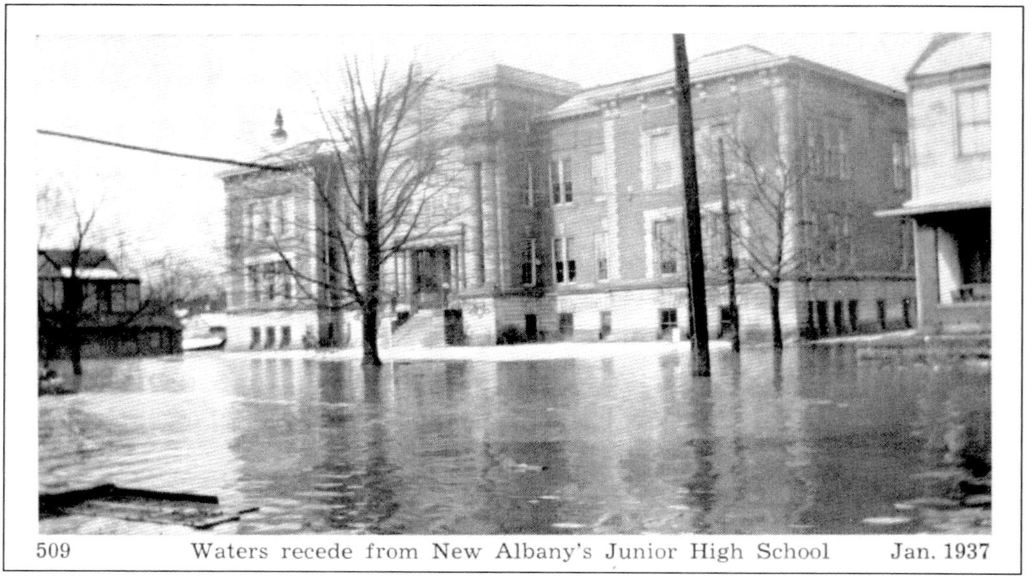

JUNIOR HIGH SCHOOL. This postcard from the 1937 flood shows water receding from what was then New Albany Junior High School. The building was first known as the People's College when New Albany High School occupied it. New Albany High moved to Vincennes Street and the Junior High School took the space. The building was torn down in 1962 for a Frisch's Drive-in Restaurant.

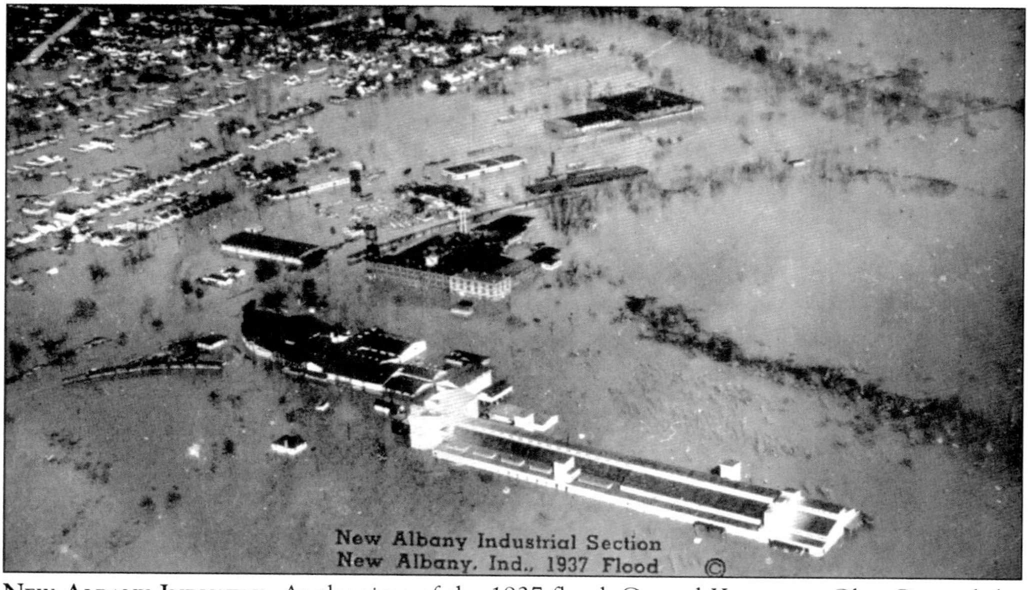

NEW ALBANY INDUSTRY. At the time of the 1937 flood, Conrad-Kammerer Glue Co. and the Tennessee Corp. fertilizer manufacturer occupied the buildings shown on the bottom of the postcard. The Indiana Veneer & Panel Co., established in 1902 and considered the grandfather of the modern plywood industry, was located just above the glue factory in this photo. To the right of those two businesses is the George Moser Leather Co. and trees lining Loop Island.

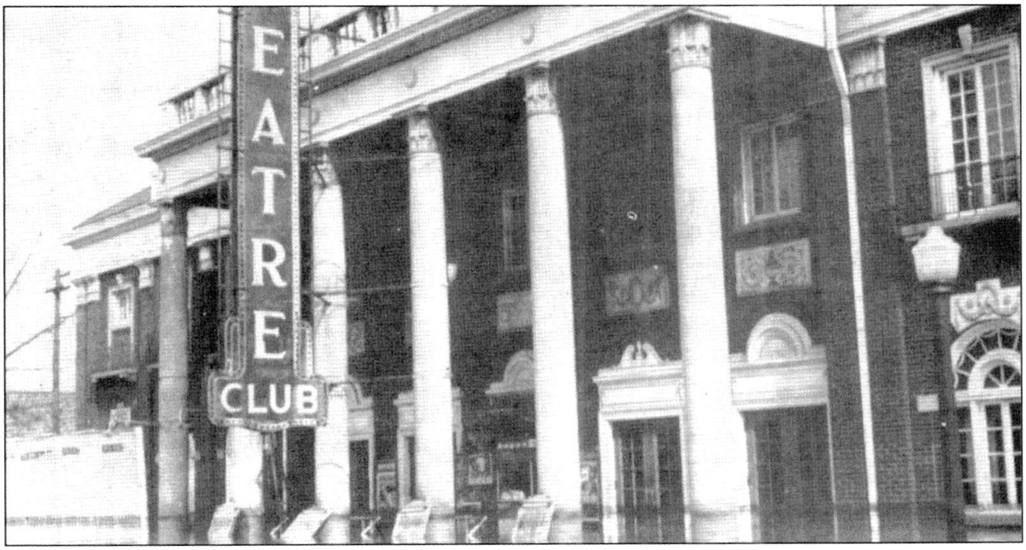

ELKS CLUB AND THEATER. Located on the southeast corner of Pearl and Elm Streets, the Elks Club and Theater took up about half of the 400 block of Pearl Street. The building was designed by Joseph and Joseph Architects in Louisville and built in 1921 at a cost of $200,000. A theater, swimming pool, gym, and meeting rooms were all housed in the building. It was flooded in 1937, as shown here. It burned down in 1962.

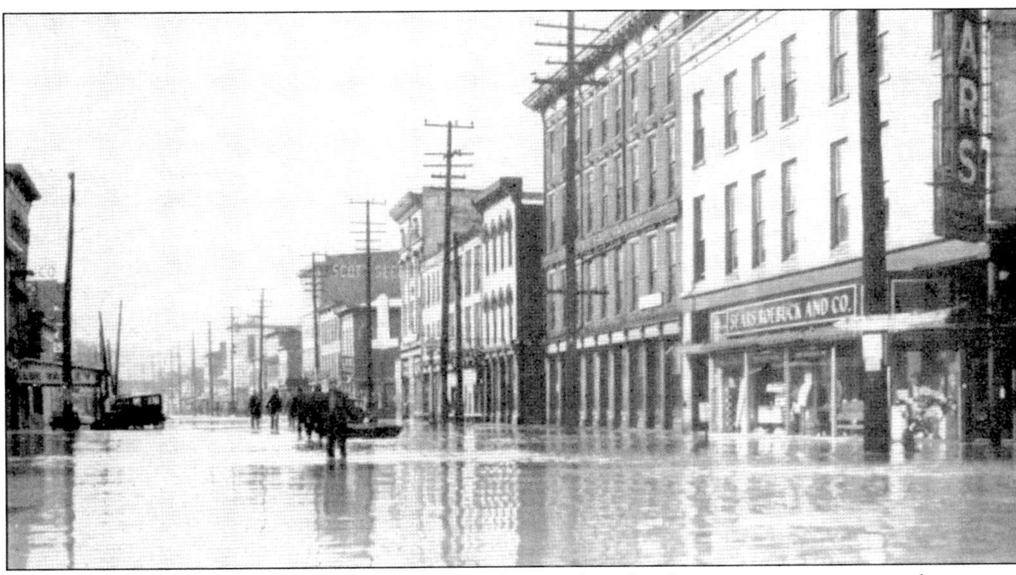

MAIN STREET. This Main Street image shows the flood waters in various downtown establishments. The John J. Morgan building is to the right. Sears Roebuck & Co. moved to this corner in April 1934. The store reopened after the 1937 flood and continued to operate at this location until September 1966. The store then moved to a suburban location.

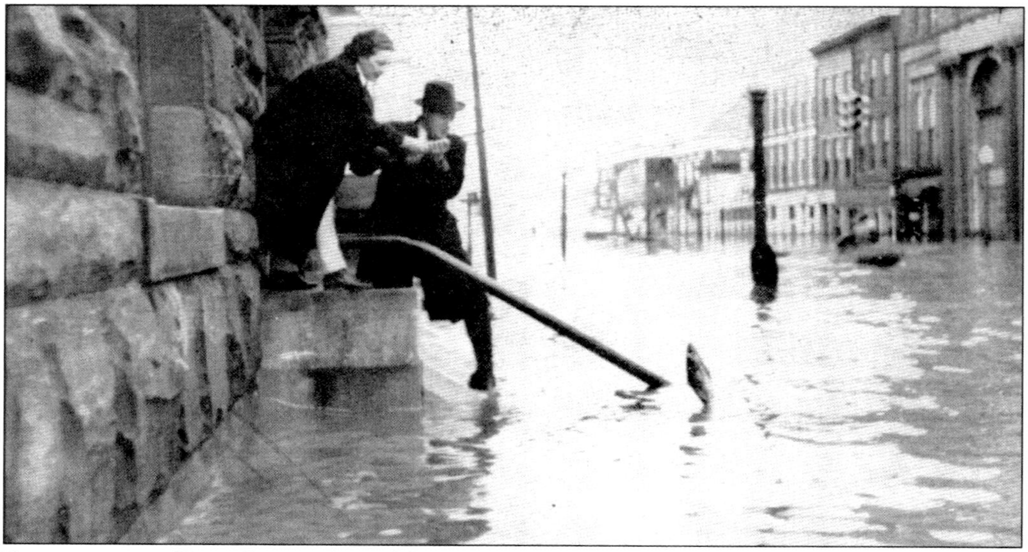

Fishing at the Post Office. One of the more whimsical images from the 1937 flood is this one of two people fishing. The people shown here are believed to be Mary Stein and Frank Edwards. They are standing on the Pearl Street side of the U.S. Courthouse and Post Office building.

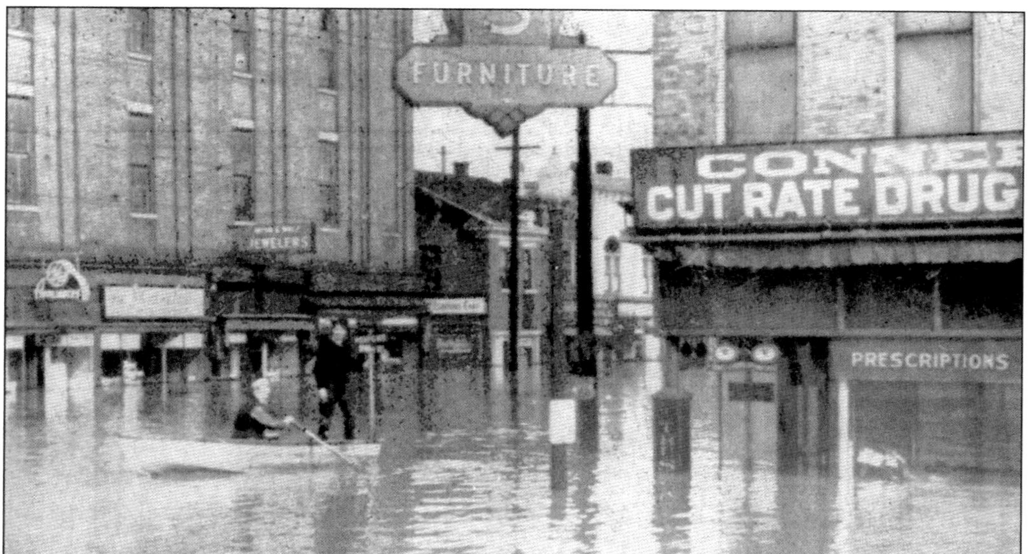

Pearl and Spring Streets. This 1937 flood postcard shows Conners Cut-Rate Drug Store and Huffs Furniture on the right in the Ledger Block building. The Opera House is shown on the left.

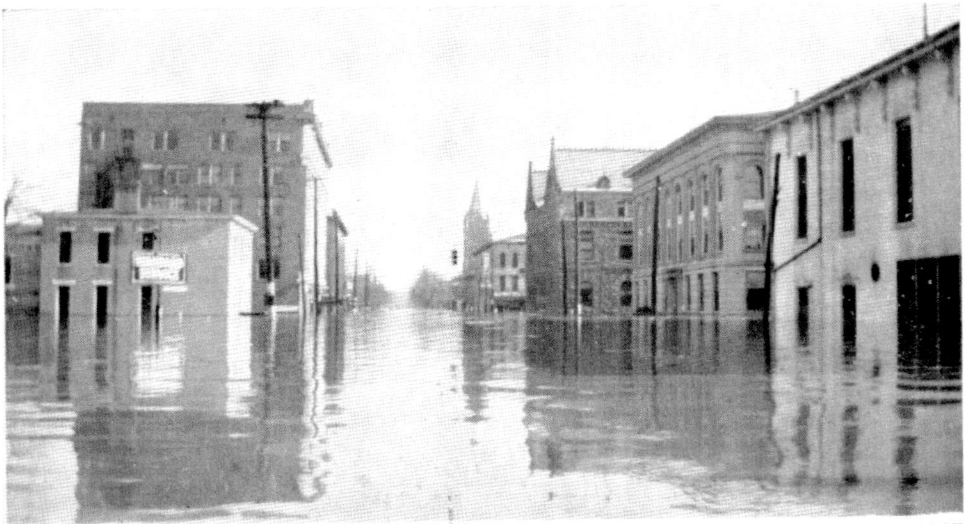

501 Office and Public Buildings, State and Spring, New Albany Jan. 1937

MUNICIPAL BUILDINGS. Among the buildings flooded in 1937 was the Floyd County Jail, which was built in 1859 and designed by Isaac P. Smith, and the Elsby Building, both shown on the left. On the right is the 1857 City Hall, the Floyd County Courthouse across State Street, and the adjacent U.S. Courthouse and Post Office.

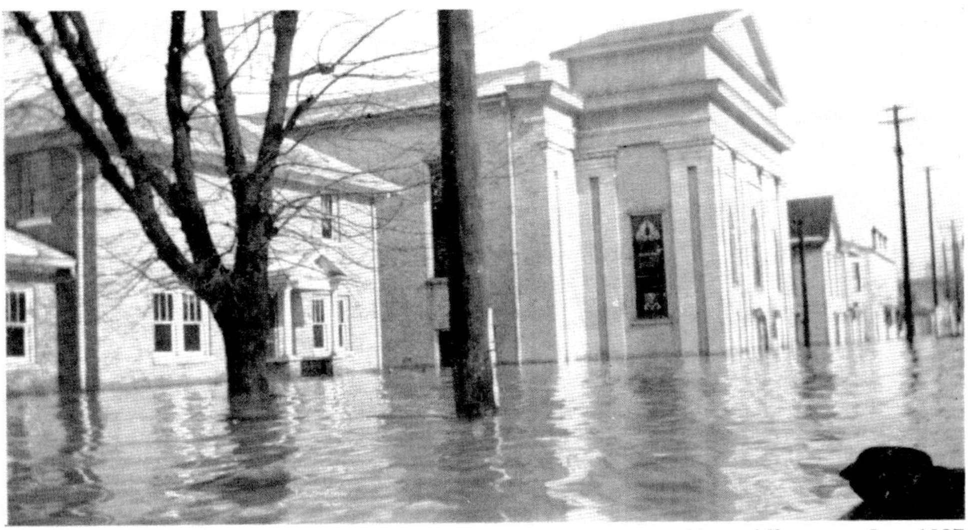

502 Centenary Church, Fourth and Spring Streets, New Albany Jan. 1937

CENTENARY CHURCH. This was one of several churches flooded in 1937. Centenary Church and its parsonage, located at East Third and Spring Streets, are shown.

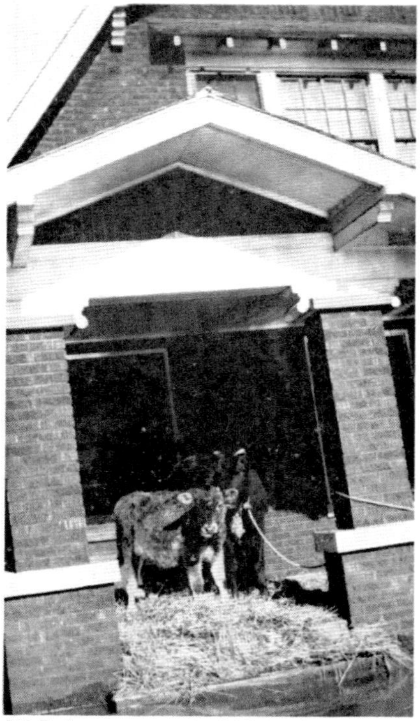

512 Refugees on porch of Methodist Parsonage

Refugees. A few cattle took shelter on the porch of the Main Street Methodist Parsonage on the northeast corner of West Sixth and Main Streets.

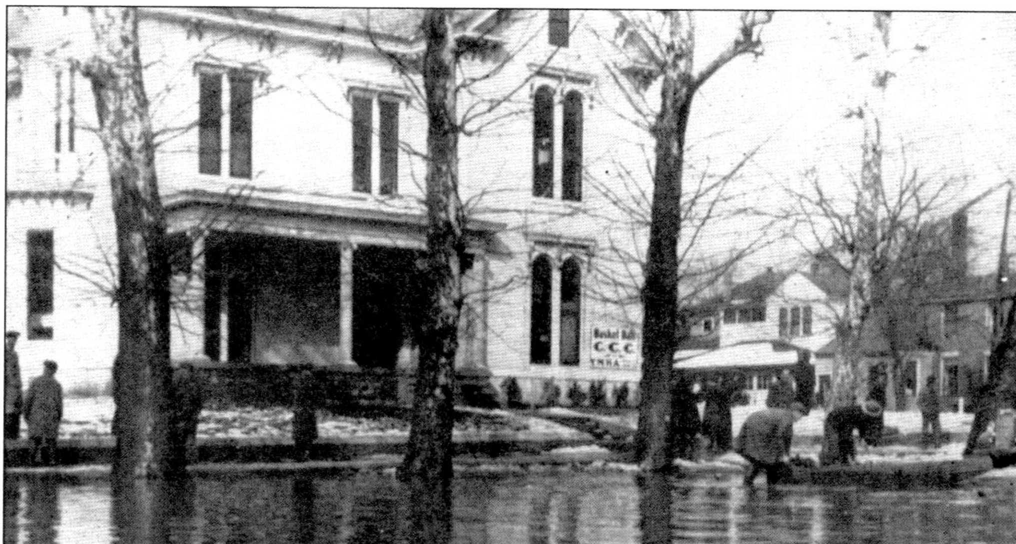

East Main Street. Flood water approached the Catholic Community Center's building, located at 805 East Main Street, in 1937. This house was originally the home of William A. Culbertson.

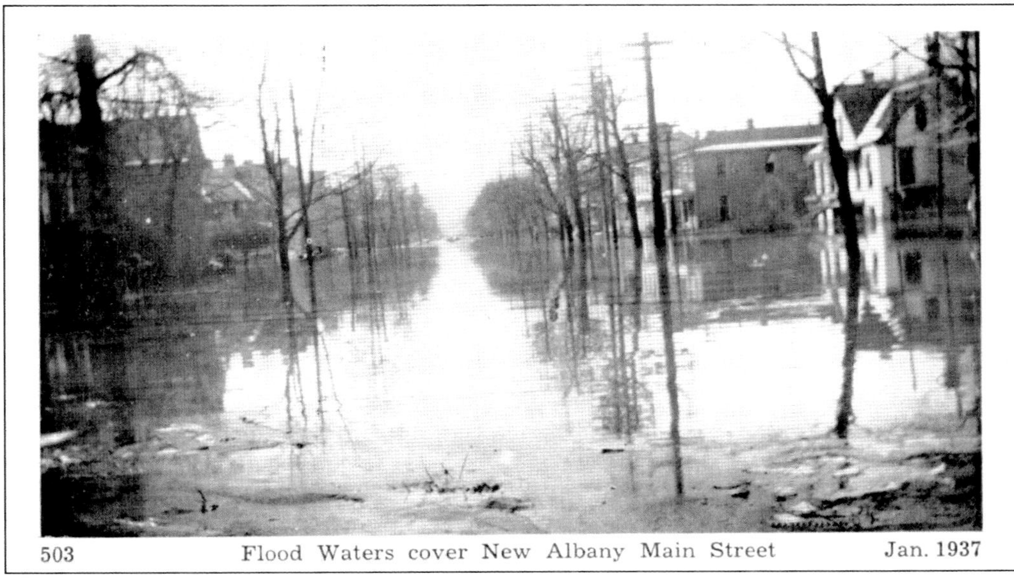

MAIN STREET. This postcard shows East Main Street looking west from the 800 block. The 1873 Culbertson Old Ladies Home is to the left and the Nunemacher-Hangary House, built in 1853, is to the right.

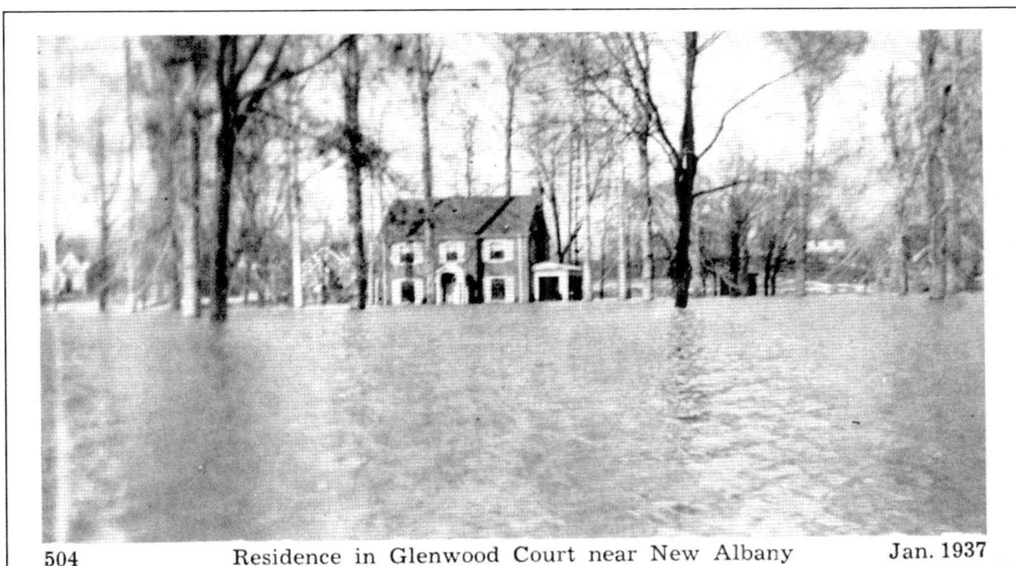

GLENWOOD COURT. Even the city's newest developments were not immune from the 1937 flood. The home shown here was built after 1935 and is actually located at 2523 Glenwood Park.

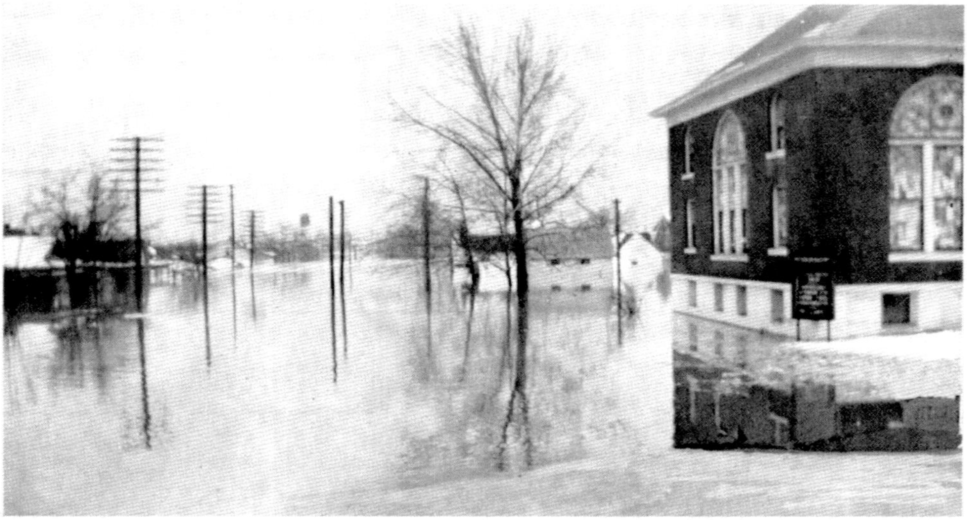

510 United Brethren Church in New Albany Jan. 1937

UNITED BRETHREN CHURCH. Another church flooded in 1937 was the United Brethren Church, located at the intersection of Silver and Elm Streets. The church is on the southwest corner.

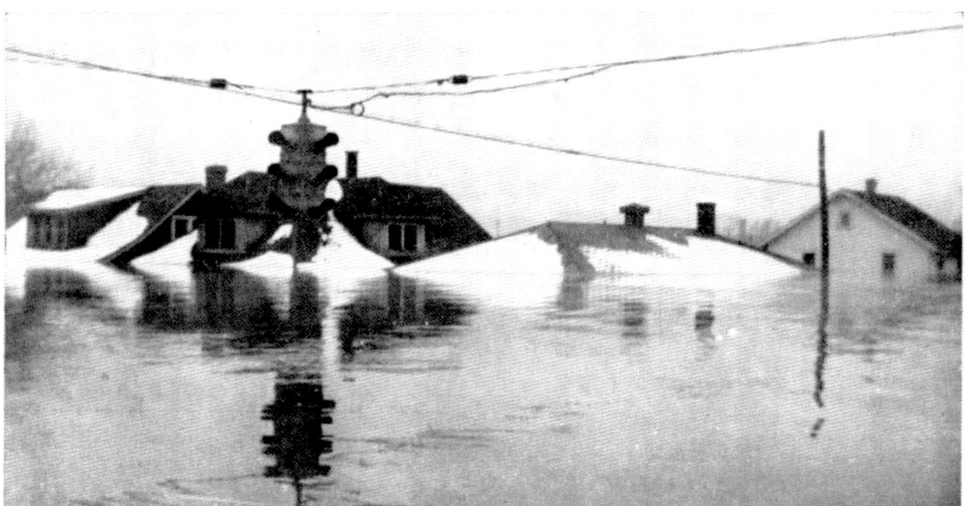

406 The semaphore stopped working at Silver and Spring Streets, New Albany.

SEMAPHORE STOPPED WORKING. This image shows the stoplight at the corner of Silver and Spring Streets, looking toward the southeast corner of the intersection.

Eight

The Tornado of 1917

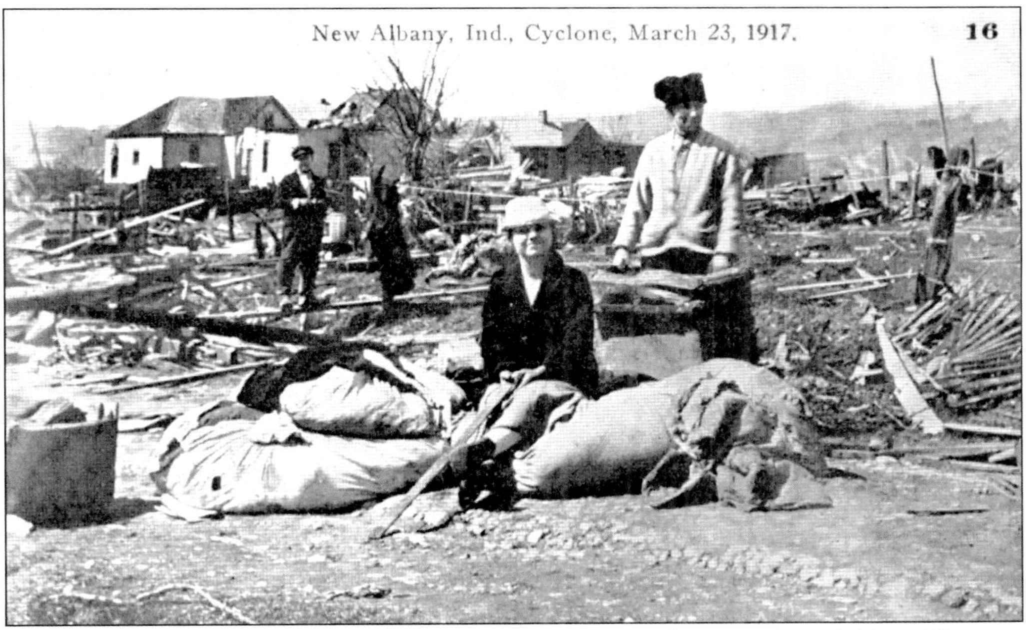

Tornado Damage. On March 23, 1917, a devastating tornado swept through New Albany at 3:30 p.m., destroying one-third of its buildings and killing 45 people. The tornado cut a path three miles long by a half-mile wide starting with West Seventh Street and winding down Charlestown Road. Five factories and 500 homes were destroyed, with another 300 homes damaged. This postcard image is one in a series that showed the devastation of the event.

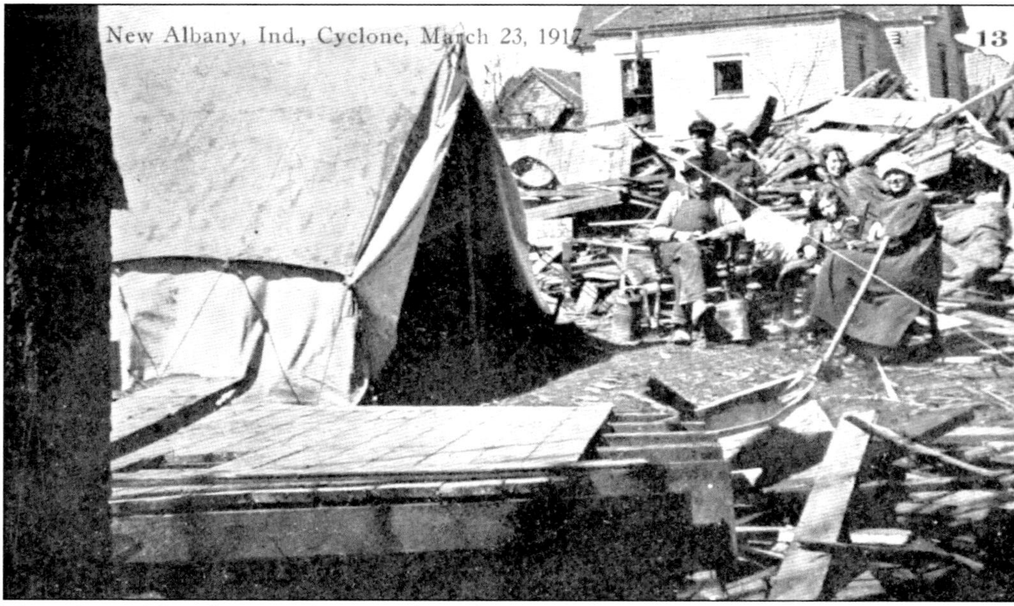

Tent Life. After the tornado came through New Albany, many families were left homeless, including the people pictured here, who were living in the tent shown in the foreground.

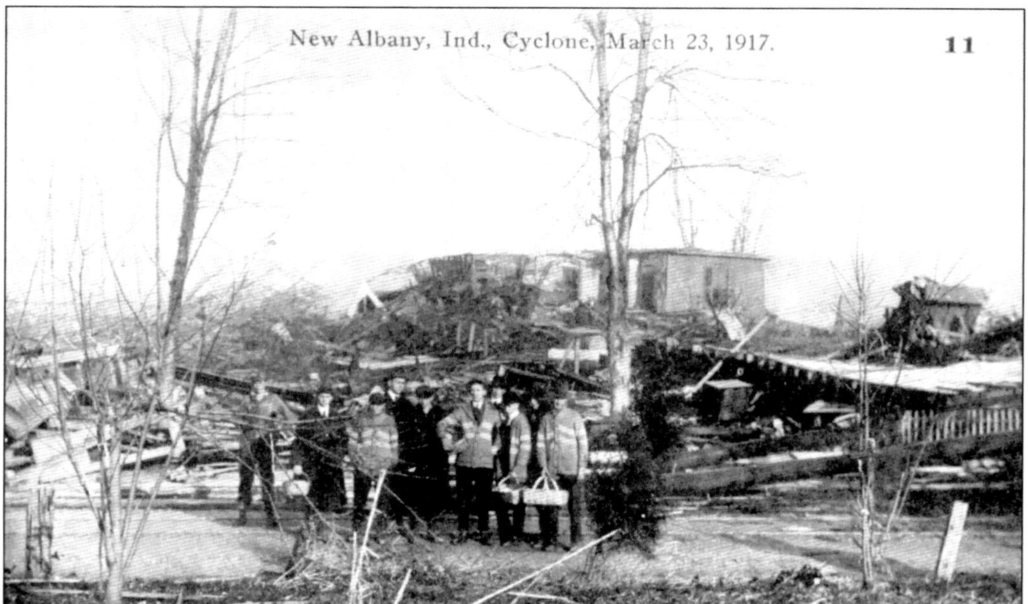

Calumet Members. The local Calumet Club, a young men's fraternal group, took to the streets of the devastated city to help people in the aftermath of the tornado. The group's trademark purple and white sweaters were said to be as good as a pass during the martial law that ruled the town as New Albany cleaned up.

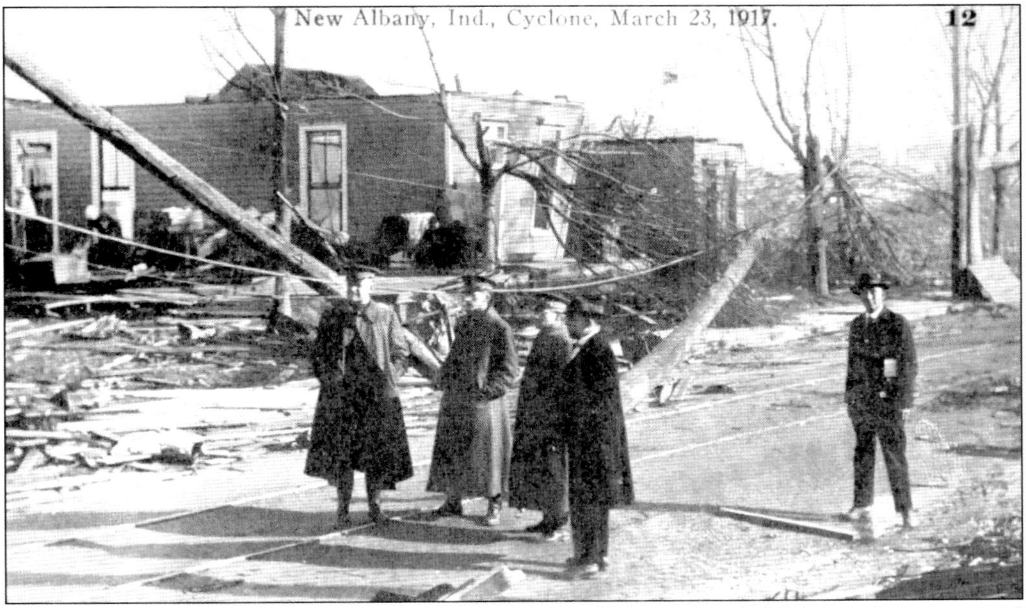

CLEANING UP. Members of the public spent months working to get rid of debris, salvage personal belongings, and try to handle the mess as best they could. In some cases, roofs were lifted off of homes completely while the walls were left standing, as shown in the background of this image.

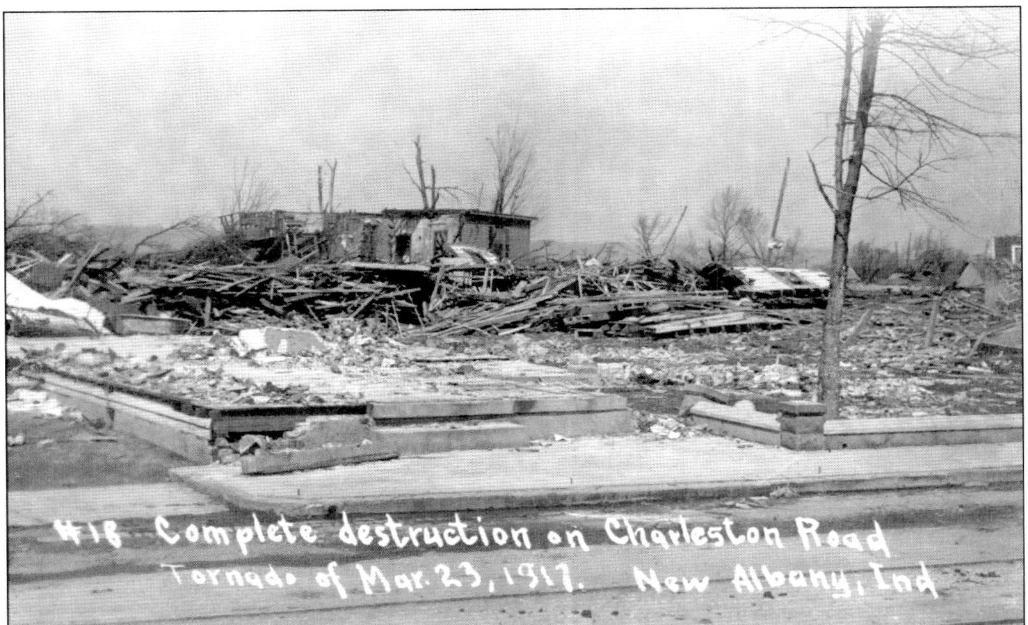

COMPLETE DESTRUCTION. One of the hardest hit areas was Charlestown Road, as shown in this image. The building pictured here is Nickel's Grocery at 1805 Charlestown Road.

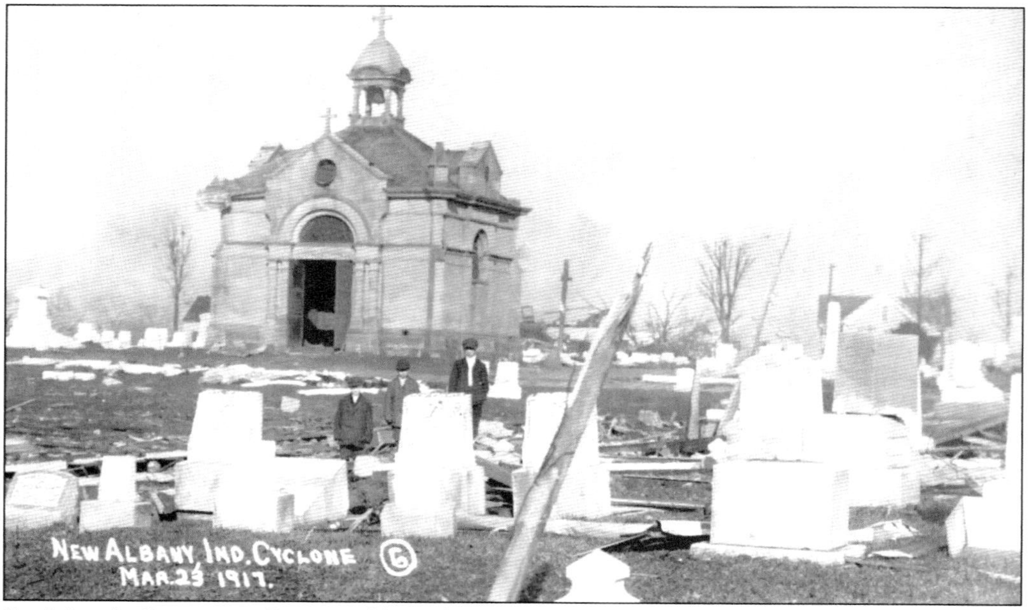

ST. MARY'S CEMETERY. Even marble and stone were prone to damage from the tornado. This image of St. Mary's Cemetery on Charlestown Road shows several stones uprooted or damaged. The chapel in the center is no longer standing.

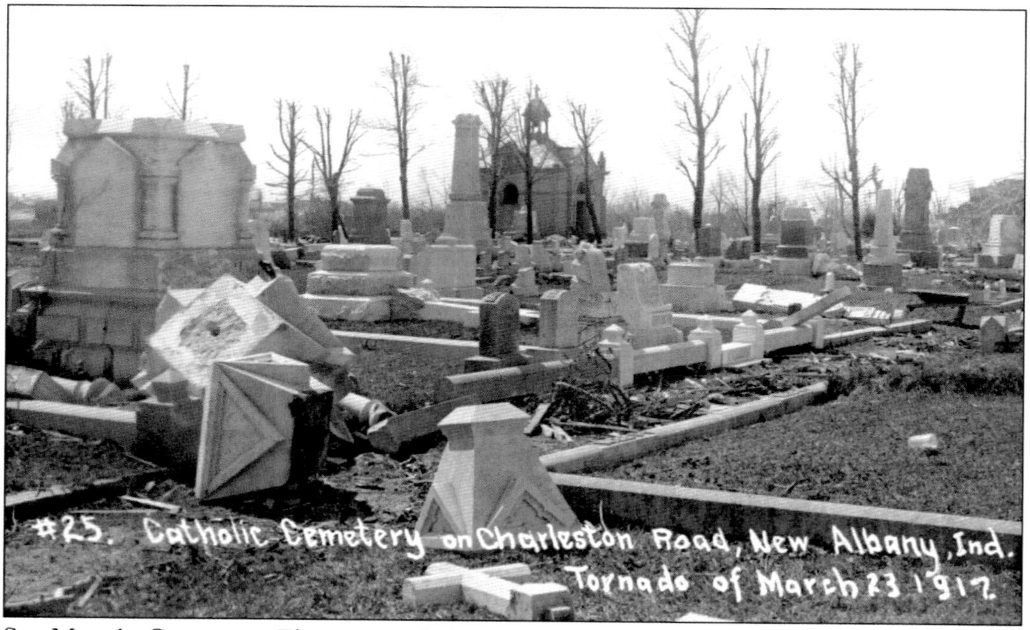

ST. MARY'S CEMETERY. This postcard shows another view of St. Mary's Cemetery, which was heavily damaged by the tornado. Note the massive size of some of the headstones and monuments that were toppled by the fierce winds.

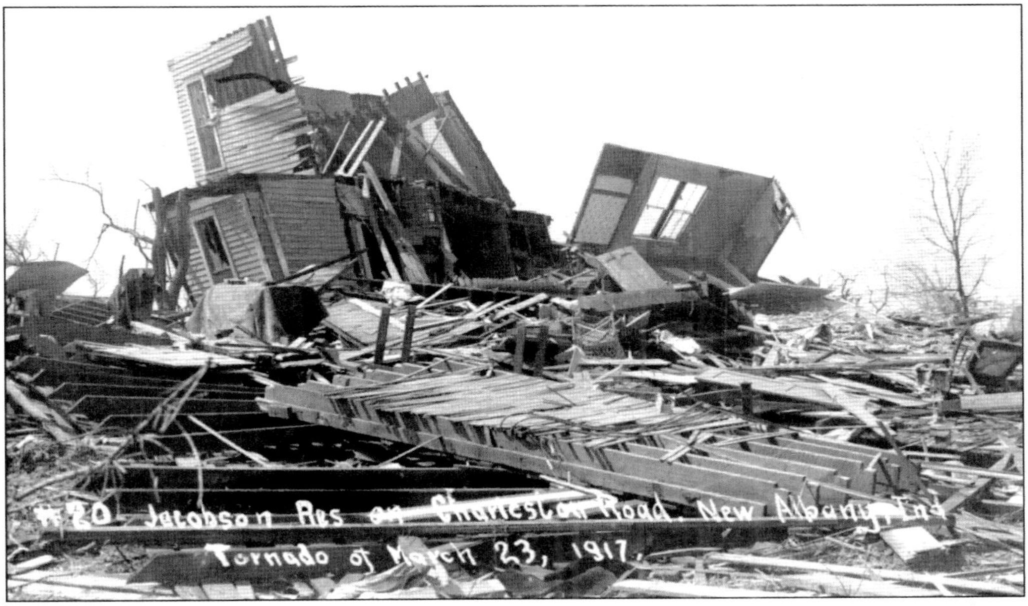

JACOBSON RESIDENCE. Located next to the heavily damaged cemetery, the Jacobson residence was destroyed by the tornado. The home, in the 2200 block of Charlestcwn Road, was the old Lafayette Frederick home. It was home to two families at the time of the tornado, the Jacobsons and Albert Marzian.

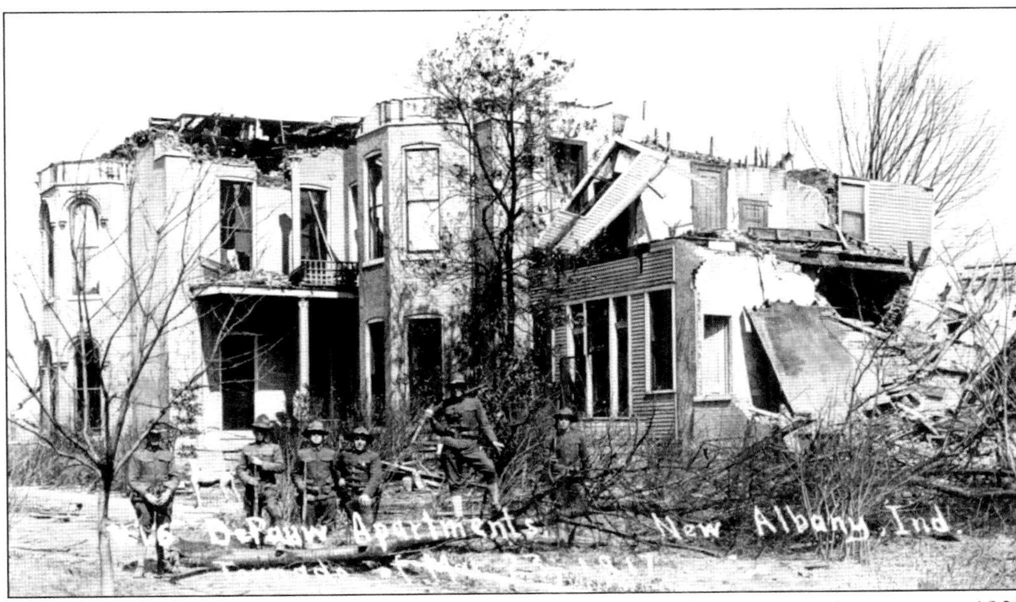

DePauw Apartments. A rear view of what was then called the DePauw Apartments, 1905 Charlestown Road, shows the enormous amount of damage done to the home. Jane Barth Anderson and her mother, Helen Krebs Barth, escaped through a window of the house and fled to get help. The Italianate house was Washington C. DePauw's summer home and was originally called Beechwood.

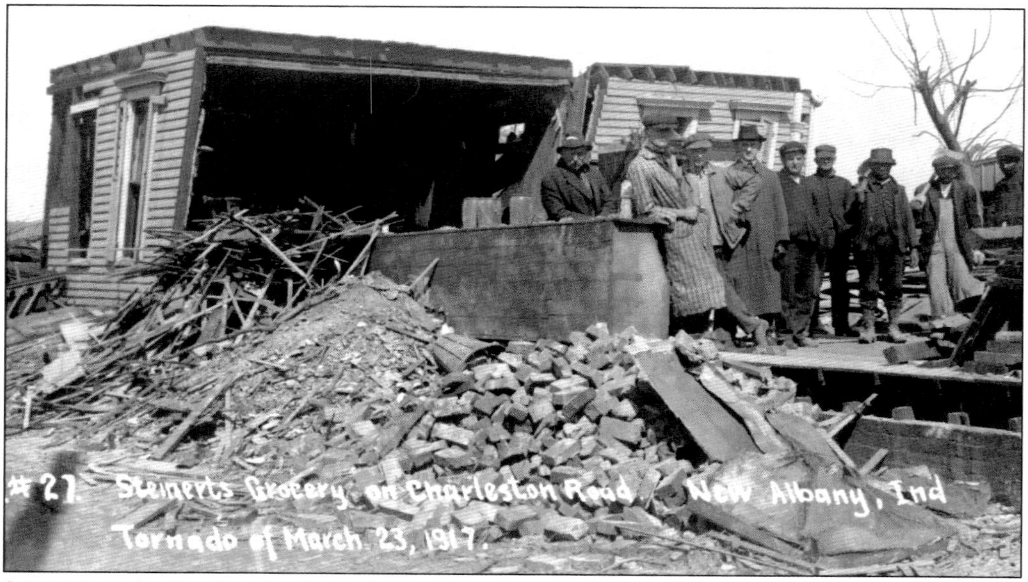

STEINERT'S GROCERY. One of New Albany's state-recognized centennial businesses, Steinert's Grocery and Saloon, was heavily damaged in the tornado. Steinert's, located at 2015 Charlestown Road, was established in 1877 at 1301 East Oak Street, and at some later point moved to the Charlestown Road site shown in this postcard. The Steinert family rebuilt the store at the same site after the tornado, and then later moved it to 2239 Charlestown Road. Steinert's is still in business, but the Steinert family is no longer connected with it.

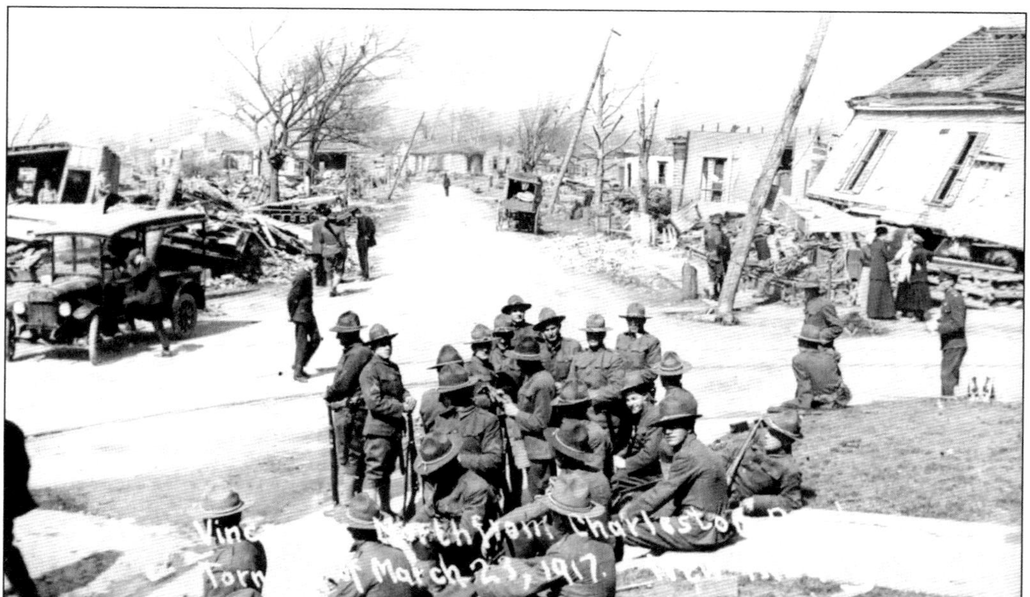

VINCENNES STREET LOOKING NORTH. Members of the National Guard Troop D gather at the intersection of Vincennes Street and Charlestown Road. Lopp's Grocery can be seen on the right. News accounts from the time indicate that one of the store's proprietors, Elsie Lopp, and a male customer were killed inside the store by the tornado.

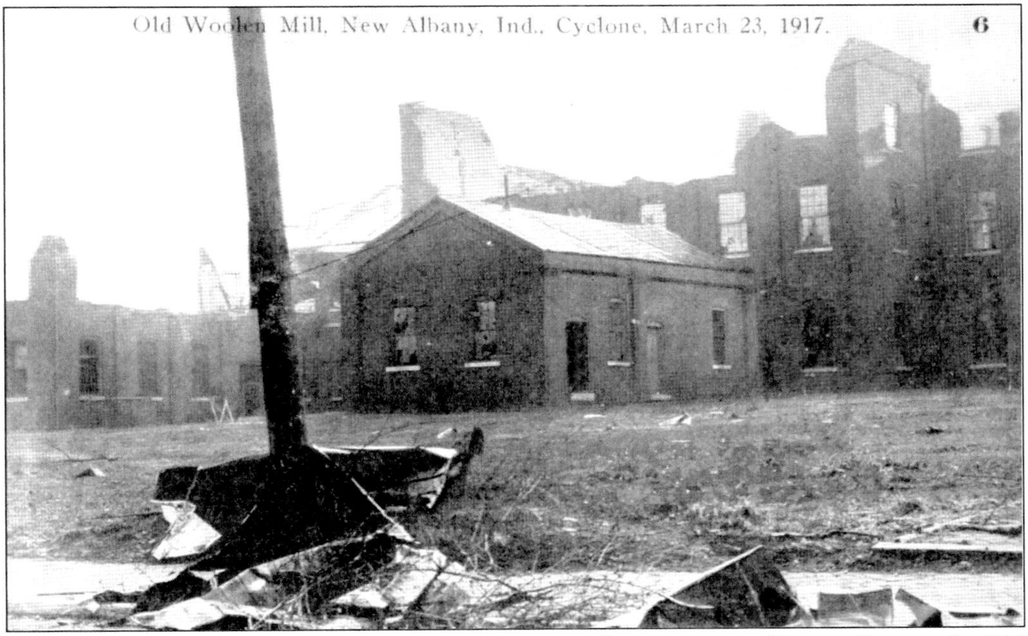

OLD WOOLEN MILLS. Located on the southeast corner of Vincennes and Locust Streets, the Old Woolen Mills building was one of several factories extensively damaged in the tornado. At the time of the tornado, the building was owned and used by Hercules Motor Works.

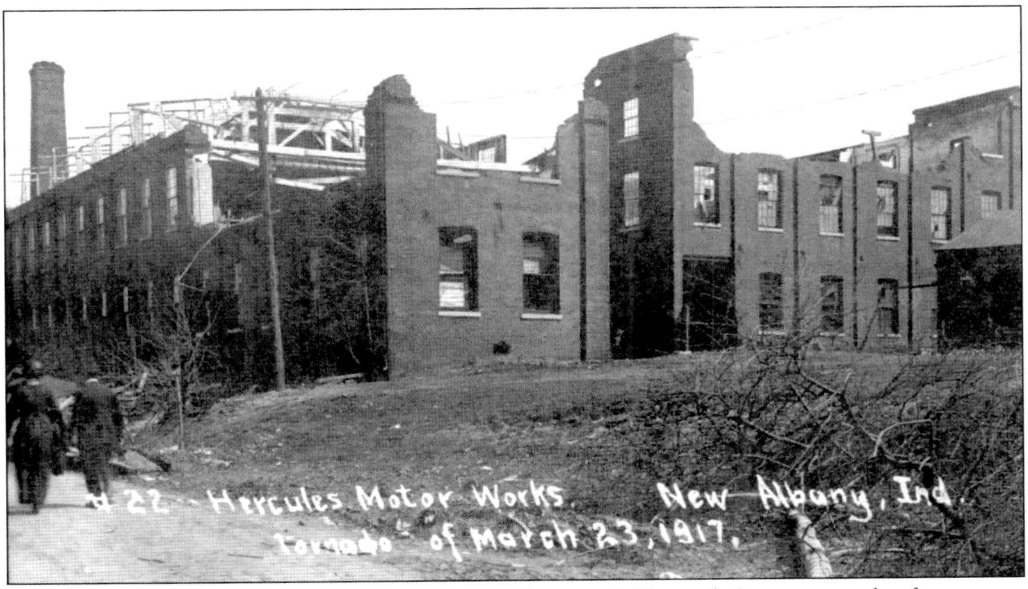

HERCULES MOTOR WORKS. Brothers Chester, Cary, and Elsworth Jones were the first to use this property, known as the Old Woolen Mills, as a car manufacturing plant. Their company was called the American Automobile Manufacturing Co. From 1910 to 1917, the building went through five ownership changes, though all companies located there made cars. After the tornado, the factory did not reopen. Eventually, New Albany High School came to be located on the property.

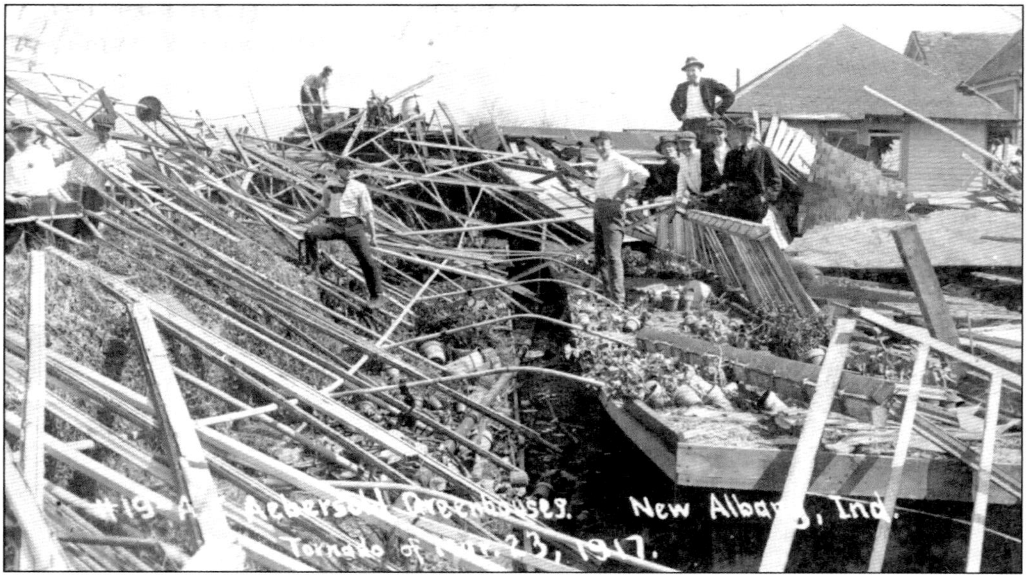

AEBERSOLD GREENHOUSES. Alfred Aebersold established his business on the west side of Silver Street, south of Charlestown Road, in 1908. He rebuilt the business after the tornado destroyed his greenhouses; today, the business is located on that same site.

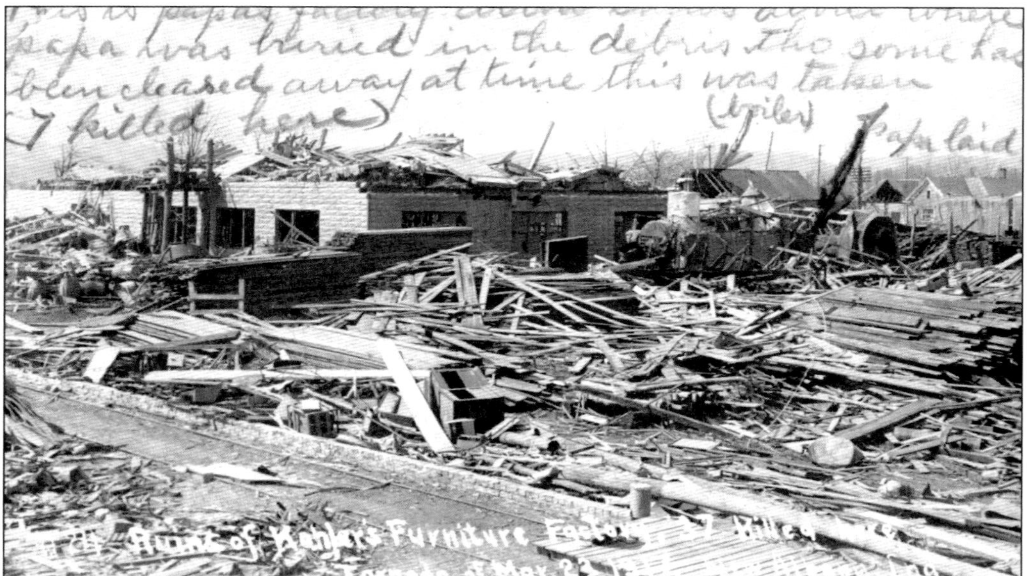

KAHLER'S FURNITURE. Ethel Smith used this postcard to write to an aunt and uncle about the factory where her step-father worked. She marked the spot on the card where he was trapped under rubble. Seven people were killed in the factory by the tornado. The factory, which was established in 1907, was located on the southeast corner of Vincennes Street and Grant Line Road and made tabletops, interior woodwork, and automobile beds. Despite enticing offers to relocate his company after the devastating tornado, Kahler elected to stay in New Albany, doubling the size of the plant and its work force.

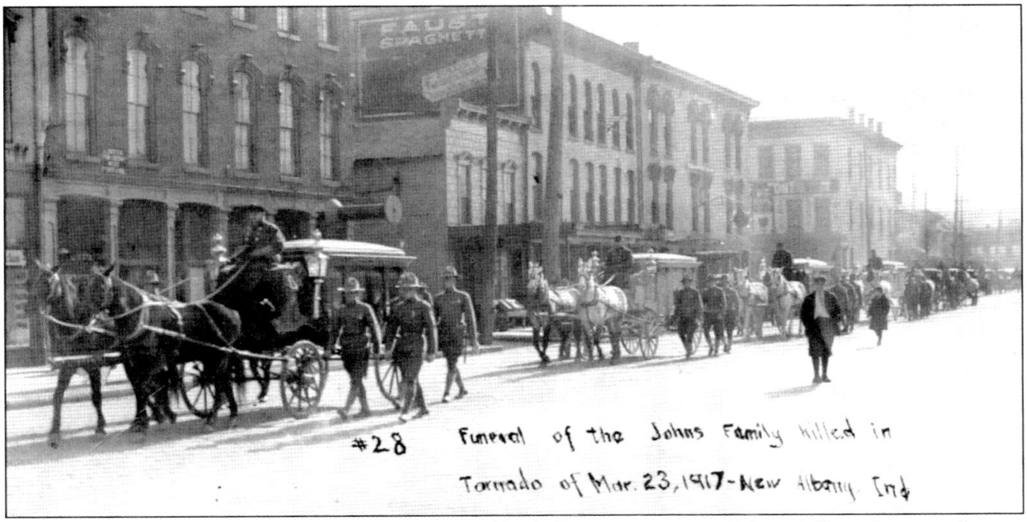

JOHNS FAMILY. One of the most tragic and publicly known stories of New Albany's tornado was the death of the Johns family. Four members of the family were killed, including the wife of the family, who was blown from her home and into another home. The funeral procession for the family wound through the streets of downtown New Albany, which was virtually untouched by the tornado. Market Street is shown in the background of this postcard. The first horse-drawn hearse contains the body of Mrs. Lomax, who was Mrs. Johns' mother. The second and third hearses carried the bodies of Mr. and Mrs. Johns, respectively, and the fourth hearse carried Mrs. Johns' small child from a previous marriage.

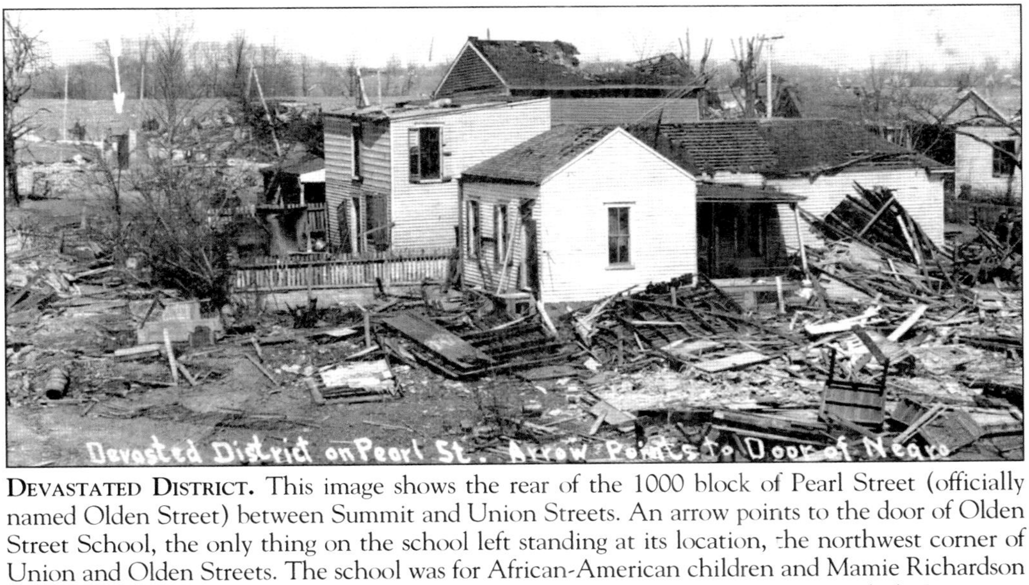

DEVASTATED DISTRICT. This image shows the rear of the 1000 block of Pearl Street (officially named Olden Street) between Summit and Union Streets. An arrow points to the door of Olden Street School, the only thing on the school left standing at its location, the northwest corner of Union and Olden Streets. The school was for African-American children and Mamie Richardson was the teacher at the school. (Richardson married in 1917 and became Mamie Starks.) Newspaper accounts tell that two African-American children rushed to the People's College, 13 blocks away at East Seventh and Spring Streets, to get help from Professor H.A. Buerk, superintendent of New Albany Schools. Oral history states that he and Mamie worked with flashlights into the night saving many of the children, but two students and a school employee died.

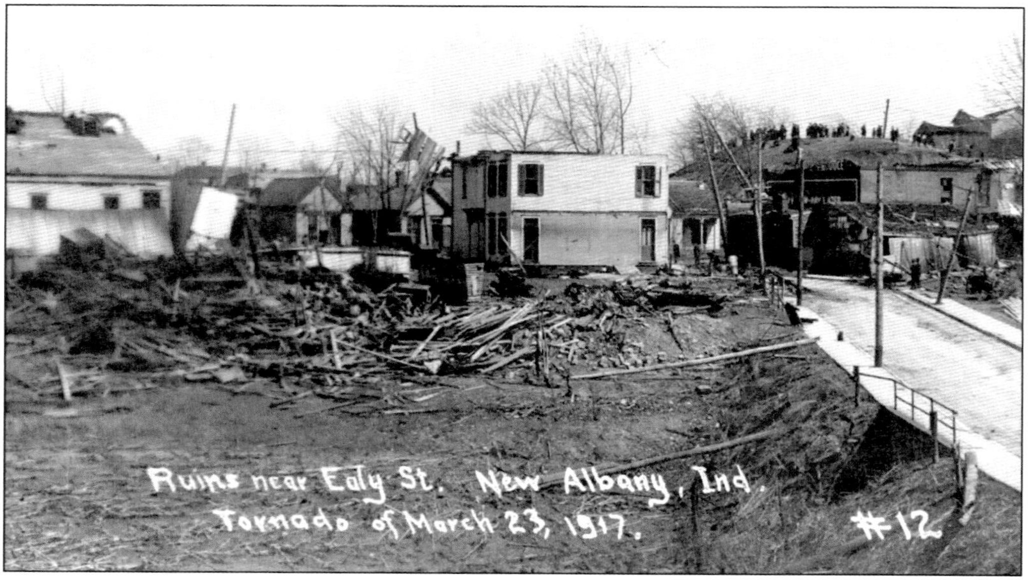

Ruins Near Ealy Street. This image looks east from Ealy Street toward State Street at the rear of Wunderlich's Grocery, the two-story white building in the middle of the postcard. Adolph Wunderlich began his business in 1888 and continued to serve the area until his death in 1941. His son Anton continued the business and was said to be so tender-hearted he gave away significant amounts of merchandise. The grocery went out of business when the Anton died in 1957. The Old Pike Inn is to the far right.

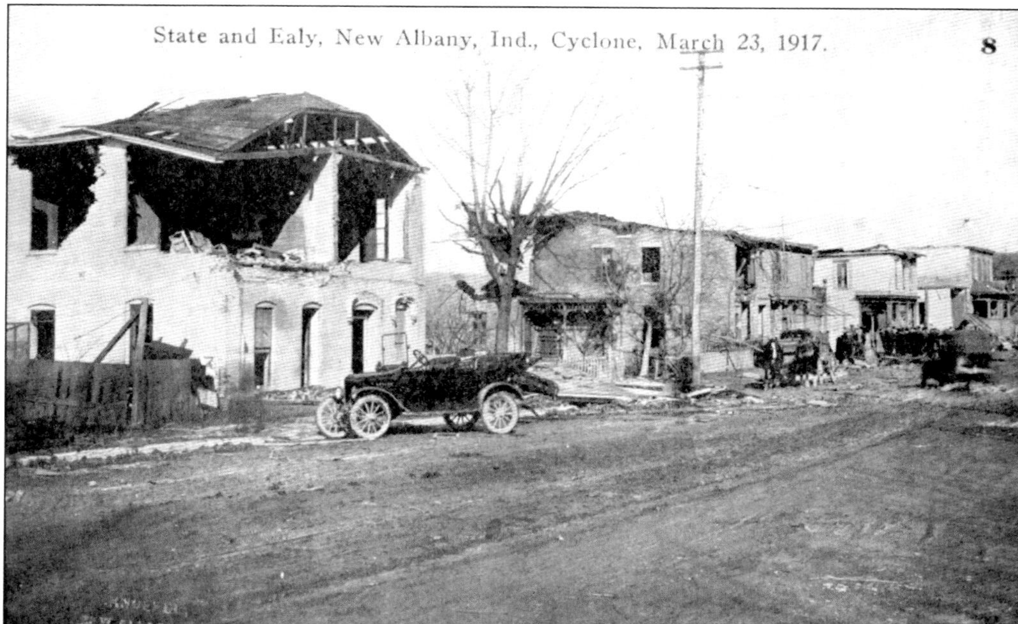

State and Ealy Streets. The heavily damaged Old Pike Inn is in the center of this postcard that shows the 900 to 1000 blocks of State Street.

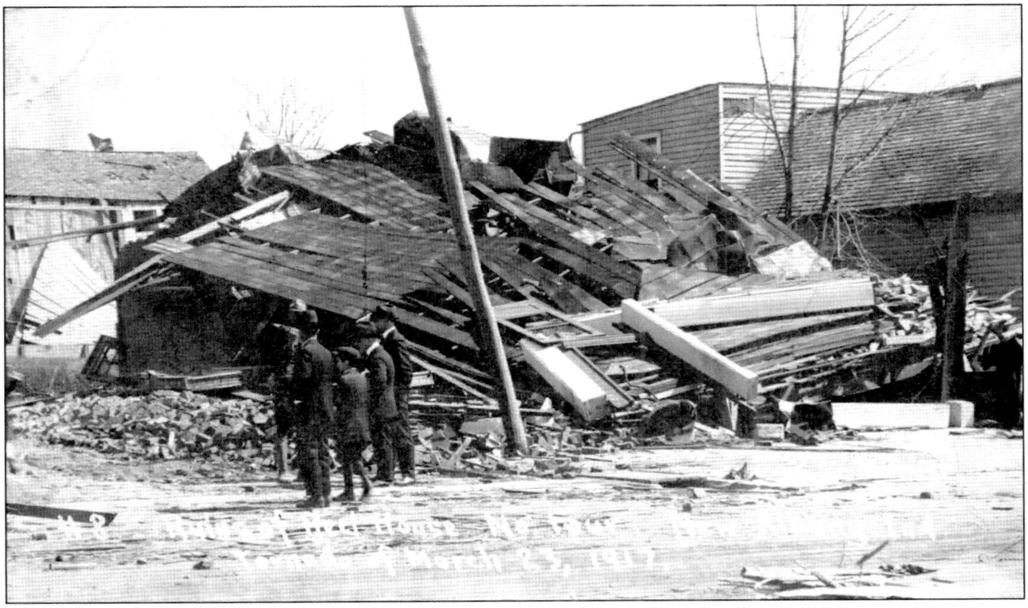

Reel House Number Four. The New Albany Fire Department's Reel House Number Four was destroyed by the tornado, and replaced the next spring with a new firehouse. It was located at the southeast corner of State and Union Streets.

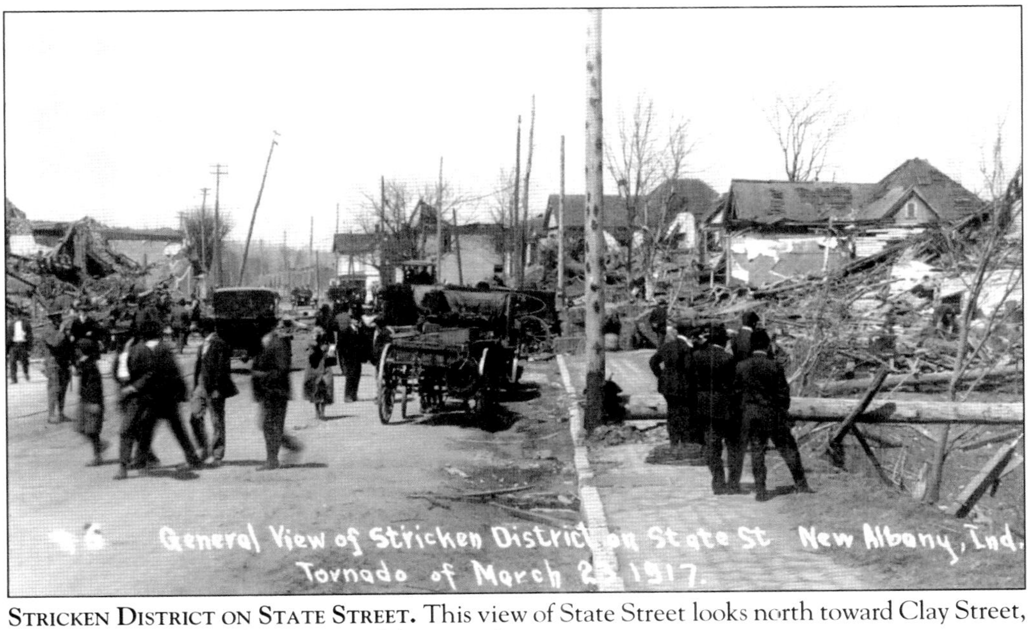

Stricken District on State Street. This view of State Street looks north toward Clay Street, showing more of the destruction of the tornado.

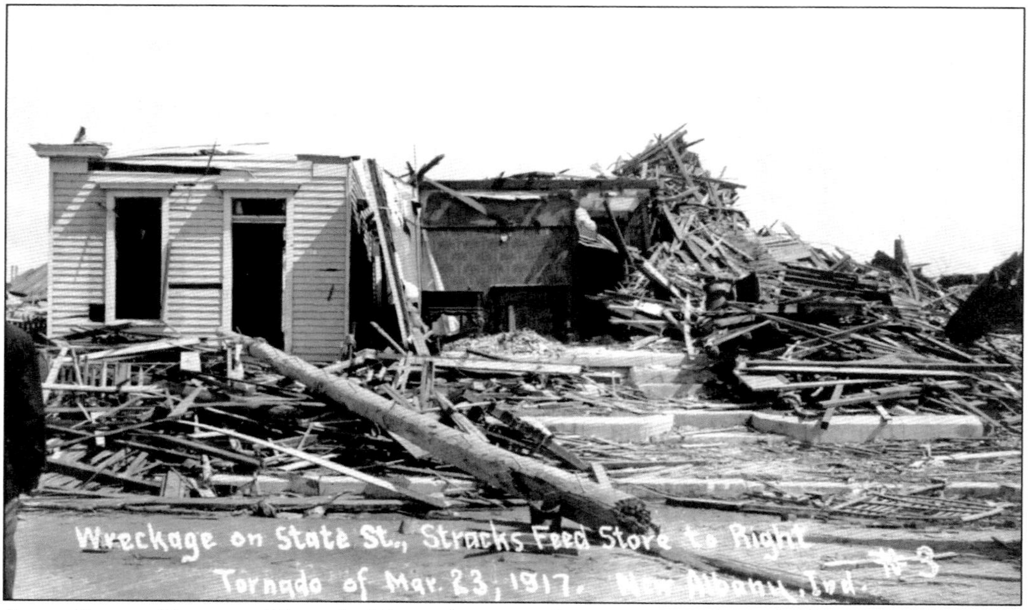

State Street Damage. Three buildings shown in this image were heavily damaged: 1218 State Street, which is the Flannery residence, 1216 State Street, which is the Vollenhals residence, and Stracks Feed Store at 1210 State Street, mentioned in the handwriting on the front of the card.

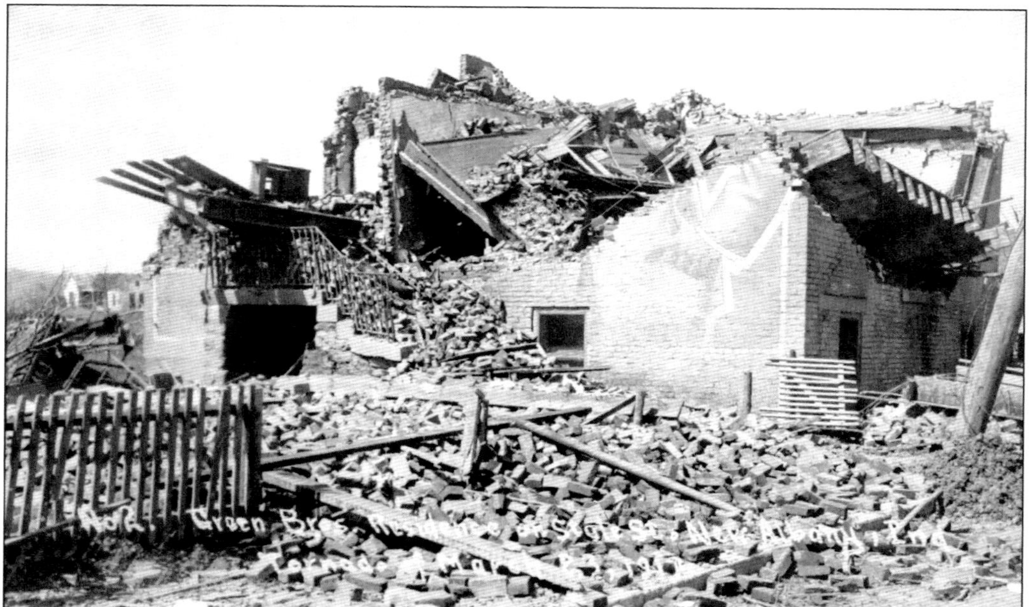

Green Brothers Residence. This brick building at 1301 State Street was originally the Bruggeman Saloon building during the late 1800s. At the time of the tornado, the building was probably an apartment building, since a 1916 city directory lists a number of people living there, including a Green.

Nine

SCHOOLS

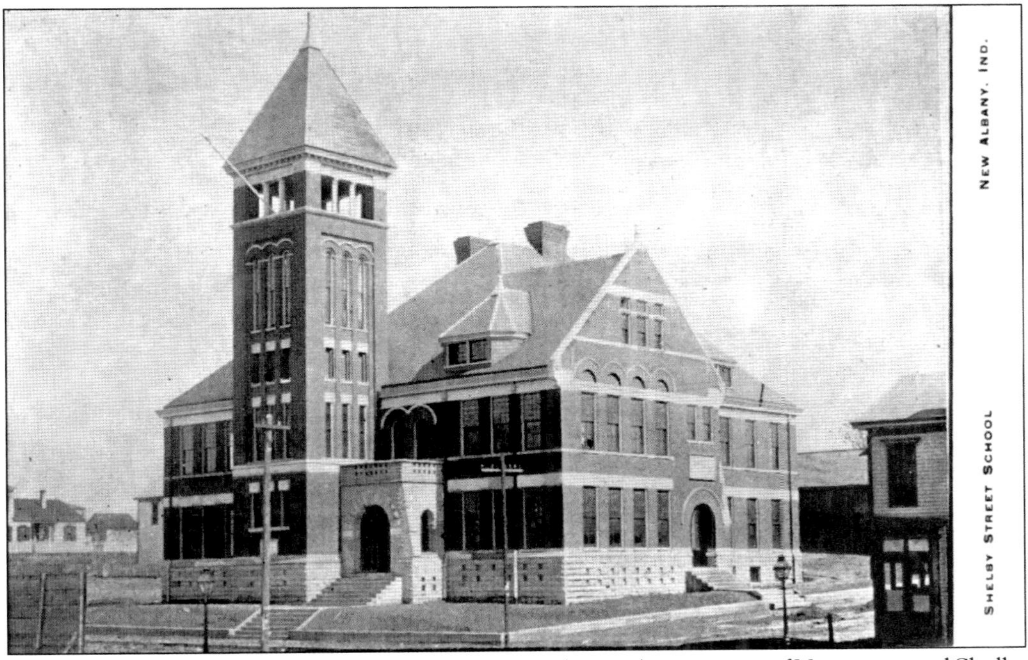

VINCENNES AND SHELBY STREET SCHOOL. Located on the northeast corner of Vincennes and Shelby Streets, the Vincennes and Shelby Street School, shown in this 1905 postcard, was completed in 1893 at a cost of about $30,000. In 1923, the school was renamed the Cora Martin School in honor of Cora Martin, a teacher who spent 27 years of her 50-year teaching career at the school. It was used as an elementary school until 1943, when Fairmont Elementary School opened. Beginning that same year, the school became an annex to New Albany High School. The building was torn down in 1979 to make way for the New Albany High School swimming pool.

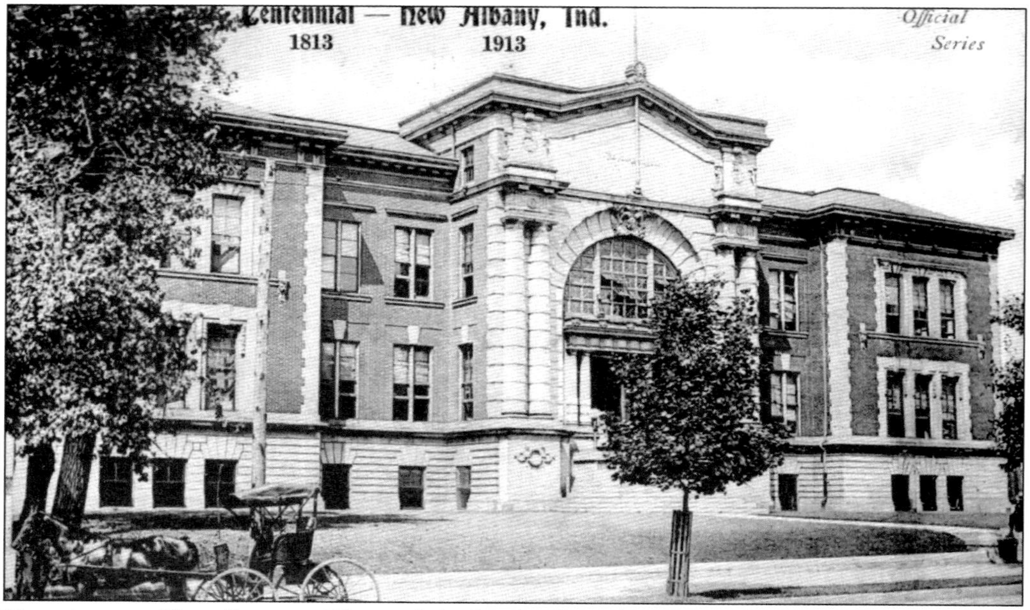

NEW ALBANY HIGH SCHOOL. The city's high school was known as The People's College when it was located on the northwest corner of East Sixth and Spring Streets, as shown in this 1913 postcard. The city's first high school was established in 1853 as Scribner High School, in honor of the founding family of New Albany, but changed its name to New Albany High School a short time later. It was the first public high school in Indiana. New Albany High School was located in this S. Day and Sons building from 1905 to 1927, after which it moved to its present location on Vincennes Street. The building later became a junior high school and was demolished in 1962 for a Frisch's Drive-in Restaurant.

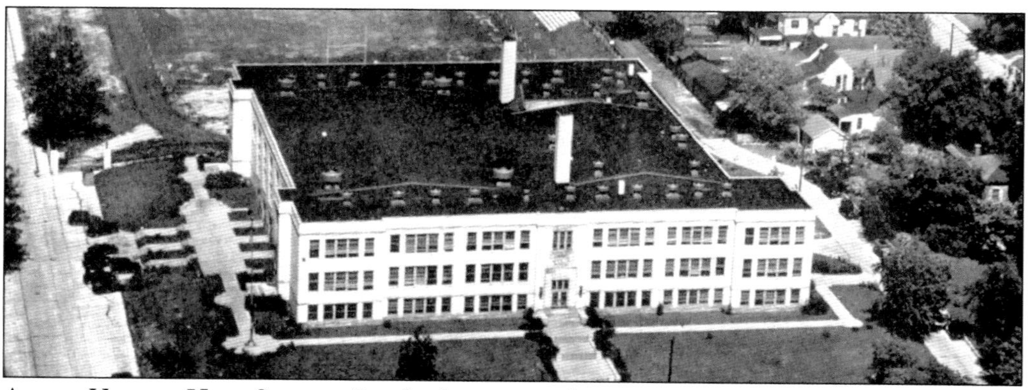

AERIAL VIEW OF HIGH SCHOOL. For the first senior class presentation after the school relocated to 1020 Vincennes Street, the class commissioned an aerial photograph of the school. This 1933 postcard shows that view. The high school was built on the site of the old Woolen Mills building, which was destroyed in the tornado of 1917. The school purchased that lot plus two others for a total of 7 1/2 acres. To secure funds for construction, the City Schools bonded itself for $250,000 and the Civil City of New Albany for $50,000. Residents and alumni together organized the New Albany Gymnasium Corporation and raised $75,000 for the construction of the gym. The school has had numerous additions since this photograph was taken.

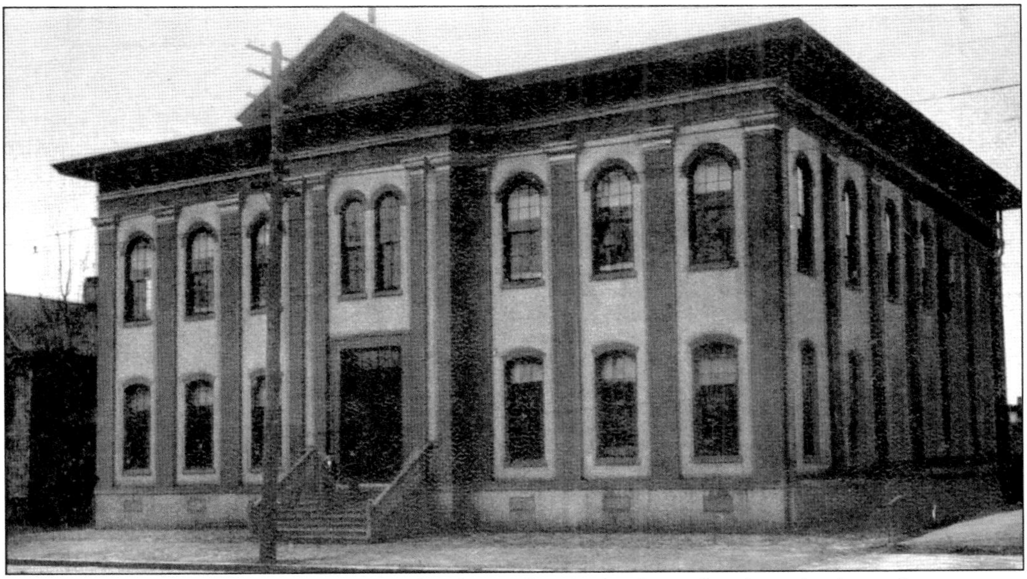

Spring Street School. Opened as School Number 8, the first school was built on the property at 1613 East Spring Street in 1868. That building, which is shown here in this 1910 postcard, was demolished in 1938. In 1939, a new building was dedicated. Its name was changed to M. Lucille Reisz Elementary School in 1977 to honor its long-time principal. It closed as an elementary school in May 1991.

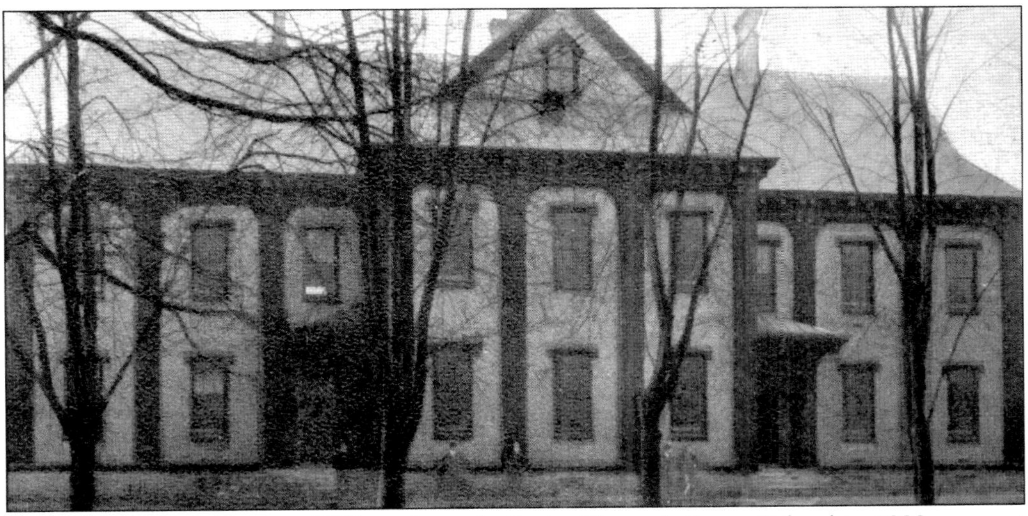

Eleventh Street School. William Banes built the Eleventh Street School in 1888 at a cost of $20,000 on the southeast corner of East Eleventh and Sycamore streets. (Sycamore was later renamed Culbertson Avenue.) Sara Ellen Jones was named principal and also taught class. The first Parent-Teacher Association in New Albany was established at the school in 1912. The school was renamed for Miss Jones, who resigned from the school in 1922 and died December 23, 1932. In 1950, the school opened a new addition with eight classrooms, an auditorium/gymnasium, and a cafeteria. When the 1973 addition was made to the 1950s addition, the original 1888 building was demolished.

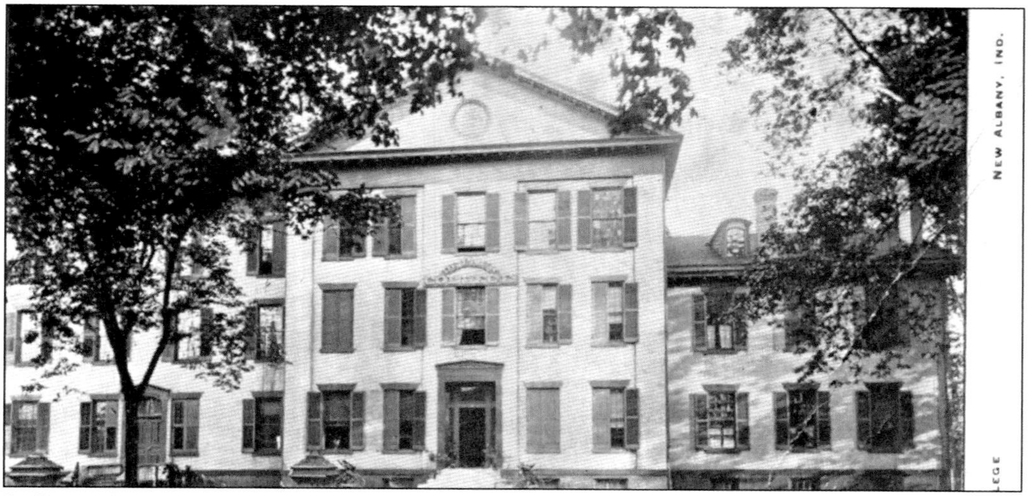

DEPAUW COLLEGE FOR YOUNG LADIES. This school for women was located on the southwest corner of East Ninth and Main Streets and was the property of the Methodist Episcopal Church. It was built in 1852 and first named Indiana Asbury Female College. The name changed after Washington C. DePauw and other business leaders came to the rescue of the financially troubled school and also after a $10,000 wing was added, paid for by Mr. DePauw. In 1908, the building became home to the New Albany Business College. The structure was razed in 1919. The DePauw Apartments have occupied the corner since 1925. This postcard is from about 1905.

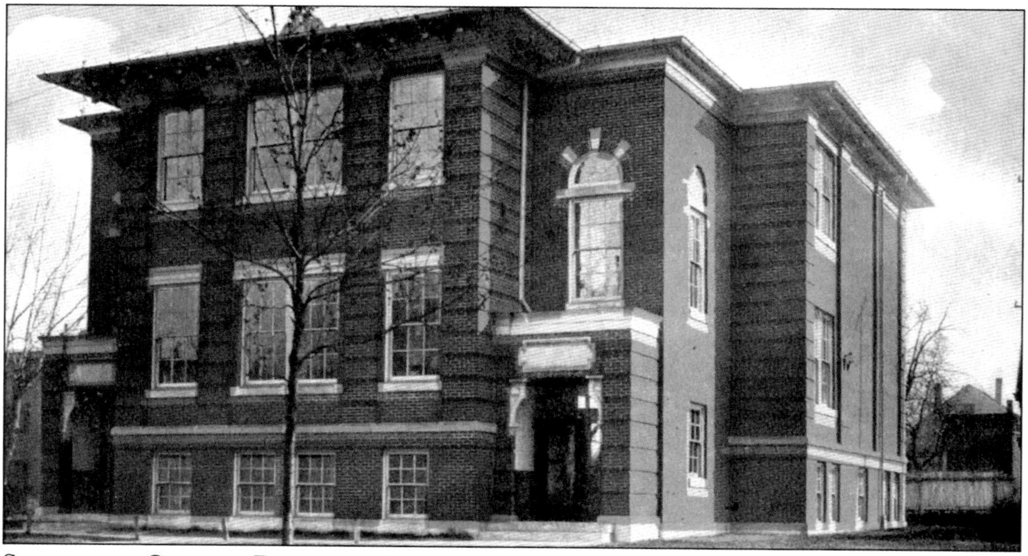

SCHOOL FOR COLORED PEOPLE. Scribner High School was established in 1880 under an 1869 Indiana law mandating public education for African-American children and allowing segregated schools. For the first 26 years of its existence, classes were held in an 1822 school building. That building was demolished in 1906 and replaced by the building shown on this 1910 postcard. S. Day and Sons built the building at a cost of $19,000. The school's last graduating class was 1951. That fall, students from grades 10, 11, and 12 were integrated into New Albany High School. The school was closed in 1952 after a 1949 Indiana law barring segregation. In 1959, the building was demolished to make way for the present City/County building for New Albany and Floyd County.

HOLY TRINITY SCHOOL. This 1905 postcard shows the 1883 Holy Trinity Convent and School building. It was located on the southwest corner of East Seventh and Market Streets. The convent was demolished in 1938 to make way for a more modern facility. Father Neyron started Holy Trinity School in 1837. In 1857, he invited the sisters of Providence to establish a school for girls. During its early years, the school was divided into two sections, one for boys on the north side of Market Street and another for girls on the south side of the street. In the 1970s, Holy Trinity and St. Mary's schools merged to form Catholic Central. Grades one through four used the St. Mary's building, and grades five through eight used the Holy Trinity building. All grades are now located in the St. Mary's School building under the name St. Mary's School.

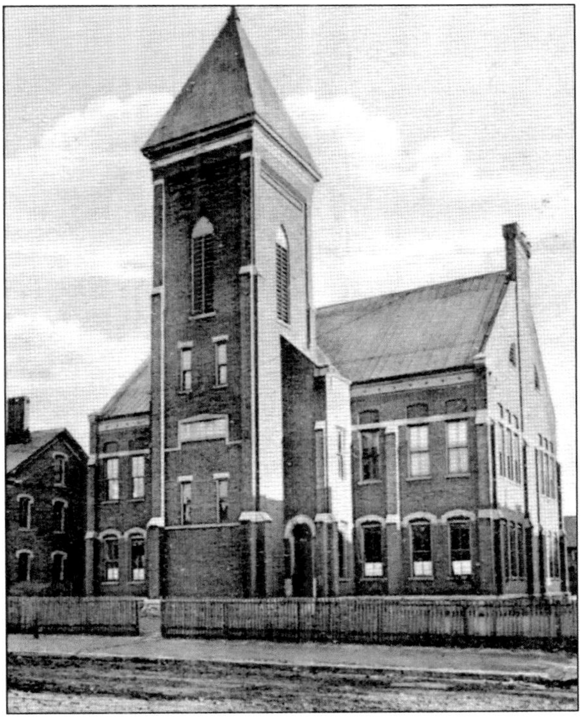

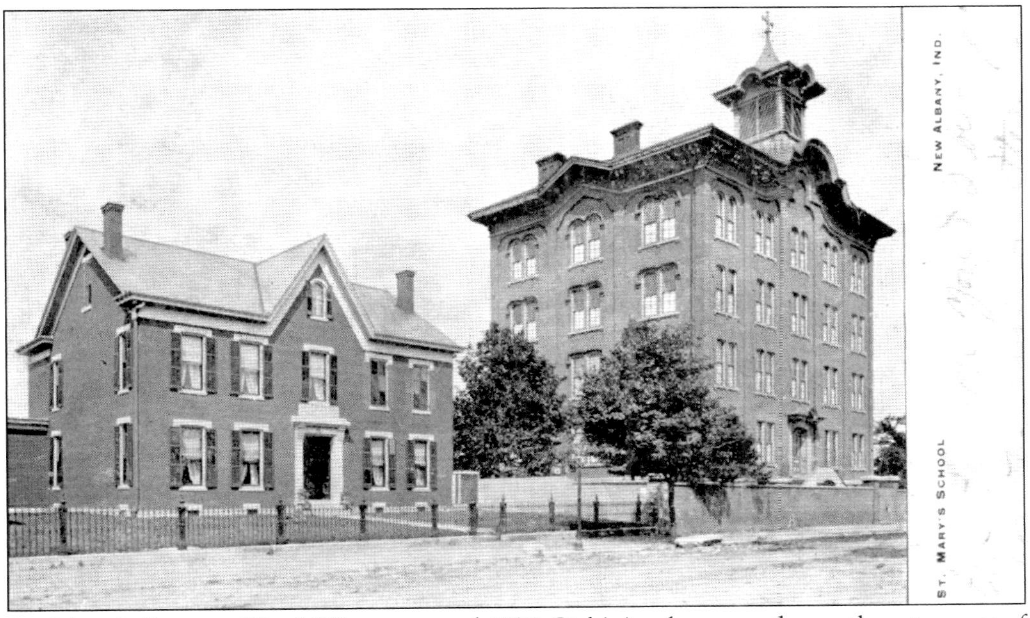

ST. MARY'S SCHOOL. The 1888 rectory and 1872 Girls' Academy, on the southwest corner of East Eighth and Elm Streets, are shown in this 1905 postcard. The boys' school was built across Eighth Street in 1879. In 1949, the present St. Mary's School building was completed, and the school became co-educational. The Girls' Academy was demolished in 1951 and replaced by a convent building.

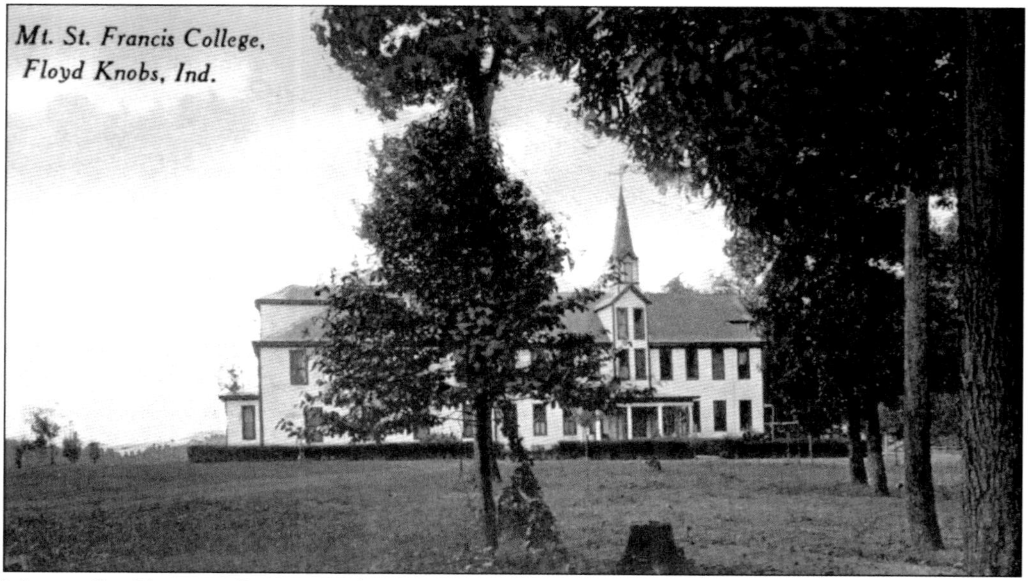

MOUNT ST. FRANCIS COLLEGE. This 1910 postcard shows the 1896 friary with its 1910 addition to accommodate a college and a chapel at Mount Saint Francis, about three miles west of New Albany. The Mount Saint Francis community started with the donation of 400 acres to the Conventual Franciscans in 1885 by siblings Joseph and Mary Anderson, who wished to honor the memory of their uncle, Fr. Anthony Mueller. By 1896, a friary had been built. In 1910, a seminary for the early training of boys who wished to become priests was instituted and christened Mount Saint Francis College. In 1932, the name was changed to Pro-Seminary, and boys entered it in the seventh grade. The school was closed in 1975.

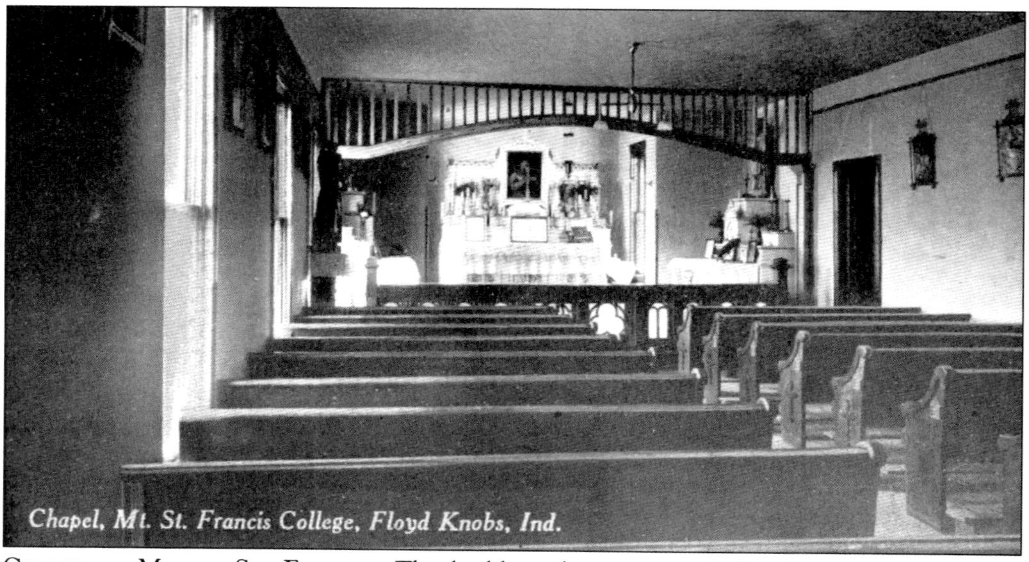

CHAPEL OF MOUNT ST. FRANCIS. The building that contained the chapel and college at Mount St. Francis was razed in 1955. Mount St. Francis still has its own post office, which was established in 1937.

Ten

Business and Industry

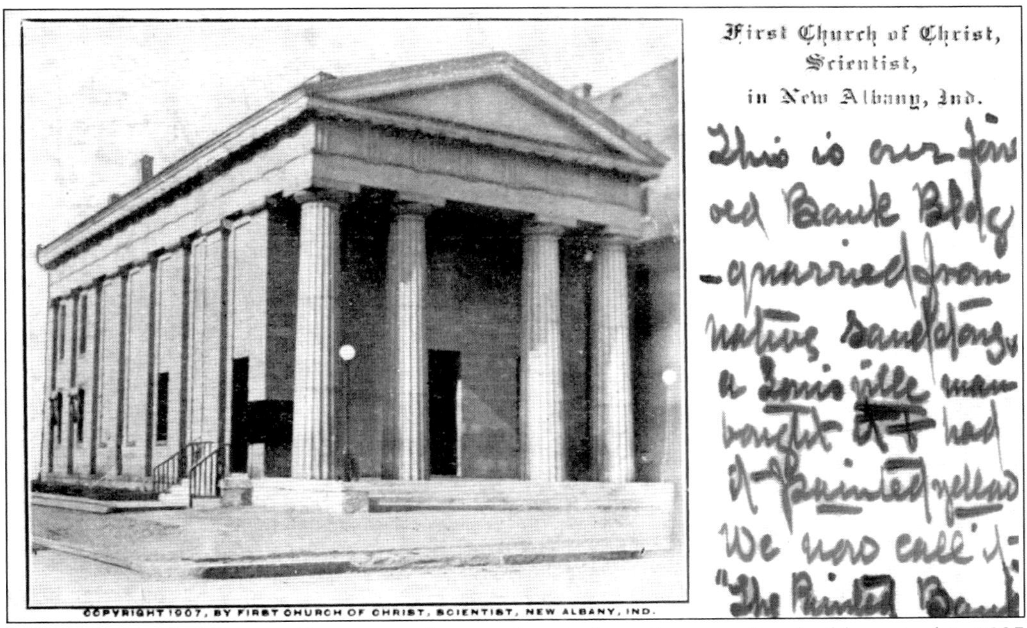

First Church of Christ Scientist. Among the city's earliest standing buildings is this 1837 Greek Revival-style bank building at 203 East Main Street. In 1834, the Second State Bank of Indiana was chartered with the main bank instituted in Indianapolis, along with 10 branches throughout the state. New Albany received one of those charter branches. It was built of native Floyd County sandstone at a cost of $50,000. The building was a bank until October 1897. Later uses of the building included serving as the First Church of Christ Scientist, the Knights of Pythias temple, and the New Albany Chapter of the American Red Cross. This postcard is from 1907.

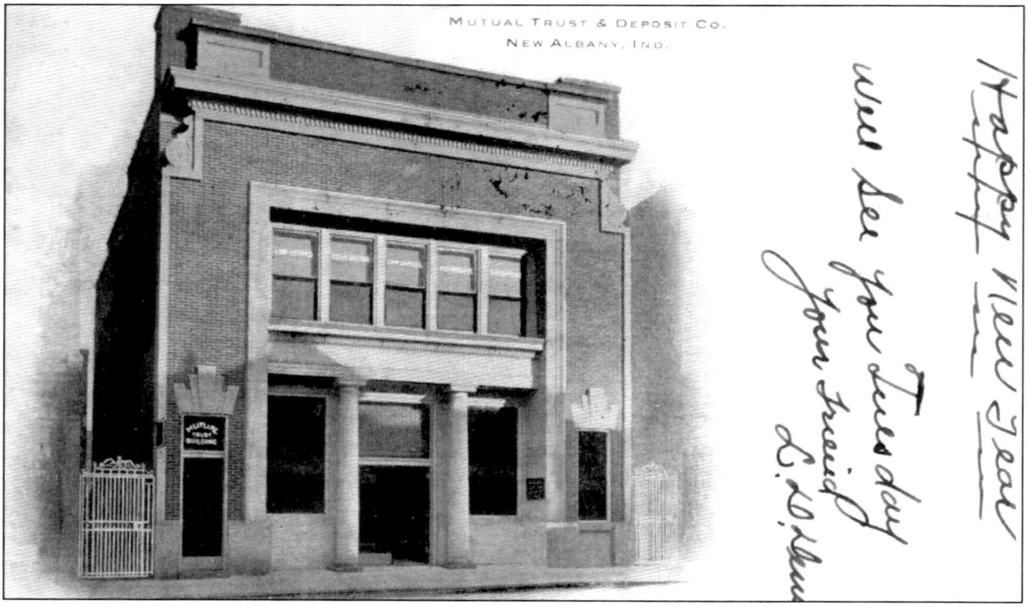

MUTUAL TRUST AND DEPOSIT CO. This 1910 card shows the Mutual Trust and Deposit Company at 322–324 Pearl Street; it was founded in 1904 just down the street in the Goodbub building. The building shown here was constructed in 1909. In 1951, the bank building expanded to the south, and a modern building replaced two older structures. It was later remodeled into an even more modern structure.

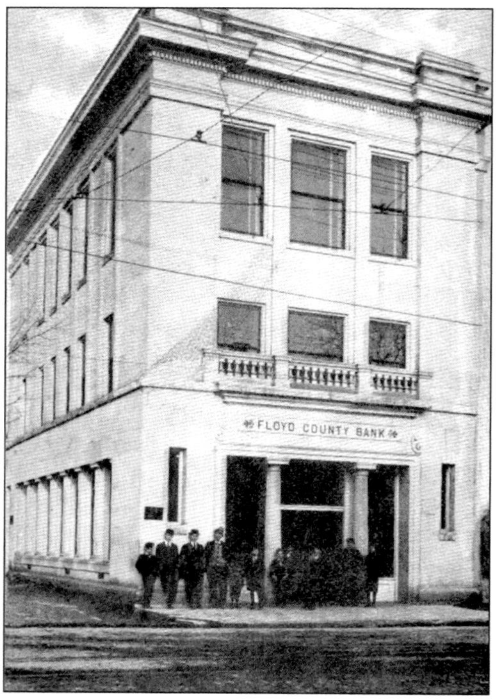

FLOYD COUNTY BANK. This 1911 postcard shows the Floyd County Bank with its staff of men standing outside. The bank was located on the southeast corner of Spring and Vincennes Streets. Its original building was completed in 1909, with an addition completed in 1929. It was torn down in 1964, and a new bank building constructed. Following the tornado of 1917, the bank extended credit to residents to rebuild the devastated city, and after the flood of 1937, the bank provided the capital to rebuild homes, factories, and businesses. The Floyd County Bank was only one of two banks in Floyd County allowed to reopen in 1933 after many banks were ordered closed due to the Great Depression.

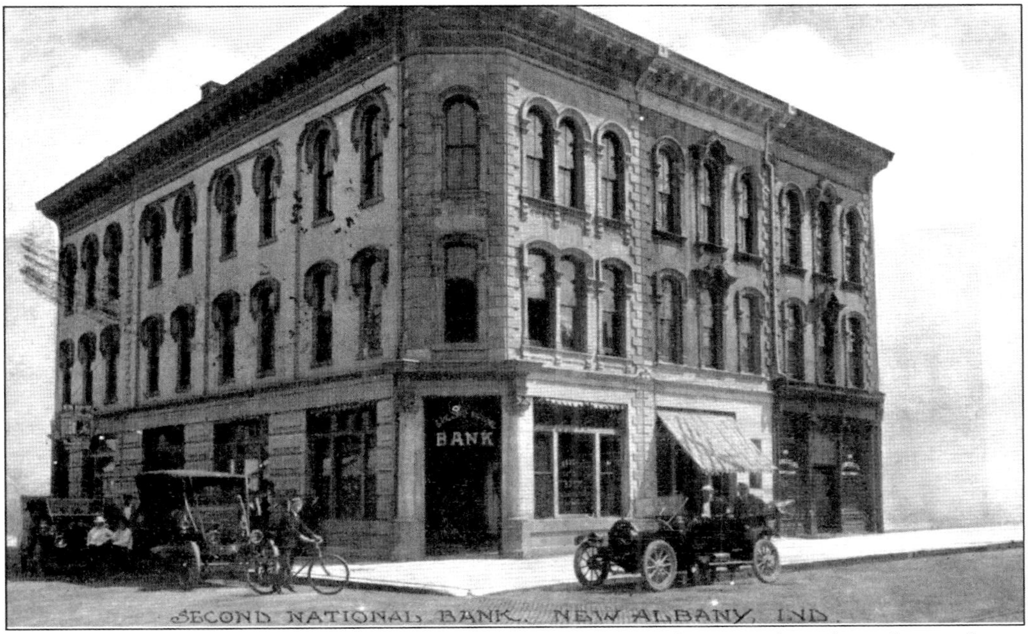

SECOND NATIONAL BANK. The building that housed the Second National Bank on the northeast corner of Pearl and Main Streets was built as the Merchant's National Bank in 1860. It was extensively remodeled in 1905. This postcard is from 1911.

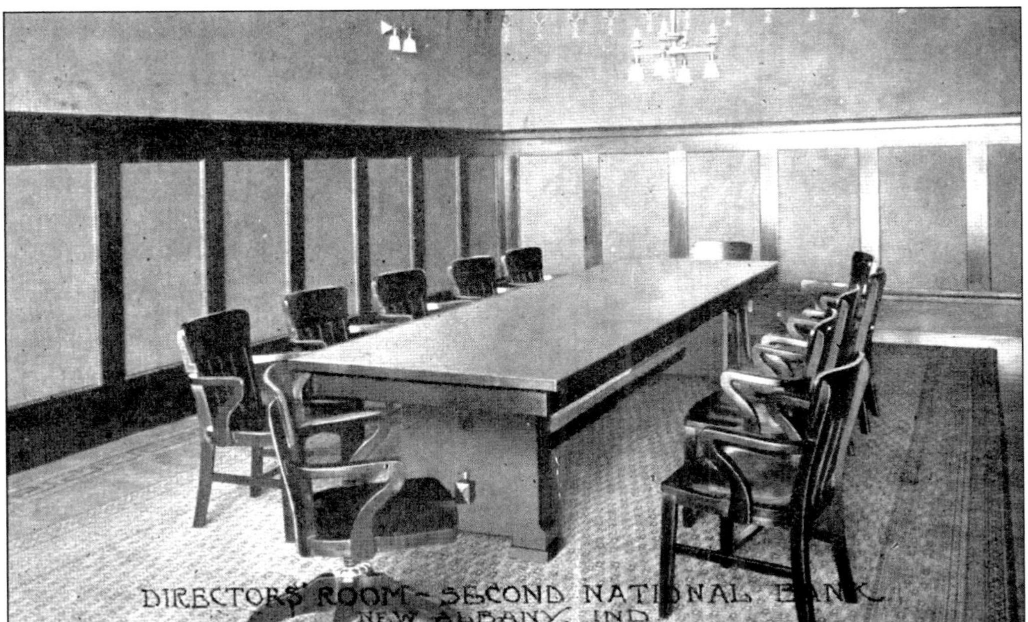

DIRECTOR'S ROOM. This card shows the director's room of Second National Bank, which was done in the Mission style of the time. This postcard is from about 1910.

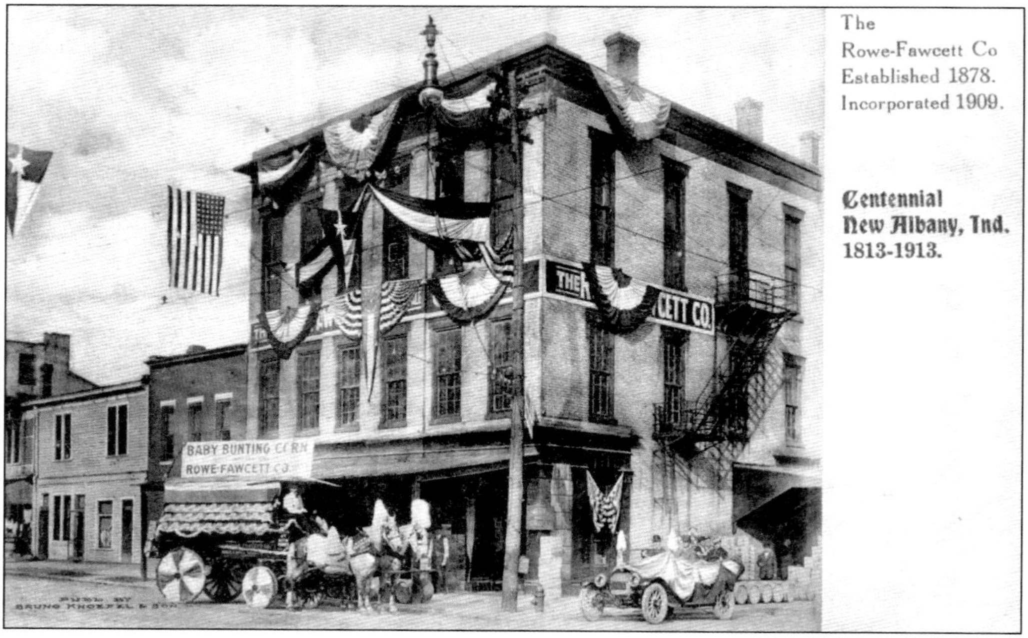

ROWE-FAWCETT. Wholesale grocery Rowe-Fawcett Co. was established in 1879 and located in what is one of the city's most important buildings. Then, the building's address was listed as 128–130 Lower High Street. Today, that same address is known as 128 West Main Street. The building was constructed in 1852 in a restrained Egyptian Revival style as Woodward Hall, with the city's first public meeting place on its third floor. A Civil War hospital was located in the building. This image is from the 1913 series of postcards commemorating the city's centennial.

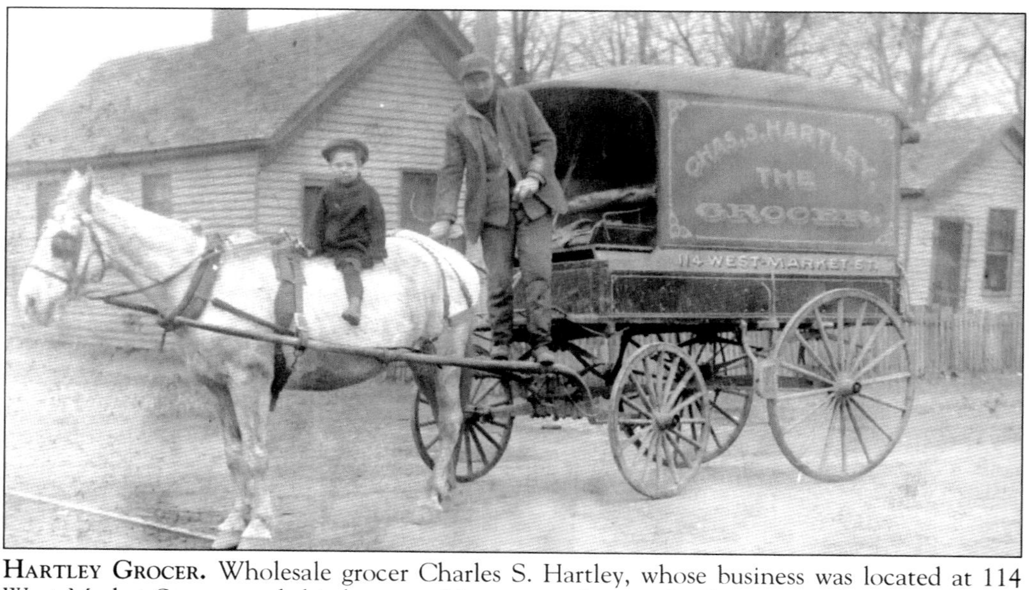

HARTLEY GROCER. Wholesale grocer Charles S. Hartley, whose business was located at 114 West Market Street, used this horse and buggy to advertise his business and possibly deliver groceries. This postcard is from 1917.

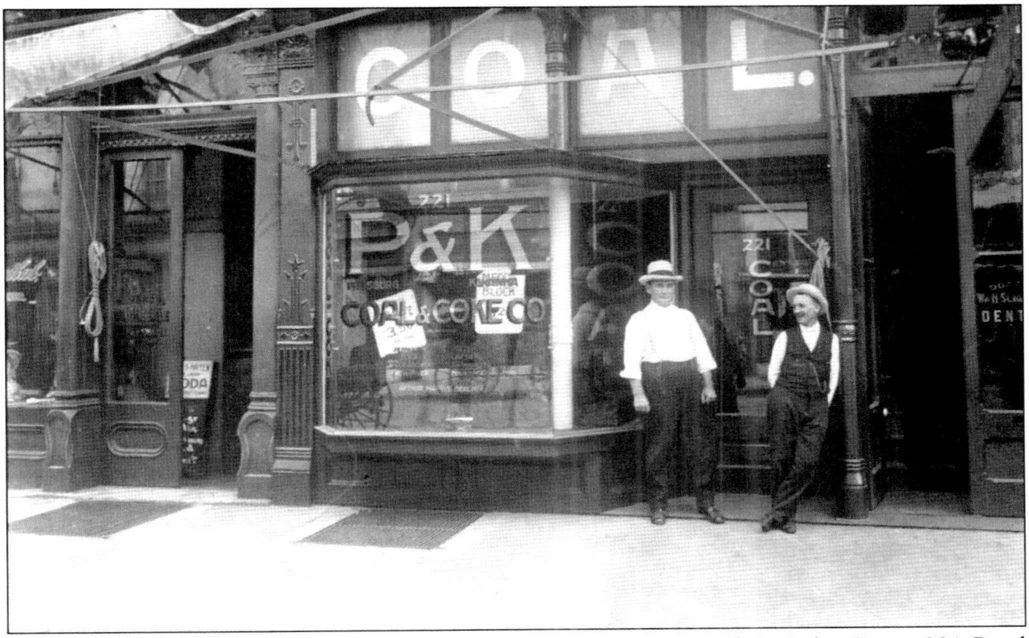

P&K Coal & Coke. The Finger Brothers operated the P&K Coal & Coke Co. at 221 Pearl Street and likely used this postcard to advertise their business. The Goodbub Confectionary is to the left of the store. This postcard is from 1911.

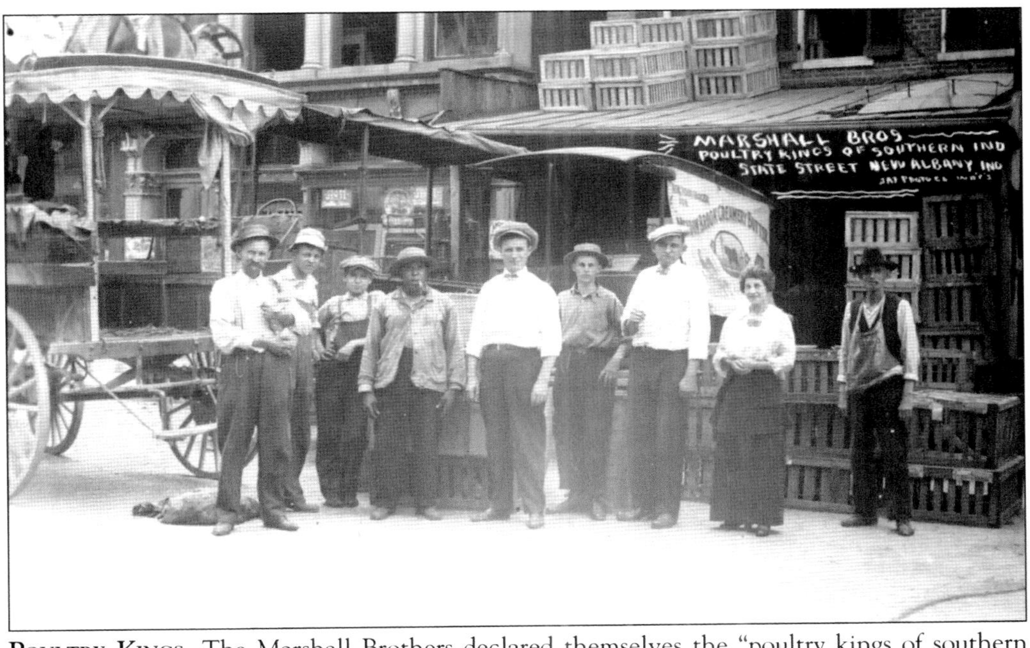

Poultry Kings. The Marshall Brothers declared themselves the "poultry kings of southern State Street in New Albany." This card, probably used to advertise the business, shows their staff in front of the store at 221 State Street around 1913.

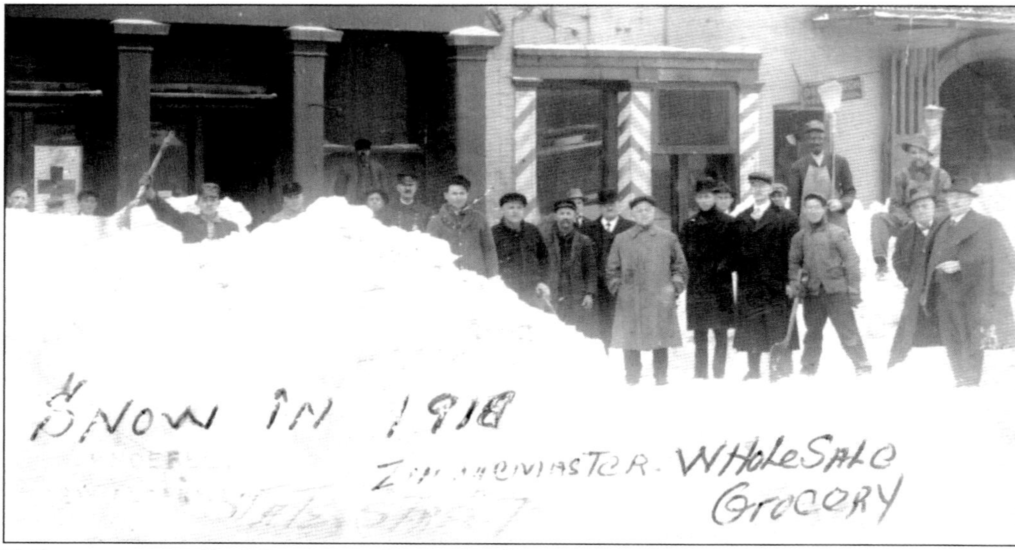

F. ZINSMEISTER & CO. WHOLESALE GROCERY. The winter of 1917–1918 was one of the coldest on record in the Ohio River Valley and worth commemorating with a postcard. National Weather Service records in Louisville, just across the Ohio River, indicate that 15 inches of snow fell in early December. Ice covered the Ohio River. Temperatures stayed bitterly cold for some six weeks after that, keeping the snow on the ground with another 10 inches of snow fall on top of that on January 14. January 12 was one of two days on record in which temperatures never rose above zero. This picture was taken on January 16, 1918. The business was located at 317–321 State Street.

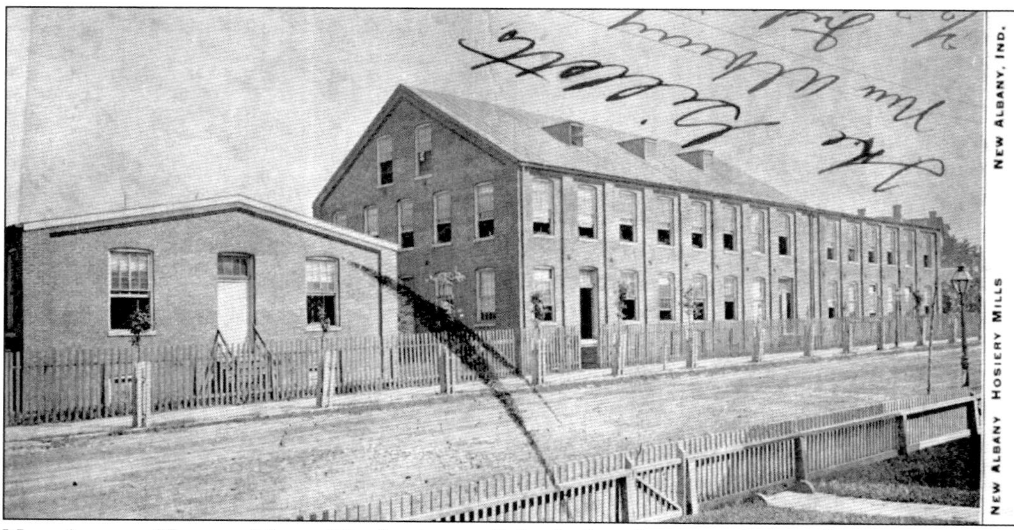

NEW ALBANY HOSIERY MILLS. The hosiery mills had a long history in New Albany. The woolen mills were established in 1864, and the hosiery mills added as part of that same company in 1879. In 1881, both mills were sold to W. A. Hedden and his partner, Richard Greuner. The building shown in this card was the new hosiery mill, completed in 1884 and located in the 1700 block of Ekin Avenue. The mill had 150 employees and distributed its products throughout the United States. The City of New Albany Recreation Department moved into the building in 1939 and still owns it today. This postcard is from about 1905.

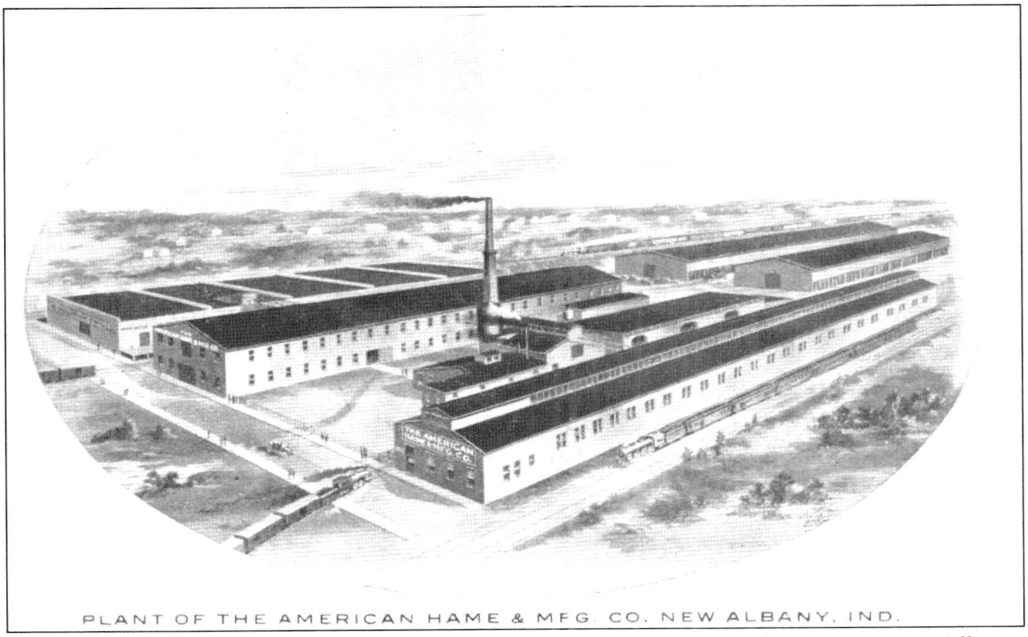

AMERICAN HAME AND MANUFACTURING CO. According to the 1908 publication, "New Albany: Its Industrial Possibilities," this was one of the largest and best-equipped factories in America making hames, chains, and single-trees. The plant was located along the Pennsylvania Railroad east of Silver Street and employed about 175 people. By 1915, the name had changed to National Hame & Chain Co., and in 1918, it was the second largest hame manufacturer in the U.S. By 1931, however, it had dissolved. In 1946, the neighboring Indiana Veneer & Panel Co. bought the old hame property and incorporated it into their own plywood manufacturing plant. This postcard is from about 1913.

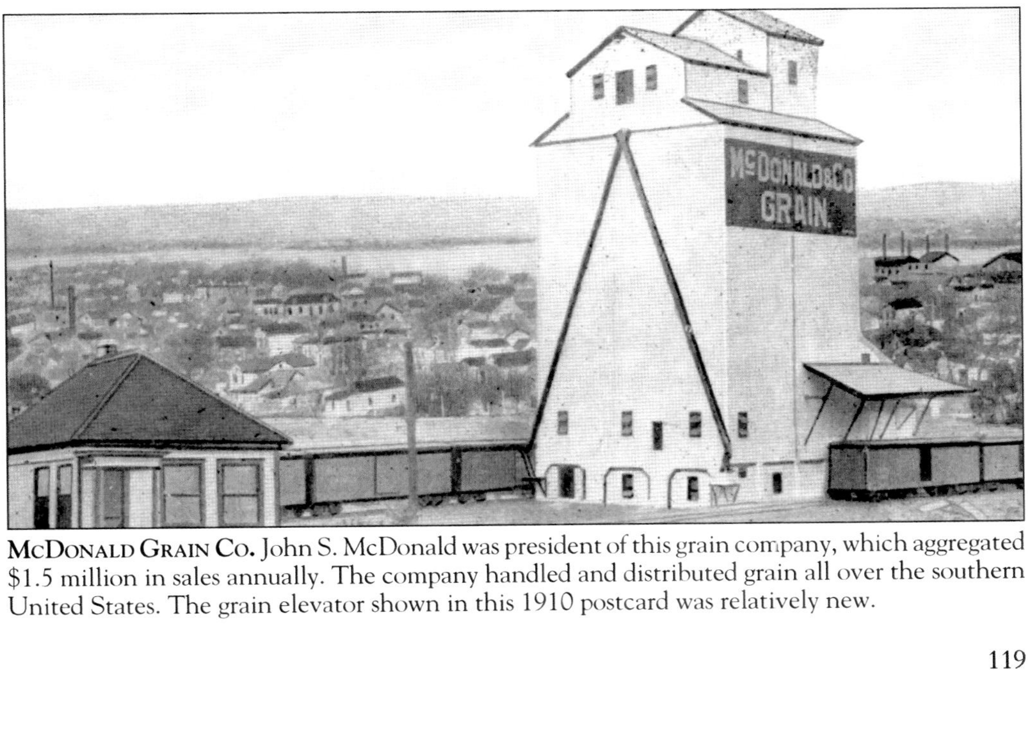

McDONALD GRAIN CO. John S. McDonald was president of this grain company, which aggregated $1.5 million in sales annually. The company handled and distributed grain all over the southern United States. The grain elevator shown in this 1910 postcard was relatively new.

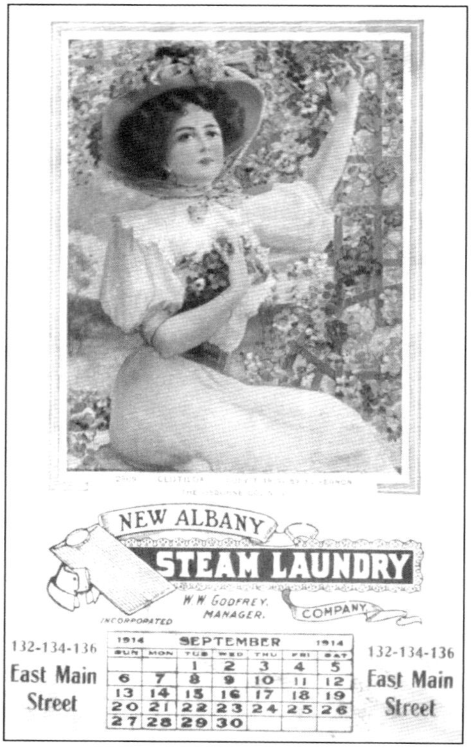

NEW ALBANY'S STEAM LAUNDRY. The laundry business, shown in this 1909 postcard, was established in 1887 and managed by Mr. W.W. Godfrey. According to the publication "New Albany: Its Industrial Possibilities," the plant was a model of scientific efficiency. This firm, still in business, is located at 1935 West Street. It is one of New Albany's state-recognized centennial businesses.

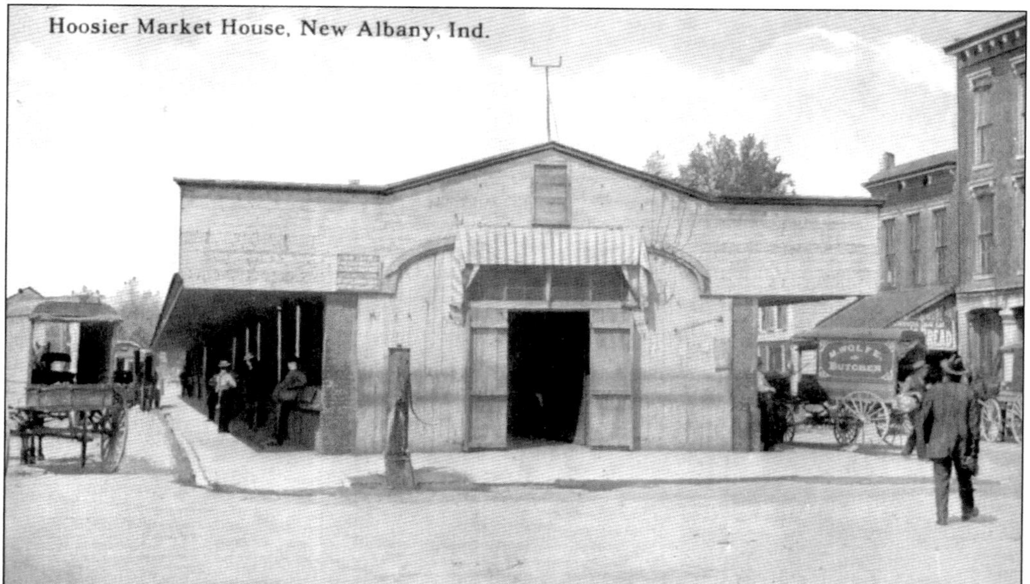

HOOSIER MARKET HOUSE. Located on Market Street between State and West First Streets, the Hoosier Market House, known also as the Lower Market House, was a general market at which customers could purchase all manner of goods. It was built in 1839 and demolished in 1937. There was also a Middle Market House that was located on Market Street between State and Pearl Streets. It was built in 1832 and torn down in 1903.

KRAFT UNDERTAKER. This 1905 postcard was an advertisement for Frank A. Kraft, funeral director and embalmer, whose business was located at 146–148 East Main Street, in what we now refer to as the Reisz building. Frank A. Kraft became associated with his father's business, which was established in 1856, at age 18. He took over the business after his father's death in 1882. The Kraft funeral business had the finest funeral livery around the Falls Cities, according to the centennial book of 1913. By 1921, the business had moved to 708 East Spring Street. This company continues today and is one of New Albany's state-recognized centennial businesses.

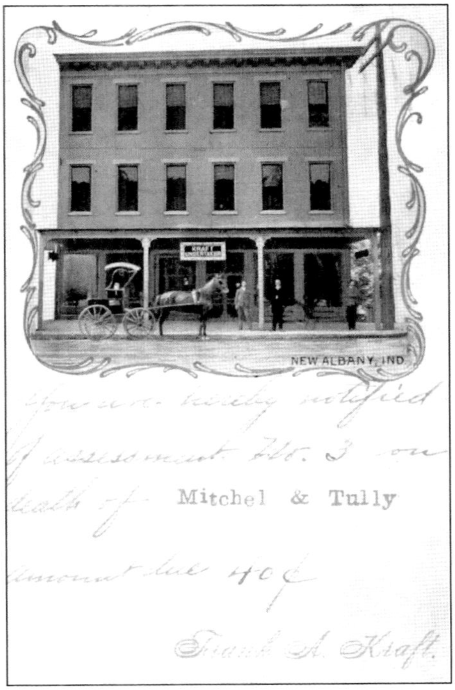

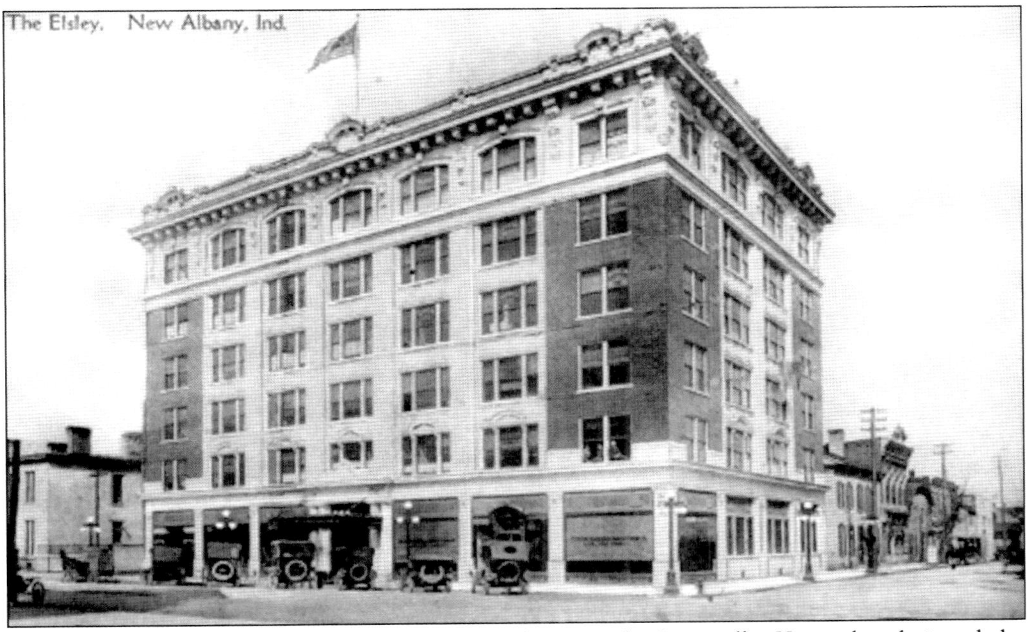

ELSBY BUILDING. Joseph and Joseph Architects from nearby Louisville, Kentucky, designed the Elsby Building, which was constructed in 1916 on the former site of P. Vernia's 1866 Masonic Temple building. Built of steel, concrete, terra cotta, and brick, the building cost $100,000 and was advertised as being fire-proof. In 1917, the name was changed from German American Bank & Trust Co. to the American Bank & Trust Co. The bank failed during the Great Depression. It later received a new charter as the American Bank. This postcard is from about 1916.

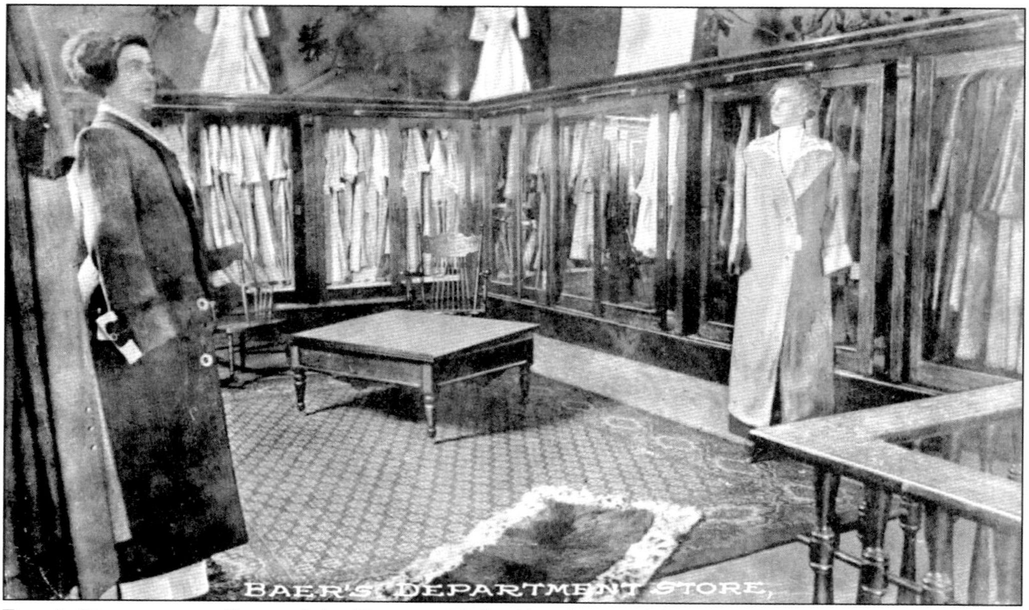

BAER'S DEPARTMENT STORE. John Baer established his dry goods business in 1871. He commissioned S. Day and Sons to construct the Baer's Bazaar building at 319–321 Pearl Street in 1900. Mr. Baer was one of the most enterprising and successful merchants of New Albany, according to the centennial book of 1913. He was an active member of the German Evangelical Church.

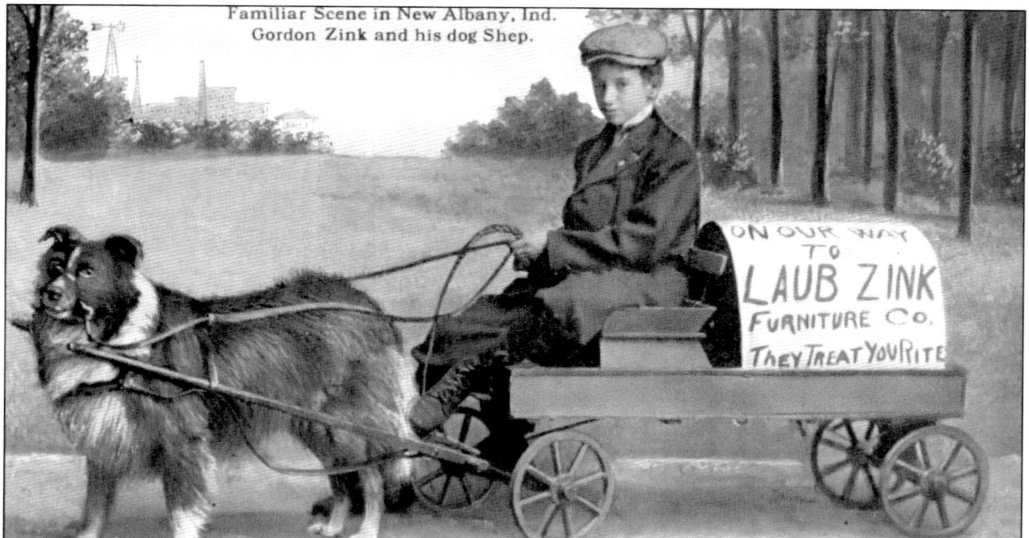

GORDON ZINK AND HIS DOG SHEP. Morris Laub established his furniture business in 1891 and retired from it in 1911. It was reorganized under the name Laub-Zink Furniture Co. Charles Zink became the manager of the new company with the assistance of his brother John Zink. They sold "Made in New Albany" items: mattresses, appliances, bedroom suits, sideboards, parlor suites, and kitchen cabinets. Gordon Zink and Shep were in the 1913 centennial parade, the same year of this postcard.

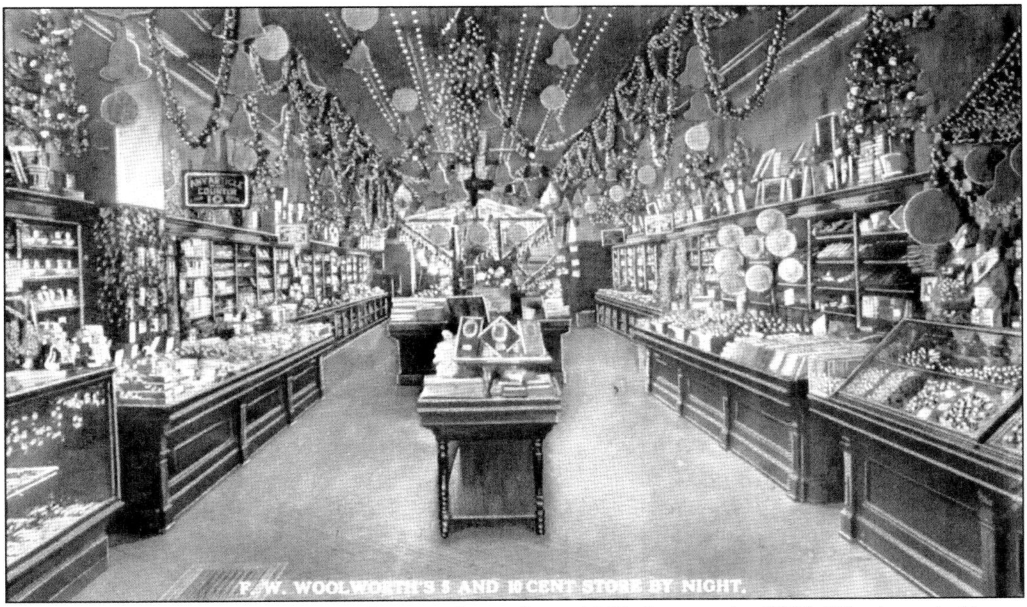

F.W. Woolworth. This postcard image from about 1913 depicts the F.W. Woolworth Co. at night during Christmastime. The store was located at 218 Pearl Street. By 1923, the store also included 220 Pearl Street.

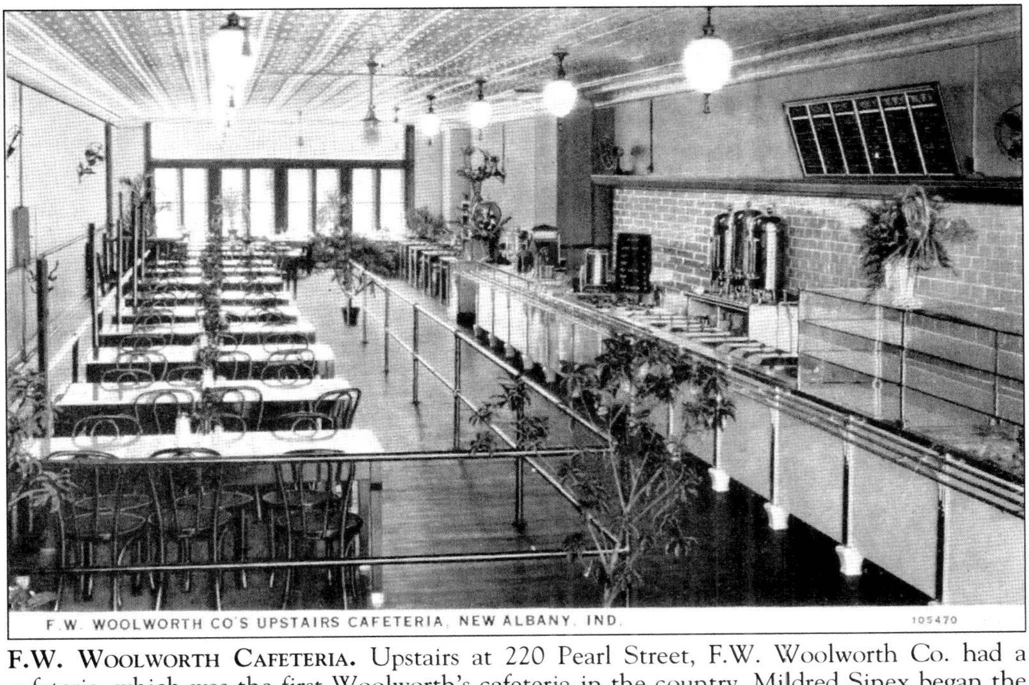

F.W. Woolworth Cafeteria. Upstairs at 220 Pearl Street, F.W. Woolworth Co. had a cafeteria, which was the first Woolworth's cafeteria in the country. Mildred Sinex began the operation about 1923. This postcard is from about 1925.

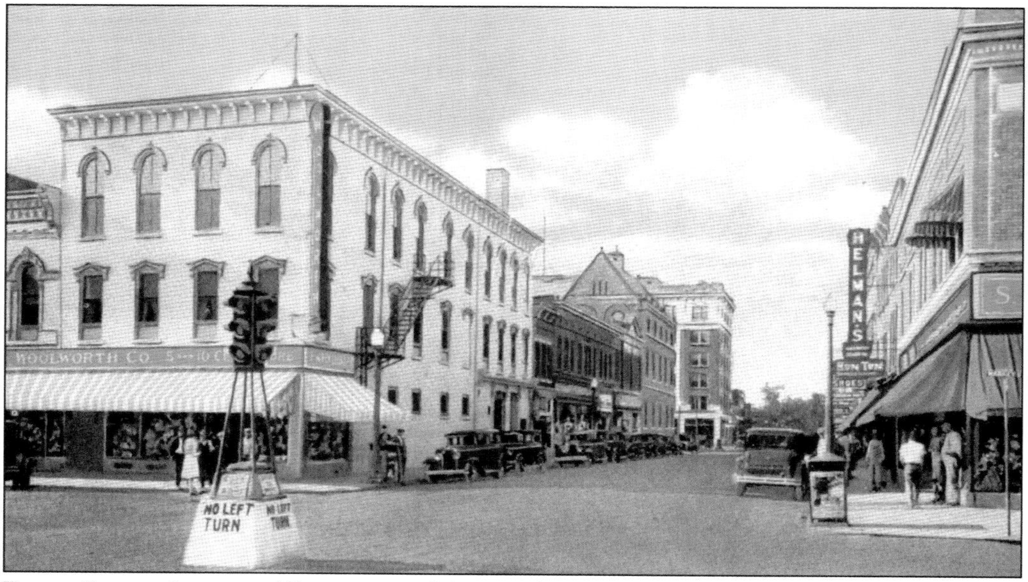

PEARL STREET LOOKING NORTH FROM MARKET STREET. On the left is the F.W. Woolworth store at 123 and 127 East Market Street. The two buildings were built for Ben Briggs and John Briggs respectively in 1891 and 1872. George W. Grosheider Grocery was in the corner building at 127 East Market Street in the late 1800s. Woolworth had moved their store and cafeteria to the corner buildings by 1931. Woolworth closed its New Albany store in the early 1970s. On the right is the S.S. Kresge building, which was built in 1930. Bon Ton Ladies Clothing, run by Clarence Benjamin, Helman's Department Store, and Stein's Shoes are further down the street.

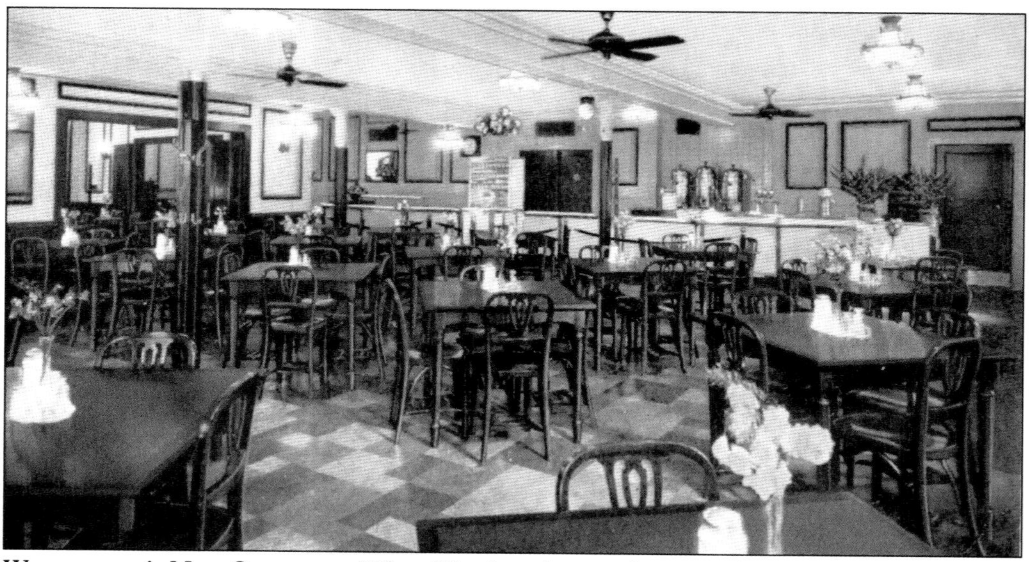

WOOLWORTH'S NEW CAFETERIA. When Woolworth moved its store from 218–220 Pearl Street, the cafeteria moved with it to the northwest corner of Pearl and Market streets. As shown in this 1931 postcard, the seating capacity was increased in the new restaurant, which occupied the upstairs of both buildings on Market Street.

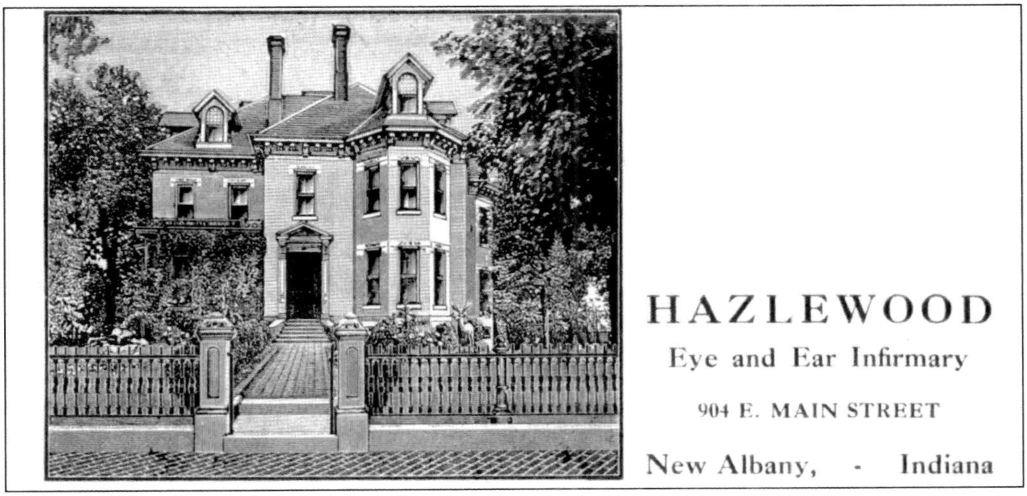

HAZLEWOOD INFIRMARY. Dr. John Hazlewood moved his Hazlewood Eye and Ear Infirmary, shown in this 1905 postcard, to 904 East Main Street sometime around 1897. By 1931, the eye and ear infirmary had ceased operations. Originally, this Queen Anne-style home was built for Samuel Culbertson by his father, William S., as a wedding gift in 1886. Samuel moved to Louisville, where he became a prominent citizen and eventually the president of Churchill Downs. During his tenure as president, he commissioned the first "garland of roses" to be placed on the winner of the Kentucky Derby, a tradition that continues today. For many years, the house was home to the Improved Order of Red Men Manzanita Tribe No. 276 fraternal organization.

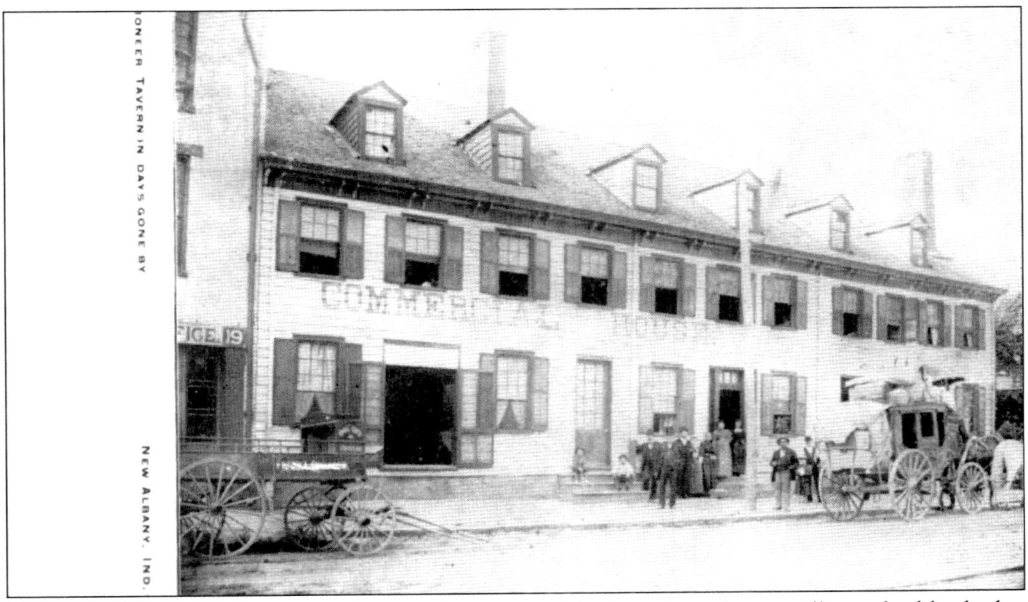

PIONEER TAVERN. Mrs. Joel Scribner, wife of one of the founders of New Albany, had built this tavern in 1817. It had numerous names throughout its 102-year history, including Hale's Tavern, High Street House, Brooks House, and Commercial House. The building even hosted a governor's ball for Jonathan Jennings, Indiana's first state governor. Torn down in 1919, it was located on the southeast corner of West First and High Streets. This postcard is from about 1905.

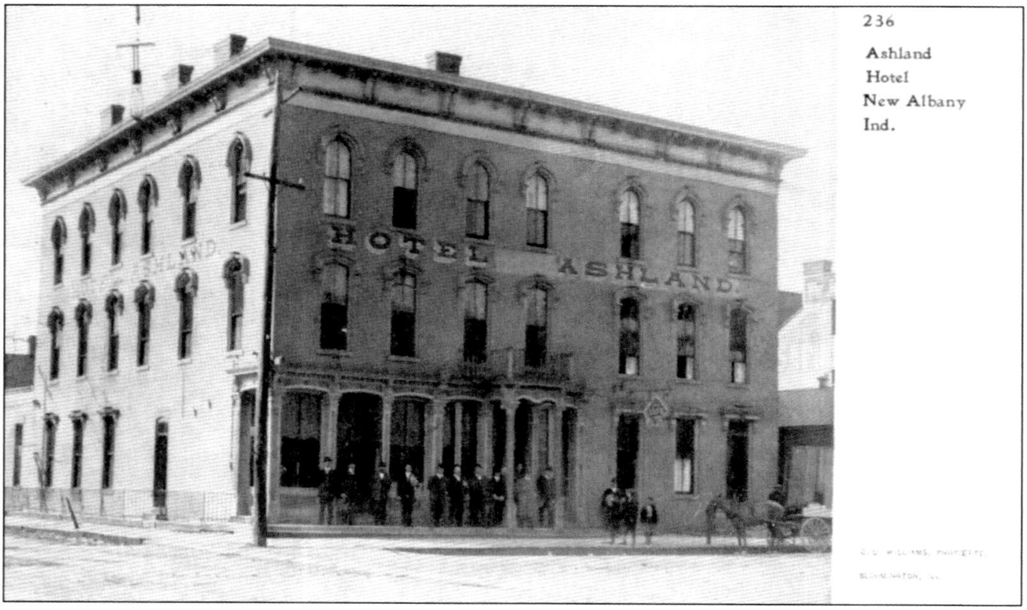

ASHLAND HOTEL. Located on the southwest corner of Bank and Market Streets, the Ashland Hotel was built in 1871 as the Monsch Hotel and operated as a hotel until 1994. It had at least 11 name changes, including the Central Hotel, the Windsor Hotel, the St. Charles Hotel, the Tavern Hotel, and the New Albany Inn. Construction on the project included brick masonry by John Anderson, stone work by John Diebold, and glass from New Albany Glassworks, all New Albany companies. This postcard is from 1910.

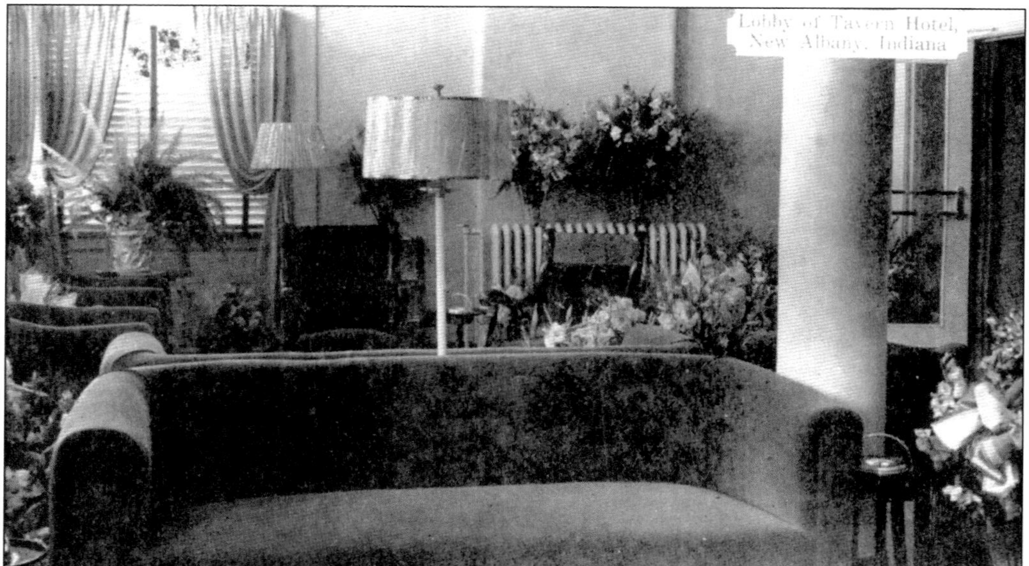

LOBBY OF TAVERN HOTEL. This mid-20th century view shows the lobby of the Tavern Hotel, as it was called then. The hotel was in the Nicklies family from 1911 through 1936. In 1937, C. Pralle Erni bought the Tavern Hotel, but wasn't until 1963 that the name changed to the New Albany Inn. The Erni family owned the hotel until 1973.

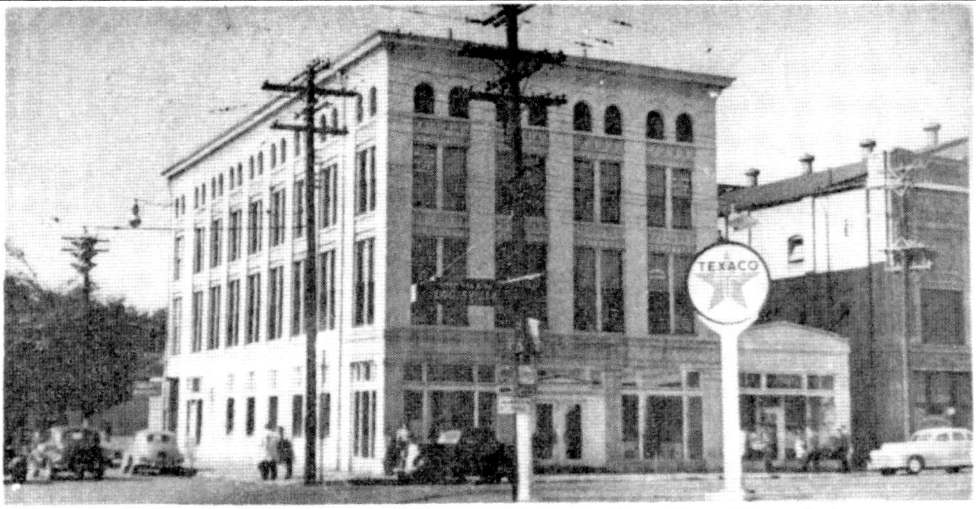

LIBERTY BUILDING. The Liberty Building was constructed in 1886 as the Fieock building and originally home to Fieock's Tavern and outdoor beer garden. Later occupants included Roy Hayden Café and Pool Room, Pfeffer's Confectionery, and Liberty Bank. Liberty Bank was one of the four banks in New Albany to fail during the Great Depression. The building was demolished in 1961.

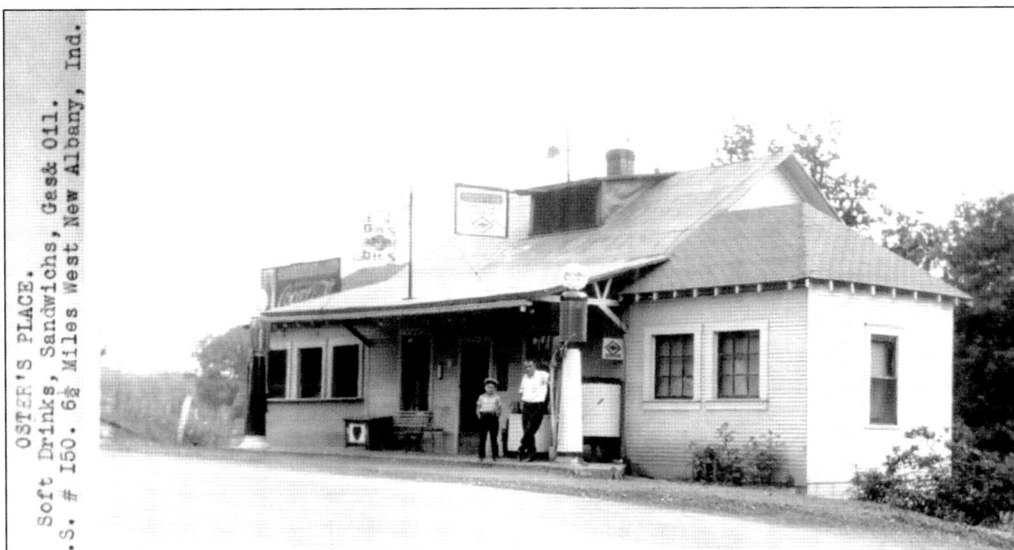

OSTER'S PLACE. Located on U.S. Highway 150, six-and-a-half miles west of New Albany, Oster's was a gas station where patrons could also buy sandwiches and soft drinks. This postcard is from about 1925. The proprietor was Bill Oster, and he was known for his delicious barbecue.

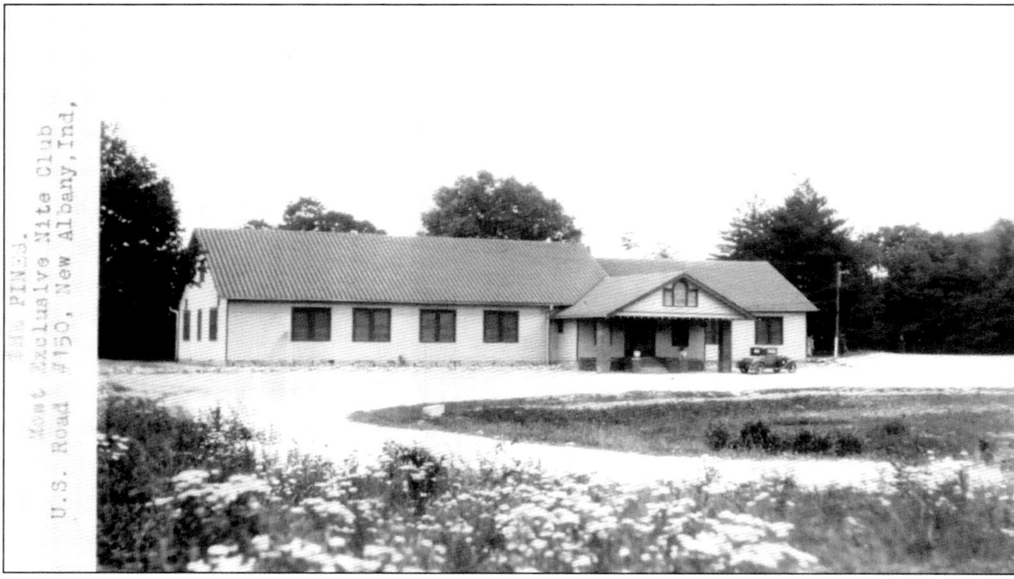

The Pines. This establishment stood at the top of a hill on Paoli Pike where the Buffalo Trace subdivision is now located. It was advertised as the "most exclusive night club" in the area. The property was sold in 1937. This postcard is from about 1930.

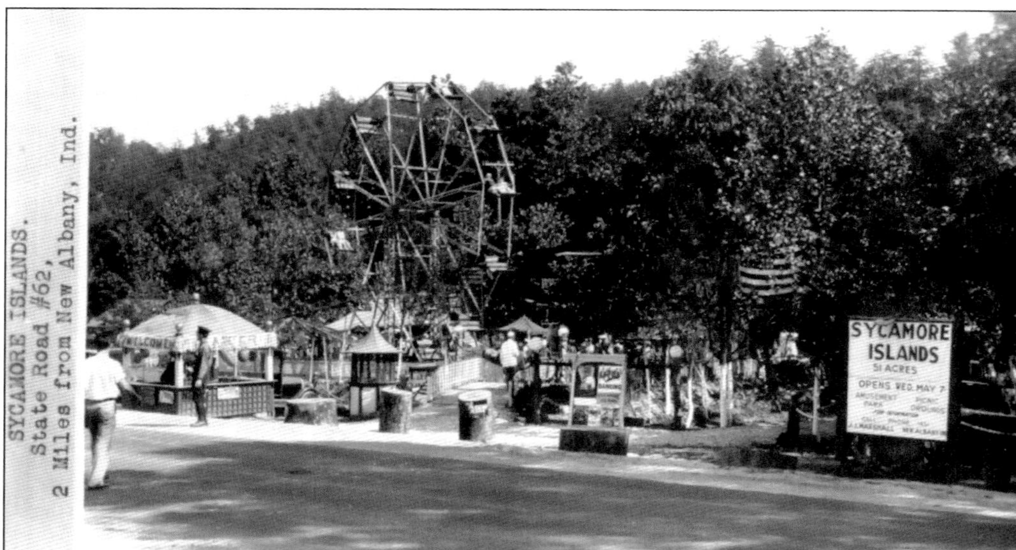

Sycamore Islands. This establishment was an amusement park and picnic grounds on 51 acres at 3239 Corydon Pike. J.J. Marshall was the proprietor. This postcard is from about 1925.